THE BRITEINU TORAH COMMENTARY
Covenant Insights from the Weekly Parashiyot

Volume 4

BAMIDBAR במדבר NUMBERS

The Covenant Community

ARIEL BERKOWITZ

TIMELESS TORAH TRUTHS
דברי אמת התורה לעולם ועד

The Briteinu Torah Commentary
Volume 4: Bamidbar — Numbers: The Covenant Community
by Ariel Berkowitz

Copyright © 2001-2025 by Ariel and D'vorah Berkowitz
Cover and Title design: Ariel and D'vorah Berkowitz
Book and cover layout: Hugo Buitenhuis
Editors: Dr. Winnie Chen, Dolly Salins and Jan Styles
Cover Picture: Courtesy of Yo'el and Tikvah Berkowitz
The picture is Numbers 34: 5–16 from a Sefer Torah.

The right of Ariel Berkowitz to be identified as the author of this work has been asserted by him in accordance with the Copyright, Designs & Patents Act 1988.

Unless otherwise stated, Scripture is taken from the NEW AMERICAN STANDARD BIBLE, Copyright © 1960, 1962, 1963, 1968, 1971, 1972, 1973, 1975, 1977, 1995 by The Lockman Foundation. Used by permission. We have changed the translations of the words "law", "Christ", and "Jesus" to "Torah", "Messiah" and "Yeshua" respectively, whenever appropriate.

First Edition 2001
Second Edition 2009
Third Edition, revised 2025
ISBN 979-82-80410-86-2

This book is produced by:
Torah Resources International
www.torahresourcesinternational.com

Published and Distributed by:
Shoreshim Publishing, Inc.
71040 Memphis Ridge Rd.
Richmond, Michigan 48062
Phone:586-588-0193
Email: ad.tri@mac.com

Published in cooperation with Kindle Direct Publishing

Dedication for Briteinu: Numbers

In many ways, the Book of Numbers is about the Covenant Community.
Because of that, we would like to dedicate our Briteinu Commentary on Bamidbar
to the International Covenant Community which we have been privileged to serve
for three decades, studying Torah together.
Thus, it is to all of you, our precious fellow Torah students in:

Australia • Belgium • China (inc. Hong Kong) • France
Germany • Hungary • Ireland • Israel • Japan • Netherlands
Philippines • Poland • Slovakia • South Africa
South Korea • Suriname • Sweden • Switzerland • Taiwan
Thailand • Ukraine • USA
United Kingdom (England, Scotland, Wales, Northern Ireland, Isle of Wright)

that we lovingly dedicate this volume of the Briteinu Torah Commentary.

Ariel & D'vorah Berkowitz
Arad, Israel
May 2025

Table of Contents

Table of Maps

Maps 1, 5, 6, 9, 10 and 11 are taken from the Satellite Bible Atlas by William Schlegel and used with permission. See Briteinu Bibliography on page 235

Maps 2, 3, 4 and 7 are made by the author using the tools provided by the Atlas program of Accordance Bible Software, www.accordancebible.com.

Introduction To Briteinu

Bamidbar: The Covenant Community is volume 4 of a five-part commentary set on the Torah, the Five Books of Moses. The entire set is called *The Briteinu Torah Commentary*. This Hebrew term *Briteinu* (בריתנו) means, "Our Covenant." This name, perhaps more than any other, most aptly describes the nature of the Torah. It is most profoundly a covenant document. That is, it is a book, which speaks about the sacred covenants of promise that God made by oath with His chosen people.

We thank you for acquiring this volume. Before it can be used to its fullest, there are a number of explanations the reader must understand.

Our Goal

Our goal in these commentaries is to help the student understand the text of the Torah in its historical, geographical and cultural context. We desire that the students gain a greater appreciation for the Scriptures as well as for the One to whom the Torah points, Yeshua the Messiah.

Our Uniqueness

Many wonderful and useful commentaries already exist on the Book of Leviticus. So, one might ask, why write another one? To be sure many excellent commentaries do exist, some of which represented in our *Briteinu* Bibliography. However, what makes this commentary unique is its format.

The Five Books of Moses (Torah) are read and studied during the course of one year in most of the Jewish world. In some places, a three-year cycle of reading and studying is practised. In fact, this was the most common method utilized in the 1st century. Yet most Jewish people today follow a one-year cycle. This means that on the day following Sukkot (usually early to mid-October) people conclude reading the final two chapters of Deuteronomy and turn the Bible back to the opening sections of Genesis in order to begin a new cycle of reading. During the course of the year, Genesis will be followed by Exodus, etc., until the end of Deuteronomy again, when the same procedure will be repeated at the end of Sukkot. This is an annual cycle, designed to follow the continuous cycle of Holy Days, outlined in Leviticus 23. We shall call this the Torah Reading Cycle. Please understand that it is more than just reading that is involved. Each passage is thoroughly studied as well, with the goal to learning how its contents can affect our lives.

When this Torah Reading Cycle is practised, each of the books of the Torah is divided into smaller sections for convenience. We call these sections in English "Weekly Torah Portions." In Hebrew, an individual portion is referred to as the *parashat haShavua*, פרשת השבוע, or more popularly, just the parasha (pah-rah-SHAH) or *parshiyot* (par-shee-OTE), the plural. The Torah is divided into 54 sections, and a specific portion, or *parasha*, is read formally each week during synagogue services. Each portion has a Hebrew name. The name is derived from the first important word of that *parasha* in the Hebrew text. In some weeks, a double *parasha* is read because the calendar year has only 52 weeks. Sometimes, others refer to a Torah portion as a *sidra* (SIH-drah). The term "*sidra*" is an Aramaic word. And is used synonymously with the Hebrew term, *parasha*. The plural of "*sidra*" is "*sidrot*" (sid-ROTE).

Briteinu does not attempt to comment on each and every word and verse. It is a commentary on each Torah Portion. This is what makes it unique. To be sure, most commentaries on the Torah in the traditional Jewish world do the same thing. However, very few attempts have been made by believers in Yeshua to provide comments according to the traditional *parshiyot*. Briteinu is just such an attempt.

Our Method

In each and every commentary, we attempt to apply faithfully sound exegetical and hermeneutical principles. This means that we endeavour to consistently seek the literal understanding of the biblical text, taking into consideration, of course, the use of symbolism and metaphor, especially in biblical poetry.

In our exposition of the text, we place heavy emphasis on the historical, religious, geographical, and cultural backgrounds of a given text. In addition, whenever possible, we try to comment on important Hebrew (or Greek, as the case may be) words, grammar, or syntax. In this, Briteinu would be classified as an expositional commentary in that it makes an effort to use a careful exegesis of the original language texts. However, the reader should note that Briteinu is not intended primarily for use by biblical scholars. It is intended to help ordinary people to understand the text — through the eyes of the scholars. Indeed, we read the scholars to produce these commentaries and sifted through their technical work to bring the best of their efforts to the everyday student.

The student will notice throughout that, for the most part, we make little use of the allegorical method of interpretation as well as the traditional Jewish interpretative method of using gematria (the use of the numerical value of the Hebrew letters for determining meanings of the text). While we cannot say that these methods should never be used, nonetheless, we are quite guarded in our practice of them and do not encourage other students of the Bible to utilize them in their interpretation of the Scriptures. Furthermore, we do not recognize the use of the Jewish hermeneutical method known as PARDES (a method developed sometime in the 13"century after Yeshua) as a valid way to interpret the sacred Scriptures. Gematria is just a part of that hermeneutical method.

The Torah is read publicly in the synagogue on Mondays, Thursdays, and Shabbat. (It is, of course, read and studied at other times during the week by countless individuals, either individually or in a group setting.) Since ancient times, at least from the late second Temple Period, the Jewish sages have chosen sections from the biblical prophets which they see as corresponding in some way with the weekly Torah reading. These sections are then read publicly following the Torah reading. After a while these readings from the prophets have become standardized into the reading schedule we have today. These prophetic readings are called the haftara (הפטרה), a word that means, "finish," "ending," "taking leave," or "parting".

Thus, they more or less serve as the conclusion of the Torah reading portion of the synagogue service. Despite the similarity in pronunciation, "haftara" does not mean "Half-Torah", as many non-Hebrew readers might think! The haftara relates either to the theme of the Torah reading or to the observances of the day.'

The reader might remember Luke 4 where Yeshua is participating in his hometown synagogue service on Shabbat. During the service, Yeshua was called up to read the haftara, which in that particular week seemed to have been from Isaiah 61. Luke does not speak of other parts of the service. He did not need to because most of his readers would have understood that the rest of the ritual, as well as the Torah reading, would have taken place. This is one of the earliest historical indications of the existence of a haftara.

Our "Friends"

Briteinu makes frequent references to commentators and other biblical scholars. These exegetes are our scholarly "friends" that we consult to help us to understand the text better. There are two types of commentators that we have used in our studies. First, there are Jewish commentators. We want the student to understand that we (as believers in Yeshua) do not submit ourselves to rabbinic authority. Therefore, just because a respected rabbi comments on a text of the Torah, does not mean that this comment is to be accepted without criticism. Having said that, however, we must also recognize that Jewish scholars have been studying the Torah ever since it was first revealed on Mount Sinai! Hence, sometimes they have much to offer.

We tend to refer to a certain group of Jewish commentators frequently. Our favorite Jewish commentary series is the *Jewish Publication Society Torah Commentary* ("JPS"). In our opinion, this is by far the most scholarly of Jewish commentaries and it tends to keep allegorizing and gematria to a minimum, seeking to emphasize the historical and linguistic background of the text.

Close behind the JPS series are the time-honored studies of Israeli commentator Nechama Leibowitz. This late professor of Bible at Tel Aviv University has been the Bible teachers' teacher for countless Israelis, especially for Israeli public school Bible teachers. Professor Leibowitz shows a mastery of the knowledge of classical Jewish texts in her endeavor to bring out the most literal meaning of the biblical text.

We also enjoy reading and using the various Chumashim, bound texts of the Torah with commentaries. Our favorite is that of the former Chief Rabbi of England, J. H. Hertz. Our least favorite is the ArtScroll Chumash, because of its practice of the wide use of allegory, gematria and PARDES. The classical commentator, Rashi (Rabbi Shlomo ben Isaac), also finds himself quoted from time to time in Briteinu.

In addition to Jewish commentators, evangelical commentators are, naturally, very helpful. However, there is a great limitation here. Sometimes evangelical commentators do not attempt to adequately apply many instructions of the Torah to our lives today since, according to many evangelicals, either Yeshua or Paul (or both!) put an end to the Torah. We do not accept that understanding. It is important for the reader to know that we accept each book of the Torah (Genesis – Deuteronomy) as divinely inspired – from the very mouth of God – as much as the rest of the Scriptures, from Genesis to Revelation. Moreover, we accept since the Torah is from God's mouth, then it cannot be done away with, replaced, or held to be in contradiction with any other part of the Word of God. For more information about our viewpoint concerning the nature of the Torah, please consult our work entitled *Torah Rediscovered* (see Bibliography).

However, despite that unfortunate theological reality among many evangelical scholars, there are, nonetheless, some very helpful works from which we have drawn excellent insights. Among such works are those by Gordon Wenham, Walter Kaiser, the *Expositor's Bible Commentary*, Francis Schaeffer on *Genesis, The Tyndale Commentary on the Old Testament* series, and James M. Boice (our former mentor in biblical training).

We will provide a complete bibliography of all of the works that we have used to make this commentary.

Our Prayer

This is just one commentary. There are countless others on the first five books of the Bible. Humans are not perfect. Therefore, we trust that the careful student will apply this adage to this commentary as he/she does to all commentaries on the Scriptures: take what is accurate and leave the rest. Moreover, since human understanding is imperfect, there will be some passages where it is possible to see things differently and remain faithful to the text. When this happens, we encourage the students to practice graciousness and respect to those who differ, as we have done the same ourselves to those who derive different conclusions than we have from the text.

The text upon which we are commenting is sacred text — it is God's Word. It (the Torah, not this commentary!) is divinely inspired by means of the Spirit of God. We pray that all who read this commentary will be brought closer to Him, the Living Torah, the One of whom the prophets speak, Yeshua the Messiah, as we attempt to elucidate the sacred text.

In Messiah's Grace,

Ariel Berkowitz

Israel 2025

Abbreviations and Translations

The following abbreviations are consistently used throughout these commentaries:

BAR   Biblical Archaeology Review

BDAG   A Greek-English Lexicon of the New Testament and other Early Christian Literature, Third Edition.

BDB   Francis Brown, S. R. Driver, and Charles A. Briggs. Gesenius Hebrew and English Lexicon. (Sometimes we have used the electronic version of this work published in Accordance by OakTree Bible Software.)

BH   Biblia Hebraica Stuttgartensia

HALOT   Ludwig Koehler and Walter Baumgartner. The Hebrew and Aramaic Lexicon of the Old Testament. (Sometimes we have used the electronic version of this work published in Accordance by OakTree Bible Software.)

ISBE   The International Standard Bible Encyclopedia

JPS   Jewish Publication Society Tanakh

NASB   New American Standard Bible

NIV   New International Version

NKJV   New King James Version

Translations

When we have quoted the Bible in these commentaries we have usually quoted from the NASB. There are times we quote from other versions of the Bible and when this is done, we acknowledge which version. However, quite often we simply offer our own translation of a text, both from the Hebrew or Greek.

No matter which Bible translation we employ, we have consistently changed certain key words that reflect a greater accuracy of the Hebrew. Such words include:

Moses Changed to Moshe

Jesus Changed to Yeshua

Christ Changed to Messiah

Church Changed to Congregation or Fellowship

Law Changed to Torah (when law is used in reference to the Scriptures)

As indicated in the text of the commentaries, we tend to interchange the names Paul and Saul of Tarsus (but not always). This is to help people to remember that he was born with at least two names, a Greek and a Hebrew name — his name did not change to Paul after he became a believer in Yeshua! All of these translation peculiarities are in the spirit of attempting to retain the Hebraic character of these commentaries.

Definitions

Throughout Briteinu, we have been careful to clarify the meaning of certain important words. These words are relatively common biblical terms, but just as commonly misunderstood. Homing in on their meaning truly does make a difference in our perception of God and His Word.

> *O Lord, the great and awesome God,*
> *who guards His covenant and loving kindness*
> *for the ones who love Him and protect His commandments.*
> *Daniel 9:4 (author's translation).*

Covenant

We are defining the word "covenant" as a legally/contractually binding relationship between two or more people, which is characterized by the giving and receiving of promises. Central to this definition of covenant is the idea of a personal relationship. *Briteinu* means "our covenant." This title for these commentaries communicates the reality that there is a personal relationship between God and His people. This relationship is governed by several covenants that God initiated with His people. After God made a covenant with Noah for all mankind, He also established a covenant of unconditional promises that He gave to Abraham and a chosen people.

These were a people chosen by The Holy One to receive His Own Word and who were called to guard that Word and to live that Word so that that Word could be shared with all the families of the earth. It is this Word that will guard humanity as The Creator created that humanity to be and to live. His Covenant was given to define good and healthy human relationships as He created them to be, and provide the protective guards for these relationships against the many forms of violation that can happen between man and his fellow man. In making a covenant with His chosen ones, God established a personal relationship between Himself, The Creator, and those who will live as they are created to live.

On Mount Sinai, God made another covenant, which instructs His chosen people how to enjoy and bear fruit within those promises made to Abraham and his descendants. That, we know as the Covenant of Mount Sinai, the Covenant with Moshe, or the Covenant of Torah. The first five books of the Bible are the contents of that covenant. This commentary seeks to explain and elucidate the contents and concepts found in these precious and divinely inspired Scriptures.

Obey / Obedience

There is no Hebrew word that corresponds directly with our English concept of "obey" or "obedience" When we see this term in most English translations, it is the rendering of the Hebrew words associated with "to hear" (shema, שמע). It is similar to the Greek word hupakuo, υπακουω, which literally means "under hearing,' yet it is almost always translated as "obey."

As often as the context permits, we have tried to render this word as "to hear,' rather than "to obey'. The reason is, first of all, "hear" is what both the Hebrew and Greek terms mean, Our Creator is always conveying the concept that we, His creation, are to be in the place of hearing. God speaks to us in His Word. Throughout His Word, He says to us: Shem'a! Hear My voice. Hear My words of life, that are your life. And in doing My words you will live the life I designed for you to live. When humanity lives as humanity is created to live, life brings forth life. This is truly living!

> Deuteronomy 30:19 says, "This day I call heaven and earth as witnesses against you that I have set before you life and death, blessings and covenant difficulties. Now choose life, so that you and your children may live" (author's translation).

Be in the place of hearing. Choose life that you and your children may live as I have created you to live. Life that is life! As our Creator He will always tell us the Truth. Let us learn to be in the place of hearing. This is very different from the religious concepts of obedience. The concepts of obedience that people grow up with do not communicate accurately the relationship that God has with His people. When He gave us His instructions for life in His Word, He said, "These are not just empty words for you, they are your life" (Deuteronomy 32:47).

In short, we understand Him to be saying, "Do you hear Me?" "Are you listening to Me?" Thus, when "obey" or "obedience" would normally appear in most English translations, we have chosen to render the Hebrew and the Greek as "hearing" or "listening to."

Soul (nefesh, נפש)

This is usually rendered "soul" in most translations. Yet, the translation "soul" truly limits the full scope of the term. We have translated nefesh as "our entire being,' everything that makes us, us. According to historical evidence, the concept of soul did not exist in Hebrew before the Hellenistic period, having been brought into the biblical world through the Greeks. Nefesh, נפש, means a living being as a whole living being. When God created man, he called us nephesh chayyah, נפש היה. Nephesh chayyah is a living being that is living as it is created to live!

Spiritual (pneumatikos, πνευματικο)

This word, associated with the Greek term, pneuma (πνευμα) is the Greek equivalent of the Hebrew ruach (רוח), which in Hebrew means "wind, "breath" or "spirit". It has been used to refer to the divine Holy Spirit ruach hakodesh (רוח הקודש), as well as the human spirit. As the human spirit, it has to do with the breath of man. In the context of passages where the breath of man occurs, the term refers to the way that person is living. At any one time, a child of God can be walking within his life here on earth from their reality as seated in the heavenlies, or they can be living in a manner that does not reflect their true heavenly realities. For every moment in time, we choose to make our heavenly reality visible, or not.

The word ruach can mean wind. Wind is invisible, yet we see the results of the reality of the wind in that which is visible. John 3:8 says, "The wind [pneuma, πνευμα] blows wherever it pleases. You hear its sound, but you cannot tell where it comes from or where it is going. So it is with everyone born of the Spirit [pneuma, πνευμα)."

The Creator created that which He created to be both visible and invisible. Because of this reality of God's Creation, we are choosing to have our translations accurately reflect the biblical reality of the visible and the invisible realms of God's Creation. That which God has created need not be separated in our minds as being merely physical and not spiritual. Therefore, we prefer to translate the Hebrew and Greek words that are normally translated into English as "physical" and "spiritual" as "visible" and "invisible" to more accurately reflect God's Word.

Acknowledgments

As the author of these commentaries, I would like to express my deep gratitude to those who encouraged the production of Briteinu. There have been several people in different parts of the world that the Holy One has led into my life that have done their best to help in the many steps it takes to bring such a commentary to publication.

In the Netherlands

A depth of gratitude goes to Mario Koester, in Nijverdal, Netherlands, for his vision and profound dedication to produce Briteinu. Years of work were lost in a series of unfortunate events when the electronic copy of the entire set of Briteinu was lost. We had only a printed copy of all five volumes. Mario invested countless hours into making electronic copies of all of the commentaries so that we could then proceed to the next phase of production. The number of hours he invested into making this possible was astounding. But for his vision this commentary would not be available for the precious many worldwide who deeply desire to learn and to be careful students of the Bible. D'vorah and I look back with wonder at how this dear friend took up the vision of what could be. We are also deeply grateful to Ton and Lineke Krijnen of Veenendaal, the original Torah Resources International board members in the Netherlands, for their delightful friendship, vision, and assistance in distributing Briteinu in Europe.

In the United States

Much gratitude goes to Jackie Garamella, in Minnesota, for her vision and enthusiasm to see Briteinu ready for print. Once the reconstructed electronic copy was ready for layout, it was Jackie who arranged the layout and the first printing. Her many patient hours of working with the printer and the investment that it was to get the commentary into print is also forever a wonder in our hearts. Special thanks to Nissim and Hadassah Lerner (now residing in Israel) and David Erber in Michigan, as well as the rest of the staff of Shoreshim Publishing for publication and distribution of these works in most of the English-speaking world.

In the United Kingdom

We have deep appreciation for the tireless work of Jan Styles of Woking, for her willingness to be a main editor for all of these commentaries. She has spent many days working on each page to help keep grammar, spelling, and non-comprehensible statements to a minimum. Thanks also to Peter Badger, also of Woking, for volunteering his input to this editing process. I must also mention the helpful input of our first Briteinu Study Groups in the Woking, UK area for their immeasurable suggestions and help. Let us not forget Pennie Cranham who has been in charge of the printing of Briteinu, and Sally Cranham (mother and daughter!) for helping to distribute Briteinu in the UK and beyond.

In Israel

This writer has used the expertise and scholarly advice of two linguistic scholars, Dr. Eldan Clem and Dr. David Friedman. Because of the volume of material being covered, it is not always possible to do the extra steps of checking for linguistic mistakes. Hence, sometimes things are overlooked. We are continually in the process of checking and re-checking for such mistakes. Any mistakes are solely the responsibility of this author, who is deeply grateful to those two aforementioned scholars, brothers, and colleagues who have tried to help to keep such mistakes to a minimum! This author hopes that as this study tool is used, the students will also gain a healthy exposure to the process of being careful students of the Word of God.

Words cannot express the gratitude we have toward Karen Berger, our "right hand woman" for Torah Resources International materials' editing and layout. She has spent countless hours learning book layout, as well as scanning the pages upon pages of words with a fine-toothed comb to bring a multitude of necessary corrections in many different areas to our attention. She has also contributed her share of some of the careful wording of texts and explanations. Thank you.

My Family

Most of my gratefulness goes to my family: my wife, D'vorah and our four (now grown) children: Beth, Rachel, Rivkah, and Yoel. Briteinu was originally written over the span of 13 years taking many hours of study, research, and writing. The years of support from my family reflects their belief in the importance of creating this study tool and their commitment to helping others know God's Word more accurately.

As a family, we are thankful that this investment of our lives is bringing many expressions of delight from Bible students from around the world. We receive many stories expressing the blessing and help that Briteinu has been in their study of the Scriptures. Without the sacrifice of my entire family, this commentary would not have been accomplished.

Before Reading the Torah

As we begin a study, we quote the traditional Jewish blessings one recites before one reads the Torah portions. May the Holy One of Israel be blessed for giving us His Word.

Blessed are You, O Lord our God, the King of the universe, who has chosen us from all peoples, and has given us His Torah. Blessed are You O Lord, the Giver of the Torah.

Barukh Atah Adonai Eloheinu, Melekh ha'olam, asher bachar banu mikol ha'amim, v'natan lanu et torato. Barukh Atah Adonai, notein haTorah. Amen.

ברוך אתה יהוה אלוהינו מלך העולם אשר בחר בנו מכל העמים
ונתן לנו את תורתו. ברוך אתה יהוה נותן התורה. אמן.

May the Holy One of Israel bless all who seek to delve deeper into the sweet honey of His Torah and may God's Words, the words of our covenant that He made with us, be to all who study them, words of our freedom and words of our song. We trust that this commentary will providemany hours of enlightenment and joy as we use it to study the Scriptures.

Psalms 119:18

גל-עיני ואביטה נפלאות מתורתך

Gal 'einei v'abbitah nifla'ot mitoratekhah

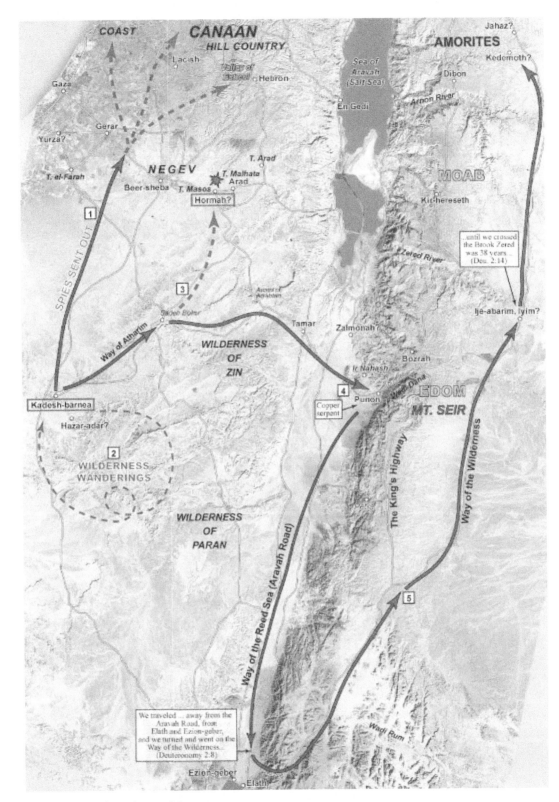

Map 1: Israel in the Wilderness

Parashat Bamidbar במדבר

Torah: Numbers 1:1–4:20
Haftarah: Hosea 2:1–22

Parashat Bamidbar במדבר

> The Torah was given to the accompaniment of three things: fire, water, and wilderness. Why was the giving of the Torah marked by these three features? To indicate that as these are free to all mankind, so also are the words of Torah free. (Bamidbar Rabbah 1.7)

Many are the words of the Torah, and many are the places in which they have been given. When God first spoke to the children of Israel He spoke through Moshe while they were still slaves in Egypt. He next spoke to them after the Exodus at Mount Sinai. This is where the teachings in the second half of Exodus and all of Leviticus originated. Now in Numbers or Bamidbar (in the wilderness), God again spoke to Israel. Only this time it was from within the Tent of Meeting. From here periodically, God would give more revelation as Israel travelled.

Once again, because this is the first parasha in this, the fourth book of Moshe, the name of the Torah portion is also the Hebrew name for the book. Consequently, in this particular commentary we will refer to the name of the book as "Numbers", and the name of the parasha as "Bamidbar".

The book of Numbers is the record of the revelation from God in the wilderness of Sinai up to the border of the Promised Land, on the plains of Moab. Numbers is a combination of history and legislation. Its legislation pertains to the sanctuary, the camp, and purification in life. It also includes many well known teachings such as the Nazarite vow, the wearing of fringes, the Aaronic Benediction, the ashes of the red heifer, and more. Its history tells the story of how the new nation of freed slaves found themselves wandering in the desert for forty years before they were permitted to enter Canaan. "But Numbers is no mere chronicle of the outstanding events during the journey in the wilderness. It interprets these events and shows forth the faithful watchfulness of God in every distress and danger, as well as the stern severity of the divine judgments against rebellion and apostasy."[1]

Numbers is quite an easy book to think through. One of the most common ways to outline it is to divide it according to the location of Israel during their wanderings. We therefore offer you this outline given by Dr. Gordon Wenham:[2]

I. Preparations to Enter the Promised Land 1:1–10:10
II. From Sinai to Kadesh 10:11–12:16
III. Forty Years near Kadesh 13:1–19
IV. From Kadesh to the Plains of Moab 20:1–22:1
V. Israel in the Plains of Moab 22:2–36:13

Our study this week will centre on the three numberings found in this parasha. Moshe counts all males twenty-years-old and over in chapter 1. Then, in chapters 3 and 4, the Levites are counted. Finally, in chapter 4 Moshe counts the firstborn males of the children of Israel.

---

1. J. H. Hertz, *Pentateuch and Haftarahs*, 567.
2. Gordon Wenham, *Numbers* (TOTC), 54.

Let us examine these numberings and the events surrounding them according to the following outline:

I.   Count # 1 — Israelite Males
II.   Count # 2 — Levites
III. Count # 3 — The Firstborn

I. COUNT # 1 — ISRAELITE MALES

The English title for Bamidbar is "Numbers". This title is derived from the title in the Septuagint translation. Undoubtedly it stems from the fact that in the first four chapters there are three censuses taken by Moshe. The Hebrew title, *Bamidbar*, means "in the wilderness". This describes the location in which the counting took place — in the desert/wilderness of Sinai.

A. Reasons for the Numberings

The first counting mentioned in chapters 1 and 2 concerns itself with finding out how many males twenty years old (or older) there were. Why did God have Moshe do this? There are several possibilities.

1. The Army

One of the most common suggestions is that God was preparing an army. Rashbam (Rashi's grandson) offers this explanation: "Take the number of all the congregation. This was on account of the fact that they had to enter Eretz Israel and those from twenty years and upwards were eligible to go forth in the army into battle."[3]

Further evidence for adopting this interpretation is derived from 1:49. Here Moshe is instructed by the Lord not to number the Levites in this particular census. We need to remember that it was their job to maintain and minister in the Mishkan — even during battle. Furthermore, chapter 2 is full of instructions about setting up a formal camp, complete with marching formations and banners. This gives the impression that a military unit is in view here. Elie Munk agrees. He states, "There is an almost military aspect to the early chapters of the book of Numbers: units are formed, leaders are appointed, marching orders are given, and instructions for encampment are issued."[4]

It is also important to see that forming Israel into an organized unit changed their appearance from that of a band of runaway slaves to a cohesive unit functioning together to serve the Lord. If the reason was primarily for military purposes, this would serve to communicate an ominous message to Israel's enemies. The message would tell them that this is no haphazard, nomadic horde. This is a formidable, disciplined fighting machine.

---

3.   Nechama Leibowitz, *New Studies in Bamidbar*, 11.
4.   Elie Munk, *The Call of the Torah: Bamidbar,* 3.

2. The Miracle of Existence

Not contradicting the first suggestion but adding to it, is another interpretation given by Nachmanides (Ramban). He suggests that the taking of the census served to demonstrate what a miracle God had performed in order to fulfil His promises to Israel.

Here were the children of Israel, only one year after their redemption from slavery in Egypt. One might have expected that because of the intense rigors of harsh servitude to the Egyptians and 400 years of exile that the children of Jacob would have emerged beaten, stricken with disease and fatigue, and dwindled in number. Instead, they were a strong, two to three million member nation. The taking of the census helped to bring to the forefront the fact that "in spite of decimation through suffering and persecution we have increased and multiplied."[5] Hence, by using numbers and figures, the Holy One was demonstrating the miracle of Israel's survival.

3. Not Just a Cog

We can learn something else from the first census in Bamidbar, which complements what has already been said. Notice that Bamidbar does not just give us sum totals such as, "and the children of Israel numbered. . . "On the contrary; the totals are very specific. For example, 1:5 tells us whom specifically were the ones chosen to help Moshe count, and then 1:20 tells us, "From the descendants of Reuben the firstborn of Israel: All the men twenty years old or more who were able to serve in the army were listed by name, one by one, according to the records of their clans and families."

The same type of wording is used for each tribe throughout the chapter. Each one was counted by head. This gives significance to each individual member of the family and the community. The census had the effect of, "impressing on us the value and sterling worth of each and every soul which is a unique specimen of divine creativity and a world of its own."[6] Therefore, by having this first census taken, the Holy One was stressing the infinite worth of each and every member of the community of Israel. The full impact of this last interpretation is somewhat lost when we remember that according to the text, only males of a certain age were counted. Nonetheless, the principle certainly holds true.

4. The Organization

One further reason for numbering the children of Israel was to facilitate the order of the camp configuration. It helped to have a relatively equal number of people on each of the four sides of the Israelite camp.

Chapter 2 describes what the camp arrangement looked like. It bore all the semblance of order and unity. Not only was their organization for the encampment, but it also functioned as a formation for moving: "They will set out in the same order as they encamp, each in his own place under his standard" (2:17). It was important for God's army to be ordered and disciplined.

---

5.   Leibowitz, *New Studies in Bamidbar,* 15.
6.   *Ibid.,* 14.

Hertz reminds us, "Israel — God's army — however great in number, is nothing, unless order and discipline reign in the midst thereof. 'Order is heaven's first law'."[7]

The order of the Israelite camp was that of a big square. Three tribes lived horizontally next to each other on each side of the square. The tribe in the middle of each three-tribe group was the leader tribe and carried the flag common to the three tribes. Thus, there were twelve tribes (counting Manasseh and Ephraim, the sons of Joseph, separately) on the outer edge of this square. On the inner layer of the square were the sons of Levi: the Merarites on the north, the Gershonites on the west, the Kohathites on the south, and the sons of Aaron on the east. The most important part of this encampment was right in the middle — the Mishkan with the Shekinah. Hence, the Shekinah was guarded first by the Levites, then by the rest of the sons of Jacob.

One of the most beautiful sights of this camp was the five main flags and banners, or *deglim* (דגלים). Each one stood for a group of three who were encamped together and the fifth was for the Levites. Then each tribe had its own smaller banner or sign, **ote** (אות). This banner was actually a sign or symbol of the particular tribe.

The *Midrash Rabbah*[8] tells us what each sign may have looked like. We use the word "may". However, the *Midrash Rabbah* is far more definitive. We are told that each tribal flag was coloured according to the stone which represented them on Aaron's Breast Piece, and had their own tribal insignia which was determined from some aspect of Jacob's prophecy for them, embroidered in the centre of the flag. According to the War Scroll of the Dead Sea Scrolls, "each unit of three tribes down to the smallest unit — whether a myriad, thousand, hundred, fifty, or ten — had its own standard."[9] Here is the description according to *Midrash Rabbah*:

1. **Judah**   A Lion on a sky-blue
2. **Reuben**   Mandrakes (a certain flower) on red
3. **Simeon**   The town of Shechem embroidered on green
4. **Levi**   Urim and Thummim embroidered on one-third black, one-third red, and one-third white
5. **Issachar**   The sun and moon on black
6. **Zebulun**   A ship on white
7. **Dan**   A snake on sapphire
8. **Gad**   A camp of soldiers on grey
9. **Manasseh**   An ox on jet black
10. **Ephraim**   A bull on jet black

7.   Hertz, *Pentateuch and Haftarahs,* 573.
8.   Bamidbar Rabbah 2.7
9.   Jacob Milgrom, *The JPS Torah Commentary: Numbers*, 11.

11. **Naphtali**   A doe on pale red
12. **Asher**   An olive tree on the colour of the "precious stone with which women adorn themselves"
13. **Benjamin** A wolf on a multi-coloured flag

The student can easily notice that the *Midrash Rabbah* does not assign a flag to the tribe of Levi. At the same time, both the sons of Joseph, Ephraim and Manasseh have their own flags. This would appear that there were thirteen tribes instead of twelve. However, it was always understood that Ephraim and Manasseh were "the tribe" of Joseph. Moreover, the Levites, represented by the three sons of Levi: Gershom, Kohat and Merari had a unique place and role among the sons of Jacob.

The midrash also continues to explain that the reason for the particular order in which the tribes were placed around the Mishkan was because, "They already have a traditional order from Jacob their father: in the same way that they disposed themselves round his bier when they carried him, so shall they dispose themselves round the Tabernacle."[10] Rashi confirms this. In fact, he tells us that it was Jacob himself who arranged the set order and assigned the family or tribal insignias.[11]

B. The Camp of the Shekinah

The most important thing about the Israelite encampment was what was in the middle — the Shekinah.

It is interesting that the Talmud mentions the existence of three encampments.[12] Dr. Epstein, editor of the Soncino edition of the English *Talmud*, tells us that the outer camp was called the camp of the Israelites, the middle one was the camp of the Levites, and the innermost one was called the camp of the Presence, or Shekinah.[13] From this we get the impression that this was not really Israel's camp. It was really God's camp! The two camps that surrounded it were guarding His Presence.

We have, therefore, a new picture or metaphor forming from these verses. Up to this point, we have been emphasizing the metaphor of a husband and wife to describe the relationship between God and His people. Now the picture changes to that of an army. Israel is the army of the Lord! God is the Commander-in-Chief who speaks from the midst of His "command post", the Tent of Meeting. To take the Promised Land there had to be war, but Israel was not able to fight this war on her own. The Divine Presence dwelt in their midst to give commands, directions and encouragement to His hosts, the people of Israel.

One more critical point needs to be made here. The war Israel was to fight was not just a physical one where people would die, and blood be shed. On the contrary, it was primarily an

10. Bamidbar Rabbah 2.8
11. Rashi: *Bamidbar*, ArtScroll Edition, 10.
12. B Sanhedrin 42b
13. Epstein, *Babylonian Talmud*, Soncino Edition, "Sanhedrin", 275.

invisible battle. Israel was commissioned by God to make Him known throughout the earth. He gave them a piece of property in which to carry out these "operations". However, there were strong unseen forces set in opposition to Israel — the gods (demons?) of the Canaanites. Therefore, the God of this universe, the Lord of Hosts ("Armies") decided to pitch His tent in the midst of Israel and direct the battle Himself. Israel needed Him to war against the powers and principalities, which were the unseen realities that the physical idols represented. Hence, having the Mishkan set in the midst of the camp of Israel was like the Commander-in-Chief dwelling right at the heart of the army.

Things have changed very little since the Israelites went against the gods of the Canaanites. Believers everywhere are commanded to, "Put on the full armour of God... for our struggle is not against flesh and blood, but against the rulers, against the authorities, against the powers of this dark world and against the spiritual forces of evil in the heavenly realms (Ephesians 6:11-12)".

Moreover, just as ancient Israel needed to have the "Camp of the Shekinah" among them, so also do we. The Divine Presence should always be in the midst of the children of Israel."[14] How can the Divine Presence rest in our midst today? We find the answer to this question in the rest of the passage in Ephesians. When we as individuals and as a community of believers, continually wear the armour that God gave us, we are allowing His Presence to dwell through us. This armour includes: the belt of truth, the breastplate of righteousness, the sandals of preparation from having the good news of Yeshua, the shield of faith, the helmet of salvation, and the sword of the Spirit which is the Word of God. Having on this kind of armour we can rest assured that the Presence of God will be with us in each and every battle into which He leads us.

II. COUNT # 2 — LEVITES

This parasha speaks of a second numbering in this parasha — the counting of the Levites. In fact, the Levites were numbered twice. The first is mentioned in 3:14f, the second in chapter 4. Why were the Levites thus counted?

A. A Levite Job Description

It appears that one reason for counting the Levites may have been to organize them for their work. In 3:7–8 we are given a three-fold job description for the Levites. This is based on the use of two Hebrew verbs in verses 7–8.

1. Guard Duty

In 3:7, the Levites are instructed to serve guard duty over the Mishkan while the nation was encamped. The Hebrew verb used here is an idiom **shamru mishmeret** (שמרו משמרת) which

---

14. Hertz, *Pentateuch and Haftarahs*, 573.

usually means "guard duty".[15] This idiom tells us that the Levites were to give themselves to the priests (the sons of Kohat) to help them guard the tent of meeting so that no one who was unauthorized or in a *tam'ei* condition could enter.

2. There's Work and Then There's Work!

The second verb in 3:7 describes the second part of the job of the Levites. It is associated with the verb, *'avad* (עבד). This word is used most of the time to refer to physical work.[16] The emphasis here would therefore be on the physical labour that the Levites had to do in assisting the kohanim (priests) in the ritual services.

3. On the Move

The final part of the job description of the Levites is delineated in 3:8. Again, the word "to guard" is used, but this time it is employed with reference to keeping watch and caring for the Mishkan and its implements when Israel was on the march. We know this because the only time the Levites would have been exposed to the Mishkan implements would have been during transportation. Otherwise, the *kohanim* (the priests, descendants of Kohat, a son of Levi) would have guarded them because they were inside the Tent of Meeting, where only the kohanim were permitted to go. This brings us to the question, why count the Levites? We know if at least two possible answers.

The counting appears to be because it was easier to divide the Levites into "watches" or work shifts. There was much work to be done and plenty of people to do it. However it all needed to be coordinated and organized, otherwise it would have been chaos! According to Munk, Moses divided the Levites and the kohanim into eight groups of families, called "watches", each to "perform the Temple service for a week. The cycle of eight watches would repeat every eight weeks. Later, the prophet Samuel and King David changed the arrangement, dividing the responsibility for the service into twenty-four watches."[17]

B. When was Yeshua incarnated?

This detail becomes rather significant to believers in Yeshua. It may provide a key in helping to solve a centuries old riddle and problem, which in this day and age is turning into a cause of grave disunity in the body of believers. The issue is when was Yeshua incarnated? Was it in December? Sukkot? Pesach? When?

We are about to take you down a path of controversy that involves examining some complicated data. The results could be rather fascinating, but do not get too excited; the end of the path is still quite inconclusive! As we take you along this road, be careful! Pitfalls abound, among which is basing conclusions on shaky assumptions. In other words, please do not jump to hasty conclusions. Take time to carefully sift through all the data. When finished and a

---

15. Timothy R. Ashley, *The Book of Numbers* (NICOT), 78.
16. *Ibid.*
17. Munk, *The Call, of the Torah: Bamidbar.*, 19–20.

conclusion is reached, please do not be dogmatic! There are so many unknowns and variables in this process. We need to stay away from hasty dogmatism. Nevertheless, having said all that, here are several pieces of information we are able to piece together which may help us in the impossible task of figuring out when Messiah was incarnated.

1. Fact

Luke 1:5 tells us that Zechariah, John the Baptist's father, was a Levite who belonged to the course ("watch") of Abijah. Luke 1:8 tells us that he was on duty when an angel of the Lord gave him the announcement that he would have a son. 1:23–24 say that his wife became pregnant after he finished serving his watch.

2. Fact

1 Chronicles 24:7 and 10 inform us that the first of the 24 watches was that of Jehoiarib, and the eighth watch was that of Abijah.

3. Fact

The Talmud, B. Taanit 29a, tells us that in the year 70 ce, the year that the Temple was destroyed by the Romans, the first watch (Jehoiarib) was on duty on the 9th Av (July/August).

4. Variable

Alfred Edersheim places this date at 5 August in 70 CE.[18] (This is the first uncertainty!)

5. Variable

From here on our travel to truth gets really uncertain. Edersheim calculates that from this point we can guess that Zechariah was serving from the 2nd to the 9th of October the year before the birth of Messiah.

6. Fact

Counting six months from October to the birth announcement of Yeshua (Luke 1:26 and 36), then nine months to the birth of Yeshua, we come up with when He was incarnated.

7. Uncertainty

Edersheim, based on all of the above reasoning, comes up with a time somewhere in late December for the birth of Yeshua. Thus, Edersheim bases much of his conclusion on some technical and historical calculations. The student needs to read his reasoning found in *Life and Times of Yeshua the Messiah* (Edersheim's one volume, 1976 edition), in his Appendix entitled "On the Date and Nativity of Our Lord".

Does this mean that we consider Edersheim's conclusion correct? We really do not know. However, we *do* know that the methodology he used to reach that conclusion appears to be sound, and it encourages us to learn how to do such research in order to discover other biblical truths.

---

18. Alfred Edersheim, *The Life and Times of Yeshua The Messiah,* Book I, 705.

Is there disappointment with the findings? There does not need to be. This conclusion is that of only one scholar (Alfred Edersheim). Many would like to have seen him conclude that Sukkot (September/October) was the time of Yeshua's incarnation — and indeed, it might just be! The last word is certainly not in yet. What is important is that Edersheim used a reasonably sound method to ascertain his conclusion — he sought out Hebraic, biblical and historical backgrounds. In our opinion, that is the correct road upon which to walk when we pursue answers to such biblical problems. It is important to remember that, in the end it really does not matter whether or not we can know for certain when Yeshua was born. The important thing is that He **was** born!

However, this exercise has served at least two purposes. One was to show how a little detail such as the numbering of the Levites in Bamidbar could contribute to a very significant biblical debate. Another purpose was to show how difficult it is to be really dogmatic on such an issue as the date of the birth of Yeshua, because there are so many historical factors to consider with so many variables along the way. However, sometimes this kind of research is necessary to be honest with the biblical data. In other words, biblical research is more difficult than many may realize. It is not for the untrained novice! Neither is it for those who desire to be dogmatic and insistent on their findings, as if they have discovered the final answer, which has eluded scores of qualified scholars.

C. The Substitutes

We believe the text strongly hints at another reason for the counting of the Levites. The numbering of the Levites falls into a context which contains two statements from the Lord concerning the firstborn. For example, 3:12 (c.f. 3:40) says, "Behold! I have taken the Levites from among the Israelites, in place of the first male offspring…." We will comment further on the concept of the firstborn son. The reason to mention it now, however, is to show that in order for the firstborn to be properly offered to the Lord, the number of Levites had to be known. Therefore, we read, "Take the Levites for me in place of all the firstborn of the Israelites, and the livestock of the Levites in place of all the firstborn of the livestock of the Israelites. I am the Lord" (3:41). Hence, it was necessary to know how many Levites there were in order to coordinate it with the counting of the firstborn.

One more note in this regard. We are told in 3:15, that the Levites were to be numbered from the age of one month upwards. This also corresponds to the criteria for numbering the firstborn. "The Levites were numbered in this manner because they were substitutes for the firstborn, who by Divine command, were to be redeemed 'from a month old'."[19]

---

19. Hertz, *Pentateuch and Haftarahs*, 575–576.

III. COUNT # 3 — THE FIRSTBORN

The third and final counting in this parasha is the counting of the firstborn males and animals among Israel. The regulations for the counting are discussed in 3:40. Essentially, every firstborn male in Israel, one month old and up was to be counted. For every such firstborn there was to be one Levite to replace him. The results of the actual counting revealed that there was an excess of 273 firstborn males over the number of Levites. The Torah provided for this by teaching that a redemption price of five shekels for each extra head was required. In order to appreciate the importance of this counting, we need to understand the reason for the setting aside of the firstborn.

A. The Uniqueness of the Firstborn

It is well known that the firstborn male in the Ancient Near East enjoyed unique status in the society. "The eldest son's special position was widely recognized in the Ancient Near East, though it was not usually extended to sons of concubines or slave-girls."[20]

Both the Tanakh and extra-biblical literature from the same approximate time period speak of a "right of the firstborn". In fact, the Hebrew words for both "firstborn" and "right of the firstborn" are from the same word, *bekhor* (בכור).[21] The Torah speaks of Israel as God's firstborn (Exodus 4:22). As such, Israel enjoys this unique position among the nations of the earth, receiving the *bekhor*, or right of the firstborn, from God. That is one reason why God granted to Israel the inheritance of Land. Other special privileges were also endowed to Israel. Paul specifies some of these in Romans 9:4–5 when he says, "Theirs is the adoption as sons, theirs the divine glory, the covenants, the receiving of the Torah, the temple worship, and the promises. Theirs are the patriarchs, and from them is traced the human ancestry of Messiah."

Among the people of Israel however, the Holy One also singled out an even more specific class of firstborn, the firstborn males. These were the ones to whom God had granted the grace of being spared death from the last plague when they were in Egypt. God took the life of every firstborn, even among the animals, except for those who believed Him and showed it by sprinkling the blood of the Pesach Lamb upon their doorposts. To them God granted mercy and life.

Because the Lord granted special firstborn status to Israel and especially to Israel's firstborn males, God then has a special right to them (c.f. Exodus 22:29–30). They belong to Him in a way that others do not. Here in our parasha, God is waiving that right of possession and service by providing the tribe of Levi as a substitute for the firstborn males. Instead of requiring all first born males to enter into full time service in the Mishkan/Temple serving Him, a whole tribe is organized to do the task.

---

20.   J. D. Douglas, organizing editor, *The New Bible Dictionary,* 378.
21.   Brown, Driver, and Briggs, *Hebrew and English Lexicon* ("BDB"), 114.

B.   At Odds with Rashi?

Some commentators such as Rashi, explain the replacement of the Levites for the firstborn on rather shaky biblical evidence. Rashi's argument is: "For originally the service (the priestly functions) was performed by the firstborn, but when they (the Israelites and among them their firstborn) sinned by worshipping the golden calf, they became disqualified, and the Levites who had not worshipped the idol were chosen in their stead."[22]

It is true that the Levites were faithful to the Lord. They demonstrated their faithfulness when Moshe told them to slay the perpetrators of sin. (See Exodus 32:25–29). It is also true that when Moshe asked who was on the side of Lord, only the Levites responded positively. Because of this, we are told that the Levites were "set apart" to the Lord. However, the text does not say that this was to replace the firstborn. It just indicates that they were rewarded for their faithfulness.

Rashi's interpretation has several more problems. For one, according to the text in Exodus, God had chosen Aaron and his sons from the tribe of Levi to be the kohanim **before** the golden calf incident. The second problem is the false premise behind this interpretation; that the choice of people to be kohanim was based on their worthiness. There is no evidence of this. God's choices are always based on His grace and His own criteria and not premised by any supposed merit that people have for the tasks that He gives. In addition, there is little evidence that the firstborn ever served as the priests in the Ancient Near East. If anything, they were the sacrifices! "Some of the early Semitic tribes believed that the firstborn belonged to the deity and had to be offered up sacrificially."[23]

C.   To Make it Smoother

Numbers 3:13, therefore, merely tells us that the Levites were given as substitutes for the firstborn in God's service. It does not offer a reason for the exchange. Keil and Delitzsch offer what seems to be perhaps the most reasonable and biblically sound explanation for this substitution. They state:

> The nation was required to dedicate to Him its firstborn sons for service at the sanctuary, and sacrifice all the firstborn of its cattle to Him. But now the Levites and their cattle were to be adopted in their place, and the firstborn sons of Israel to be released in return. Not only was a more orderly performance of this service secured, than could have been affected through the firstborn of all the tribes, but so far as the whole nation was concerned, the fulfilment of its obligations in relation to this service was undoubtedly facilitated. Moreover, the Levites had proved themselves to be the most suitable of all the tribes for this post.[24]

Although the Levites were to be offered in exchange for the firstborn in service to Lord, this does not diminish the significance and importance of the firstborn in Israel. It is important to understand the whole concept of the "firstborn" in order to help us to appreciate some

---

22.   Rashi, *ArtScroll Edition*, 11.
23.   G. Bromiley, ed. *The International Standard Bible Encyclopaedia*, vol. 2, 308.
24.   F. Delitzsch, F. and C.F. Keil. *Commentary on the Old Testament in Ten Volumes*. volume 1: *The Pentateuch*, 20–21.

significant truths in the Apostolic Scriptures. For one, in conjunction with Numbers 8:15–19, we can now understand the reason why Yeshua was presented before the Lord in the Temple in Luke 2:22–24. Beyond this however, Yeshua is declared to be the firstborn in the new creation, by being raised first from the dead, and is thus, Lord over all His Body (Colossians 1). In other words, Yeshua is God's firstborn. As such He enjoys special leadership status in God's kingdom. There is no one else who is in such a high and honoured position. Therefore, He is declared to be Lord over all His believers, including us.

ADDITIONAL NOTES

Chapter 1

Verse 1
"**tent of Meeting**" — The Tent of Meeting is referred to by several names in the Hebrew. Here in Numbers 1:1, it is called *ohel mo'ed* (אוהל מועד), "tent of meeting". Elsewhere it is called *ohel ha'edut* (אוהל העדות), tent of testimony; *mishkan ha'edut* (משכן העדות), tent of dwelling; or simply *mishkan* (משכן), dwelling.

Verse 1
"**In the desert**" — The Hebrew word translated "desert" in the NASB is *midbar* (מדבר). However, there is a difference between a desert and a wilderness. A wilderness, although quite arid, can still support life, such as providing grazing area for animals. In fact, some even suggest that the very word, "midbar" denotes a pasture land.

Verse 2
"**community**" — The Hebrew word for "community" is *'adah* (עדה).It could also be rendered "assembly" or "congregation". It is of interest to note that the Septuagint renders this word with the Greek equivalent of the English word "synagogue". Hence, the concept of synagogue was born in the Torah, although the modern concept of synagogue is a little different and did not exist back that far in history.

Verse 2
"**take a census**" — The command in 1:2 is in the plural in the Hebrew, indicating that Aaron was also to help Moshe. This phrase in the Hebrew means literally, "lift up the head". In other words, Moshe and Aaron were instructed to simply "count heads".

Verse 3
"**divisions**" — The Hebrew word is *tsava* (צבא) and is also the modern Hebrew word for "army". Sometimes this word is rendered "hosts" but in reality, this clouds the essential meaning of the term, which is "army." The phrase *Adonai Tsevaot* (יהוה צבאות), is often used in the Tanakh to depict the Lord as the God of Israel's army.

For interest's sake, the military conscription age in ancient Sparta was 20, 18 in Athens, and 17 in Rome. Here we are told that it was 20 in ancient Israel. It is 18 in modern Israel.

Verses 5–15

It is interesting to note that none of the names listed in this census is a compound name with part of the tetragrammaton (יהוה) in the end, as was the practice during the period of the monarchy and onward. We also find this phenomenon in Genesis. This would bear testimony to the antiquity of at least both Numbers and Genesis.[25]

Verse 20

"**descendants**" —The Hebrew word is *toledot* (תולדות) and has to do with creating or keeping track of ancestry through recording genealogies. Sometimes it has been translated as "generations". The word can also be used in a broader sense than merely a genealogy, such as in recording a family history. See our comments in the Genesis commentaries. Genealogies were important in other Ancient Near Eastern societies as well in Israel. They were valuable to determine tribal membership and inheritance claims.

Verses 20–47

The order in which the names of the tribes appear in this census reflects the order in which they were encamped.

Verses 44–46

Opinions vary concerning the reality of such a large figure as 603,550 fighting men for Israel. Such a figure (interestingly corresponding with that in Exodus 12:37; 38:26) would make the total population of Israelites approximately 3,000,000. Some people think this is too large. Other suggestions include taking the Hebrew word for "thousand" in this passage *elef* (אלף), to mean "families". However, there already is another more common word for family. "Another suggestion, based on a related Ugaritic term was to re-vocalize the word to read אלוף (*aluf*), "captain". If understood this way, the total Israelite army could be computed at approximately 18,000 soldiers coming from a total [male population] population of about 22,000."[26] We realize that 603,550 is rather large, but why not?

Verse 49

Jacob Milgrom notes,

> The separate mustering of the Levites (chapters 3–4) is illustrated by the Mari documents. One of its censuses is divided into three separate registrations: soldiers, those exempt from military service, and the aged. Since the Levites were exempt from the regular militia, they would have been separately mustered in accord with ancient practice (3:15; 4:2, 22, 39).[27]

---

25. Milgrom, *JPS Numbers*, 6.
26. Harrison, *Numbers*, 32.
27. Milgrom, *JPS Numbers*, 10.

Chapter 2
Verse 2
"**under his standard**" — The Hebrew word for "standard" is *degel* (דגל). It could mean a large flag (modern Hebrew usage), or the flag of the army corps itself. The latter is the meaning attached to the word in the recently discovered Jewish papyri at Elephantine.[28]

Chapter 3
Verse 1
"**this is the account of**" (*tolodot*, תלדות) — Some translations read, "these are the generations of". This is a familiar literary device in the Ancient Near East. It was common in the early chapters of Genesis. A similar use was also found in ancient Babylonian records as well. The phrase points back to the previous material and serves as a literary summary of what was just recorded. Hence, Hertz is off (a very rare occasion!!) in his interpretation of verse one, assigning it to the next body of material.[29] This 3:1 should be 2:35 instead.

Verse 3
The fact that the sons of Aaron were anointed, entitled them to the priesthood and to have authority over the other Levites.[30] According to Numbers 8:16, the Levites were "dedicated" to God, using the Hebrew verb *natan* (נתן), (given), possibly signifying that they were given for service to the Lord. However, the position of the priests is somewhat different. They are pictured as being anointed.

This word (anointed) is from the Hebrew *mashach* (משח). This is the same term from which we get the word "Messiah", or "Anointed One".

In addition the priests are described as being "ordained". Ordained is from a Hebrew idiom that reads literally "fill up their hands". There are various grammatical forms of this idiom. The one that appears in Numbers 3:3 reads *mille yadam* (מלא ידם). The use of hands in this word picture can signify service. Combining that with the term " to fill", can picture the fact that one of the things ordination means is that the one ordained is to be a servant and he will be fully equipped for that service. Perhaps that might be one reason that ordination since ancient times has always been conducted by the laying on of hands.

Another commentator suggests that the Levites were dedicated to the Lord's work, while the priests were sanctified to it. The same commentator says this is demonstrated by the use of the Hebrew root *kadosh* (קדוש) in relationship to the priests. However, we cannot find that distinction in the text. Yet, in case we are missing it here is his note about it. "This distinction is consistently maintained in the priestly sources, emphasizing that only the priests — but never the Levites — are authorized to have access to the most sacred sancta."[31]

---

28. Milgrom, *JPS Numbers*, 11.
29. Hertz, *Pentateuch and Haftarahs*, 574.
30. Milgrom, *JPS Numbers*, 15.
31. *Ibid.*, 17.

Verse 6

"**bring… present**" — The Hebrew word *hakrev* (הקרב) rendered "bring" in the NASB would better be translated as "bring near". It is associated with the same word for "sacrifice". When used to mean a sacrifice, it denotes the fact that through offering a sacrifice, a sinner is brought near to God. Here in 3:6 we could say that by using this word, in a sense the Levites were living sacrifices in their service to the Holy One. Moreover, through the Levites, sinners, when they brought their offerings, were brought near to God.

Verse 9

"**given wholly**" — This English phrase is literally "given, given" in the Hebrew. "The repetition is emphatic, and expresses complete surrender."[32]

Verse 10

"**keep their priesthood**" (NASB) — The word for keep is *shomer* (שומר). Like its usage in verse seven, it can have the thrust of being a watchman or a guard. The Levites were to "guard their priesthood", in the sense of making sure that no one else performs what has been designated to them by the Lord.

Verses 23 ff

Just to provide a helpful summary of the delegation of work duties, we have:

1. **Gershonites** — Camped on the west; carried the tapestry.
2. **Kohatites** — Camped on the south; carried the furniture.
3. **Merarites** — Camped on the north; responsible for boards, pillars, sockets.
4. **Moshe, Aaron, and Aaron's sons** — Camped on east; the most honourable place in the camp with easiest access to Mishkan.

Verse 47

"**shekel**" — Today, the "shekel" is the name for the basic monetary unit in Israel. In the time of Moshe many scholars doubt that nations used currency per se. They merely weighed out amounts of valuable metals. Hence this word is from a verb in Hebrew that means "to weigh (*shakel*, שקל). Harrison informs us that the shekel, "was a basic unit of weight familiar throughout the Ancient Near East, although it varied in size, and therefore in value, from place to place. A "heavy" shekel such as those in use at Ugarit weighed nearly half an ounce, as did similar ones from Megiddo, Gezer, and elsewhere.[33]

Chapter 4
Verse 3

"**to serve**" — The Hebrew word here is the same word used for army. Could this mean that even the Levites were not exempt from warfare? If so, it shows that the entire nation was being

32. Hertz, *Pentateuch and Haftarahs,* 575.
33. Harrison, *Numbers,* 5.

organized for battle: the Israelites were to fight the physical battles, and the Levites were to fight the spiritual battles. Both kinds of warfare are very real, necessary, and go hand in hand.

Verses 8 ff

The covering for the ark —The Hebrew word *tachash* (תחש) is very difficult to translate. Translations vary from sealskin, porpoise skin, badger skins, goatskins, to just leather. Those who translate it as some kind of a sea mammal do so because of a closely related Arabic word. However, there are several problems with this translation. For one, there is no indication in the text that the Israelites were close enough to any sea to catch the mammal, nor is there any indication of trading with locals. Moreover, did the Israelites even know how to cure such a skin?

However, the biggest problem is that whatever skin was placed over the Ark had to be a kosher one! It is inconceivable that they would have covered Israel's most sacred object with something that was *tam'ei* (ritually unclean). If protection from rain was in view, it should be noted that even in modern Israel, the Bedouins are able to produce a goatskin tent cover which is perfectly waterproof! We can only assume that the ancient Israelites also knew how to do it without the use of a non-kosher animal skin. For an unexplained reason, Milgrom suggests that the word tachash refers to a colour rather than to the animal or plant from which the cover is made. He says that tachash is really "yellow-orange".[34]

---

34.   Milgrom, *JPS Numbers*, 26.

STUDY QUESTIONS

1. Why do you think that God now spoke from the Tent of Meeting instead of from elsewhere as He had been doing up to this point?

2. Why do you think that God instructed Moshe and Aaron to take a count of the Israelites?

3. Why do you think it was necessary for all the specific names to be mentioned in this parasha? Why not just give us a sum total of how many there were?

4. Why were only the males twenty-years old or older counted?

5. Describe the order in which the tribes were placed in the camp. Was there any significance to this?

6. Why do you think that each tribe had its own banner?

7. Why were the Levites placed between the Israelites and the Mishkan?

8. Why were Moshe, Aaron, and Aaron's sons placed separately from the rest of the Levites and on the east side of the Mishkan?

9. What is the significance of the firstborn?

10. Why did God give the Levites in place of the firstborn? What did that mean?

11. Why were there two numberings of the Levites?

12. How did God protect the Kohathites from death upon contact with the Ark?

13. What, if any, is the significance of the different colours for the covers of the contents of the Mishkan?

14. In what way(s) was Israel moulded into a military unit by God?

15. Why was the Mishkan placed right in the middle of the camp instead of, for instance, in front of it?

PARASHAT NASSO נשא

Parashat Nasso נשא

"May the Lord make His face shine upon thee and be gracious unto thee." This is the light of the Torah that He should enlighten your eyes and your heart in Torah and grant you children learned in Torah, as it is said: "for the commandment is a lamp and the Torah a light." (Bamidbar Rabbah 11.6)

One of the interesting features of the Torah is that the writer does not use any literary device to differentiate what we might label a sublime passage from what seems like a more mundane section. This week's parasha is a great example of that. We are led into some of the greatest of spiritual heights when Moshe teaches Aaron the so-called "Aaronic Benediction" in chapter 6, when only a few verses before we learned how to handle a jealous husband.

Quite often a new teaching may be introduced with a phrase such as, "And the Lord spoke unto Moshe saying..." This literary device only marks off new revelation, it does not tell us if it has a specific connection with the previous one or not. Because of this, it is sometimes difficult to find a common thread upon which to hang all of the content of a given parasha. This is especially so with our present one. Several commentators have tried to find common threads, but we find most of their efforts wanting.

Perhaps the only way we can see a common denominator is to examine the content in the larger context of the whole book. According to the general outline of Numbers that we are following, this parasha comes in the section entitled, "Preparations to Enter the Promised Land". If this analysis is accurate, then we can explore all of the content in this parasha to see what relationship it has to preparing Israel for life in the Promised Land. Accordingly, we will see that the Lord provided more judicial principles, more provision to govern their spiritual lives and finally, He finished the instruction for the transportation and dedication of the Mishkan.

Let us, therefore, outline our parasha accordingly. Unfortunately, we will only have space to comment on the first two sections. The Matters of Housekeeping are concerned with a continuation of the details about which family of the Levites will carry which part of the Mishkan (4:21–49), maintaining camp purity (5:1–4) and the initial offerings of the tribal leaders. (Chapter 7).

    I.   Matters of Justice – Chapter 5
    II.   Matters of Spirituality – Chapter 6
    III. Matters of Housekeeping

I. MATTERS OF JUSTICE

This passage discusses two judicial matters. They are both found in chapter 5. We shall examine them separately.

A. To Catch a Thief

The first judicial issue is in 5:5–10. It has to do with people who sin against each other. The Hebrew however is quite vague. It reads literally in 5:6, "When a man or woman do any from all the sins of men." It then proceeds to explain the consequence. A natural question that can be asked is, "Which sins are being referred to?" Since one of the consequences is restitution, the scholars assume that the sins implied here are those that involve some sort of lying or theft. Thus, most commentators, both Jewish and evangelical, relate verses 5–10 to Leviticus 5:20–26 and 6:1–7. They assert that the passages in Leviticus and Numbers complement each other.

Along these lines, the *ArtScroll Chumash* suggests an important hermeneutic principle for us. It says "the Torah sometimes repeats a law in order to add something to it."[35] In this case, Numbers supplies several new features the Leviticus passage does not mention. These features have to do with the judicial process the offender must travel through in order for restoration to take place.

1. Regret

The first part of that process is described in the Torah as, "that person shall become guilty" (5:6). Some think that real admission of guilt has little or nothing to do with one's feelings; that it is just a formal statement of the wrong committed. They insist that a person does not need to "feel" guilty or remorse for his sin. Such thinking is based on the idea that feelings have very little place, if any, in our spiritual life. However, we need to remember that God gave us feelings. When we are angry, we feel angry. When we are happy, we feel happy. Subsequently, did not God also give us feelings that express the sense of guilt?

Furthermore, biblical scholars have done much research on the different connotations of biblical words. One such word is that which is found in our text: "to be guilty" (Hebrew: *ashmah*, אשמה). Hebrew students would be quick to notice another form of this word, *asham* (אשם), is the term which is used to describe the guilt offerings of Leviticus 5. Permit us to quote Timothy Ashley at length on this matter as his remarks are so helpful with regard to this term.

> The insistence that the word "guilty" in this passage to mean only a state without the remorse behind it, is rather redundant. It seems hardly necessary to add, however, that the one who commits sin and trespasses against [the Lord] is, or becomes, guilty. It can hardly be conceived that such a person would be innocent. A different translation of the term is in order. J. Milgrom's research has given a new translation to all occurrences of the root. Here it means, "to feel guilty".[36]

Thus, the text seems to be saying that the first step along the way of restoration from a lie or theft against someone else in the holy community is remorse for that wrong. Dennis Prager comments on this feeling of guilt when he asserts, "This quote is extraordinary. A body of law for dealing with expiating guilty feelings ("realizes his guilt") may well have been a new idea in the moral development of mankind."[37]

---

35. *The ArtScroll Chumash*, 752.
36. Timothy Ashley, *Numbers* (NICOT), 113.
37. Dennis Prager, *Numbers: God and Man in the Wilderness* (*The Rational Bible*), 42.

2. Agreeing with God

The judicial process is more than mere admission of guilt and the remorse of a repentant heart. The text also teaches us to confess that sin (5:7). Nechama Leibowitz, quoting the **Sefer Ha-hinukh** tells us that "the verbal confession of guilt provides an indication that the sinner truly believes that all his deeds are revealed and known to the Lord, blessed be He. Again, by verbally specifying the sin and regretting it, he will be more careful in the future not to stumble thereon."[38]

We wonder if concerning this particular point, Professor Leibowitz might agree with the definition of confession found in the Apostolic Scriptures. This definition is based on the Greek word translated "confess" in 1 John 1:9, *homolegomen* (ομολογωμεν). This Greek word means literally, "to say the same thing". Hence, confession of sin means to say the same thing about that sin as God does. The one who sins agrees with God that he wronged another person. He also agrees with God that when he wronged that other person, he ultimately offended God Himself. This is what Numbers 5:6 tells us. It says that when we sin against someone else, we are "unfaithful to the Lord". The word "unfaithful", *ma'ol* (מעול), could also be rendered "treacherous".

Since the sin against the human was unfaithfulness to the Lord, Rabbi Hirsch elaborates on this by comparing man's sin to a debt that he owes both to the one against whom he sins, and to the Holy One against whom he also transgresses. He says, "HaShem is the invisible third party Who is present at all transactions of His creatures. He is the guarantor of human relations. When the debtor denies his debt, he utters HaShem's Name in a false oath."[39] However, having said that, Prager notes an important principle in Judaism. He notes that "One cannot obtain forgiveness from God for a crime against a fellow human being without first obtaining forgiveness from the wronged human being."[40] Yeshua would agree with that. He taught in Matthew 5:23–24 saying, "Therefore if you are presenting your offering at the altar, and there remember that your brother has something against you, leave your offering there before the altar and go; first be reconciled to your brother, and then come and present your offering."

3. Twenty Percent

The Torah elaborates on yet another detail in the judicial process if someone sins. This is the concept of making restitution. Biblical restitution is the principle of not just returning a stolen object or money to the person from whom it was taken. It also requires that the offender gives 20% above the value of the object stolen. That is rather straightforward. The question, however, is "Why is restitution necessary?"

R. K. Harrison suggests that it was a means of deterrent. He writes, "As a result of presenting the restitution directly to the offended party and not by means of a substitute, the transgressor

---

38. Nechama Leibowitz, *New Studies in Bamidbar,* 46.
39. Elie Munk, *The Call of the Torah: Bamidbar*, 41.
40. Prager, *Numbers,* 43.

would be less likely to commit such an offense in the future, because his behavior would become public knowledge."[41]

Rabbi Elie Munk, on the other hand, suggests that the payment of the restitution was, along with the offering of a sacrifice, part of the actual atonement process itself. He writes, "The extra fifth and the associated sacrifice are not punishments but means of absolution."[42] This viewpoint (it did not originate with Munk!) gives rise to a rather interesting interpretation of the restitution process. The Rambam teaches in his *Mishnah Torah* that the one who feels guilt, freely confesses his sin, and seeks to make amends, needs also to make restitution. Whereas the one who is not truly repentant continues to claim he is not guilty, but is found guilty by a court, only needs to pay back what was taken, but not the restitution. Summarizing Rambam's views, Munk explains, "Rambam teaches that the *asham* [guilt offering] absolves only those who have repented. Thus, if the sinner does not change his attitude and show his sincere desire to redeem himself, neither the offering nor the extra fifth is of the slightest value."[43]

4. No Relatives

The last new piece of information this passage provides us, over its counterpart in Leviticus concerning the judicial process for sin, is 5:8–10. These verses speak of a case where restitution needs to be made but the offended person has died leaving no relatives to whom the payment can be made. In such a case the money is given to the Lord through the Kohanim.

However, some commentators have made a valid point about this principle and ask: When is it that a Jewish person has no relatives, especially at that time when family genealogies were being solidified? Rashi typifies this objection. He states, "Is there a person in Israel who has no redeemers? Either a son or a daughter or some related kin from his father's family, tracing the relationship upward until our forefather Jacob? But this referred to a convert who died, and has no heirs, for he had not fathered children as a Jew."[44]

Hence, the standard Jewish viewpoint is that 5:8–10 refers to a convert to Judaism, the one who has no physical heirs in Israel. We can only add that the other possibility is that the offended one was not a convert but just a non-Jew who lived among the people. The word used in the text is *ger* (גר), which we have noticed before did not refer to a convert in the time of Moshe. That concept came later, in the Second Temple Period. Rather a ger was a resident foreigner among the people of Isreal. In either case the midrash's remarks on this subject are equally applicable. It says, "The Torah laid down equal treatment for the native Israelite and the proselyte [foreigner], and taking by violence from either must be expiated by payment of a fine and an atonement offering.[45]

---

41. R. K. Harrison, *Numbers* (TOTC), 104.
42. Munk, *The Call of the Torah: Bamidbar,* 42.
43. *Ibid.*
44. Rashi: *Bamidbar*, ArtScroll Edition, 43.
45. Bamidbar Rabbah 8.2

B. The Law of Jealousies

This parasha contains a second judicial matter. It is found in 5:11–31. The text itself calls it "the Law of Jealousies", (5:29) or more accurately, "the Torah [teaching] of Jealousies".

This teaching is about a case where a woman is suspected by her husband of committing adultery, but he has no proof. The Hebrew term for such a woman is *sotah*, meaning "one who strays."[46] This section is clearly connected with the previous one about making restitution by the repetition of the word translated either "treachery" or "unfaithfulness". In 5:1–10, we looked at a case where a person, who defrauds or robs someone else, commits unfaithfulness against the Lord. Here, in these verses, we see a case where a wife is thought to be unfaithful to her husband. The same Hebrew word is being used in both cases: *ma'ol* (מעול). Hence, "Fraud and false oaths break faith with God and the defrauded person(s); adulterers break faith with God and their spouses."[47] This case has two fascinating aspects about it but also leaves us with a curiously unanswered question.

1. The Sensitivity of the Torah

The first interesting point about this passage is that its teaching shows compassionate sensitivity toward both the husband and the wife's needs. The need of the husband in this case is to calm his jealousy. Here is a situation where his wife may have committed unfaithfulness with another man. Should the husband passively ignore the sin? The Torah answers with a resounding, "No!" It staves off a potentially harmful situation caused by unchecked jealousy of the husband by outlining a judicial process to see if his fears are justified or not.

God is making an important point here. By making provision for the proper expression of a husband's jealousies, the Holy One is teaching us that jealousy for the right reasons is not wrong. In fact, He Himself tells us that one reason we are not to pursue other gods is that the Lord is a jealous God! The husband-wife relationship, with all of its dynamics, is to picture the relationship God has established with us. We hurt and offend Him when we are unfaithful. We provoke Him to jealousy, just as an unfaithful partner provokes the other to jealousy.

2. The Trial

As far as the need of the wife is concerned, if she was innocent, she needed to have her name cleared of any suspicion. This ritual provided for such justice. Moreover, this trial also protected her against a hot-tempered husband who merely was angry with her with no sufficient cause. He was allowed to take his case to the community, instead of taking out his unjustified anger against her. Here is the procedure for this trial:

---

46. Prager, *Numbers*, 48.
47. *Ibid.*

1) A husband, out of suspicion of his wife's immorality, brings her to the kohen.
2) She brings a meal offering without oil or frankincense.
3) The kohen presents the woman before the Lord.
4) The kohen makes her a mixture of "holy water".
5) The kohen uncovers her hair (a possible sign of shame).
6) The kohen makes her recite an oath agreeing to the conditions that if she was guilty, the water mixture would be a curse for her.
7) The kohen writes this oath and causes its words to be dissolved by the water.
8) The kohen waves the meal offering and then offers it up in smoke.
9) The woman drinks the water.
10) God performs due justice.

3. Holy Water!

An integral part of the judicial process used to determine the guilt or innocence of the accused wife, is the ingestion of a curious concoction comprised of a cup of "bitter waters that cause a curse" (5:16–18). The kohen mixed this brew by putting some of the dirt of the floor of the Mishkan into an earthen vessel filled with water. Just before she drank this stuff, the kohen was to write the oath that she agreed to on a little scroll, put it into the water and let liquid dissolve it.

The purpose of this drink seems to be that it was a "symbolical action to indicate that the curse is in this manner conveyed to the potion."[48] The accused was to drink it. If she was innocent, nothing happened. If she was guilty, "When she is made to drink the water that brings a curse, it will go into her and cause bitter suffering; her abdomen will swell and her thigh waste away, and she will become accursed among her people" (5:27). when it says that "her thigh will wase away" Jacob Milgrom suggests that the text is "probably is a euphemism for the procreative organs (e. g., Gen. 24:2, 9), thus referring to the physical inability to beget children (cf. v. 27)."[49]

If this was a "symbolical action," what are some of the pictures we can learn from it? For one, Rashi suggests the waters were, "holy through being in the laver and were called 'bitter' . . . because of their final effect, viz., that they proved bitter for her."[50] That is of course, if indeed she was guilty. Secondly, the water was drunk from an earthen vessel. This, done in conjunction with the offering she was to bring, was both "cheap and coarse", like the sin she may have committed. Furthermore, the kohen removed her head covering, "as a sign of mourning (Leviticus 10:6), or as a token of her shame, as it was a sign of lack of morality for a woman to appear publicly with her hair unloosed."[51] If it was a sign of mourning as Hertz suggests, it was because of the distress her sin caused in the whole camp. If it was because of her shame, as he

48. J. H. Hertz, *The Pentateuch and Haftarahs,* 591.
49. Jacob Milgrom, *JPS Torah Commentary: Numbers*, 41.
50. Rashi, *ArtScroll Edition*, 51.
51. Hertz, *The Pentateuch and Haftarahs*, 590.

also says, that is self-explanatory.

Lastly, when the scroll was put into the bitter water and the writing was erased, it most likely "was a symbolical action to indicate that the curse is in this manner conveyed to the person."[52] The Mishnah tells us that at any point the woman, if she was guilty, could confess her sin, thus avoiding the bitter results this ordeal would bring. On the other hand, if she were innocent, this would publicly be sufficient to declare her acquittal.

The instructions of jealousy were a very unusual teaching in the Torah. J. H. Hertz affirms this and adds, "This law is the only explicit instance in Scripture of trial by ordeal, an institution that was well-nigh universal in antiquity and a regular feature of Western European life down to the late Middle Ages."[53] After the House of God in Jerusalem was destroyed, the ritual was abolished. However, we can learn a great deal about how the law was practised during the Second Temple Period by reading *Sotah*, a whole tractate in the Mishnah and Talmud specifically discussing this passage in Numbers. Moreover, Prager writes, "Though some have portrayed the sotah ritual as hostile to women, the purpose of this ritual was to provide a way for a) protecting women from a husband's jealous rage and b) reconciling the couple and saving the marriage."[54]

Commentators point out several interesting nuances about this strange ritual. First, there is very little evidence that it was actually carried out in the First Temple Period, and it was suspended during the Second Temple Period. Secondly, when we compare this ritual with other Ancient Near Eastern methods to handle a suspected unfaithful wife, this ritual is by far the most merciful. For example, sometimes in ancient Babylon the accused tongue was touched by a red-hot iron. If there were burned marks, she was considered guilty! In contrast, "The ordeal of the bitter water allows a fairly simple, safe way for a woman to clear her name with divine approval, sanctioned by the priest and the Temple ritual."[55]

4. An Unanswered Question

It is relatively easy to see the wisdom of this Teaching of Jealousy, especially as a deterrent against unfaithful or careless wives. However, there is a question that we are not totally able to answer at this point: What about the unfaithful or careless husband? Did not the wife also get jealous? Did the husband have rights and privileges that the wife was not permitted to have? We do know for example that the Torah permitted multiple wives for the husband. Therefore, seeking an additional sexual partner was permitted for him. Under such circumstances, if there was a sexual relationship, the Torah commanded that the husband should marry that woman. However, that is the only reason we can think of as to why the Law of jealousy did not apply to the husband as well as to the wife.

---

52. Hertz, *The Pentateuch and Haftarahs*, 591.
53. *Ibid.*, 589.
54. Prager, *Numbers*, 53.
55. *Ibid.*, 55, quoting Rachel Biale in *Women and Jewish Law*.

We will leave the issue with this question. Perhaps the students, can furnish some biblical answers. We have just one word of clarification about our question, however. We do not in any way mean to imply that God is not fair and just. Nor do we mean to suggest that He treats men better than He does women. Let it be clearly stated that we believe that the Lord loves and treats equally both men and women. Our question, therefore, is not one of protest, just one of seeking more information!

As we leave this subject let us make one final statement about this Law of Jealousy. Rather than focusing on an apparent inconsistency, favouring the husband over the wife, we need to see the total wisdom behind this strange ritual. R. Laird Harris, perhaps best sums up our thinking regarding this teaching when he reminds us of that.

> The gravity of the ritual for a suspected faithless wife shows that the Torah regards marital fidelity most seriously. Such was not just a concern of a jealous husband; the entire community was affected by the breach of faith. Hence the judgment was in the context of the community. Contemporary attitudes that suggest that sexual infidelity is a minor, personal matter are far removed from the teaching of Scripture... The importance of marital fidelity in this passage should not be lost on modern readers in a time in which such ideas are quaint but irrelevant.[56]

II. MATTERS OF SPIRITUALITY

Immediately following the teaching about the Law of Jealousy and the Torah of Restitution, the text in Numbers chapter 6 discusses another unusual practice — the Torah of the Nazarite. This is followed by what is commonly known as the "Aaronic Benediction". Where the teaching about restitution and jealousy were instructions about judicial matters, chapter six seems to focus its attention on the issues of spirituality within the camp of Israel. Let us examine this more closely.

A.   MATTERS OF SPIRIUALITY — THE NAZARITE VOW

Numbers 6:1–21 teaches about an unusual practice where a person — male or female — could "consecrate himself unto the Lord" by abstaining from grape products, having physical contact with dead things, and by letting his hair grow without cutting it for an unspecified period of time. The Mishnah states that an unspecified Nazarite vow is for thirty days.[57] A natural question to ask here would be: Why? What purpose would all this serve? Why would a person undertake such a vow?

1.   To Do Something Extraordinary

At first glance, the Scripture seems rather silent concerning these questions. The Torah assumes that the listeners knew more about the nature of the Nazarite Vow than we do. Indeed, they did. However, the Hebrew text does provide a strong hint about its purpose. We are told in 6:2 that the vow was made in order to "consecrate himself to the Lord". The Hebrew wording here is

56.   R. Laird Harris, *Numbers* (*The Expositor's Bible Commentary*, "EBC"), 744, 748.
57.   Nazir 2.7

difficult, yet enlightening. The Hebrew uses the word is *yafli* (יפלאי), which is usually translated as "consecrate". However, this is a word that normally speaks of wonderful, marvellous acts, acts that are totally impossible for mere man to do, acts that only God can do.[58] In 6:2 the verb form is in the causative force (*hiphil*). All of this leads us to translate 6:2 like this: "If a man or woman desires to cause something extraordinary to happen, or to do an impossible thing, he may vow a vow of Nazir to the Lord."

In other words, the purpose of the Nazarite vow seems to be that there could be instances when a person wishes to accomplish something that is beyond mere human ability. Presumably, this would be something done for the Lord's glory. In order to accomplish that extraordinary task for the Lord, the person would abstain from that which the text dictates.

2. The Nazarite — Sinner or Saint?

If this is correct, it would seem, therefore, that the taking of the Nazarite vow was something good. Indeed, "The Nazarites were established by God as an example of commitment to Him and to the disciplines of their order. The consistent emphasis upon the vow to God was characterized by the seriousness of the undertaking, which made both the participants and their vows sacred."[59]

However, not everyone thinks that taking the Nazarite Vow was such a wonderful undertaking. According to the Encyclopaedia Judaica, "Taking the vow was severely discouraged by the rabbis because asceticism was against the spirit of Judaism. The rabbis even designated the Nazarites as sinners."[60]

However, some sages also felt that it was good to undertake such a commitment. They say that it has positive benefits. To more fully understand this vow from a Jewish point of view, we must first know that, like the *Sotah* (the compromised wife of Numbers 5), the Nazarite also has its own tractate in the Mishnah and Talmud. In fact, they are placed right after each other — the first is tractate *Nazir*, then followed by *Sotah*. This is somewhat of a message in this from the Sages. They see a connection. Some suggest that one reason why a wife may compromise herself and become a "sotah", is that she was under the influence of wine and therefore she should avoid drinking wine.

Professor Leibowitz most aptly summarizes this viewpoint for us. She says that many sages suggest that the vow was designed as a deterrent against the sin of excess. For they note that when a person finished the vow, he was required to bring a sin offering. Why? What sin did he do while under the Vow? Let Leibowitz tell us:

> The sin is not in becoming a Nazarite or in ceasing to be one. The sin referred to, concerns that which preceded the Nazarite vow. Previous inability to control and discipline his desires, within the bounds imposed by the Torah, and made it necessary for the person concerned to restrict

58. BDB, 810.
59. Harrison, *Numbers*, 122.
60. *Encyclopaedia Judaica,* vol. 12, 910.

himself even further and vow himself to abstinence. The Nazarite vow was thus a necessary but extreme medicine for spiritual ills.[61]

That sounds plausible, but the examples of real Nazarites from the Scriptures speak against such a negative assessment of the Nazarite vow. These examples are not exhaustive. The Bible contains more. We just cite some of the best-known examples.

3. Real Live Nazarites:

Samson

The most famous Nazarite in the Tanakh was Samson. In Judges Chapter 13 we are told that even before birth he was destined by the Lord to be a life-long Nazarite. Because of this, the vow to him was not in response to some uncontrollable problem. Instead, his vow meant that his life was to be spent totally consecrated and separated to the Lord in order to accomplish some extraordinary, superhuman tasks, such as delivering the Israelites from the hands of the Philistines.

Yochanan

The most familiar Nazarite in the Apostolic Scriptures is John the Baptist (Yochanan ben Zechariah). In Luke 1:15 we are told, "He is never to take wine or other fermented drink." Moreover, we know that he needed to be totally concentrated and consecrated on the critically important and equally superhuman task of preaching repentance to his people and preparing them for the Messiah.

The Men of Acts

The Apostolic Scriptures provide us with at least one other example (there are probably more) of the Nazarite vow in the Newer Covenant Scriptures. If we did not know about the vow, we would not be properly equipped to interpret Acts 21:23–24. Here, in response to false reports that Paul was living and teaching against the Torah, he was instructed to join in the purification rites and pay for the expenses of securing the specified sacrifices of four Messianic Jews who were under the Nazarite vow. We know this because it says that they also needed to have their heads shaved, i.e. have a haircut in completion of the vow.

Modern Nazarites

The Encyclopaedia Judaica tells us that there have been other Nazarites through the centuries, although there is no recorded example from the Middle Ages. However, we do know that the former Chief Rabbi of Israel, A. J Kook had a disciple, David Cohen, who observed the Nazarite vow while living in Jerusalem.[62]

4. The Handsome Shepherd

We will conclude our discussion of the Nazarite vow with a story from the Babylonian Talmud. This story illustrates some of the positive purposes for the vow. It shows how a godly man used the vow to accomplish a superhuman task — that of curbing his own flesh.

---

61. Leibowitz, *New Studies in Bamidbar,* 57.
62. *Encyclopaedia Judaica*, vol. 12, 910.

Only once did Simeon the Just, a Kohen and Sage, eat the trespass offering brought by a Nazarite when he concluded his vow. This was when the Nazarite was an extraordinarily handsome man, a shepherd from the south of Israel. He had especially beautiful curly hair and other handsome features. He came to Simeon the Just who asked him why he wanted to cut off his comely locks. The Nazarite responded, "Once I went to draw water from a well, gazed upon my reflection in the water, whereupon my evil desires rushed upon me and sought to drive me from the world [through sin]. But I said unto it [my lust] "Wretch!' I will shave thee off [this beautiful hair] for the sake of Heaven."

The Talmud then relates Simeon's reaction, "I immediately arose and kissed his head, saying, 'My son, may there be many Nazarites such as you in Israel! Of you says the Holy Writ; When either a man or a woman shall separate themselves to vow a vow of a Nazarite, to separate themselves unto the Lord'."[63]

B. MATTERS OF SPIRITUALITY — THE AARONIC BLESSING

In our commentary on this parasha, we said that this section of Bamidbar was concerned with matters of spirituality. The first matter was that of people wanting to serve God in special way by taking upon themselves the Nazarite vow. Numbers 6:22–27 records a second spiritual matter. These verses are commonly known as the "Aaronic Blessing". We conclude this week's commentary by examining this blessing.

An Amazing Find

In 1979 a group of students led by the eminent Israeli archaeologists Dr. Gabriel Barkay were exploring some Tanakh period tombs near the Hinnom Valley in Jerusalem. They came across what seems to be two amulets supposedly intended as protections for the dead ones who occupied those graves. They are tiny silver scrolls, measuring 2.5 cm. Because of the old Hebrew script, unlike the script commonly used since for the last 2,000 years, and because of where they were found, scholars date these 2 small silver amulets to be before the Babylonian captivity, probably about 600 BCE. The contents of these tiny scrolls were finally deciphered in 1989.[64] It was astonishingly discovered that they contain two similar passages of Scriptures, one from Numbers 6:24–26 and the other, a parallel passage from Deuteronomy 7:9. Besides the fact that they were somehow seemingly miraculously "microscopically" incised onto the silver jewellery (which is also why it took so long to decipher them), they also are some of the oldest texts of the Bible found outside of the Bible, including one of the oldest uses of God's sacred name Adonai (יהוה). For that reason alone, this section deserves special comments.

I. THE PURPOSE OF THIS PASSAGE

"To bless" is one of the most difficult words to define in English. Nechama Leibowitz attempts to deal with the difficulties in understanding the meaning of the word "bless". In doing so, she quotes from the trusted medieval commentator, Abravanel, who defines "blessing" thus:

63. B. Nedarim 9b
64. This information is beautifully summarized in the popular book *Evidence for the Bible*, by Clive Andersen and Brian Edwards, 19.

"Blessing" is a homonym referring both to the good emanating from God in His creatures… and the blessing proceeding from man to God in the sense of praise.[65] Abravanel seems to be saying that a blessing from God is something that He gives to us, usually in the physical realm, but not limited to that. In contrast, since people really cannot give God something He does not already possess, a blessing from man to Him is merely the praise and honour He rightly deserves for Who He is.

We have more to say about it. Generally, to bless someone is to wish upon them different kinds of material advantages, such as those listed as blessings in Deuteronomy 28:3–14. However, without contradicting that thought, we would like to further explain a possible dynamic involved in giving and receiving a blessing. The Hebrew verb we translate "bless" seems to be associated with the word for "knee." If it is not formally and linguistically associated, because it is spelled the same, it reminds us of the word, "to bow down" on one's knee. That as similarity might help us to understand a little more about what it means to give and to receive a blessing.

Perhaps we can say that to bless might mean to take the position of a humble servant who takes the knee to his/her master, thereby indicating to the master "I, am at your service. What is it that I can do for you." Hence, if we are correct, when we want to bless another individual, that is essentially what we are saying to them: "How can I serve you?" This is what Paul also says in Ephesians 5:21 when he writes, "Be subject to one another in the fear of Messiah." Moreover, if we carry that thought over to our relationship with the Lord, when we want to bless Him, we are saying to Him, how can I serve you?

When we express this attitude of servitude, another famous Hebrew expression comes into play, the term *hineini* (הינני). This is often translated as "here I am." Abraham said this to God in Genesis 22 when God called him to offer Isaac. Moshe also said it to the Lord in Exodus 3, and we can find other examples throughout the Scriptures. In essence, the term is like a military term when we say to the Holy One, "I am at attention. You speak and I will do, thereby offering our full service." That is how we bless the Lord. Since we cannot give to God anything He does not already have in terms of physical material, the best way to bless God is both to give Him praise and adoration and to give Him ourselves in terms to dedicated service.

However, we also know from Scripture that God wants to bless us. That is the thrust of this passage in Numbers. This is truly amazing. Sometimes God says to us, His children, "hinnei." We see this at least twice in Isaiah for example (Isaiah 52:6 and 58:9). When we see this, it is the Holy One figuratively getting on His knee and saying to us, "How can I serve you?" The greatest example of this blessing from God is in the Messiah, who Isaiah calls "The Servant." He humbled Himself by becoming a person for 30 some years, then did the ultimate serves by voluntarily being crucified to take our sins away and dying in our place.

---

65. Nechama Leibowitz, *New Studies in Bamidbar*, 63.

Hence, when God teaches Aaron and the kohanim to bless Israel, all of that is included. The ultimate blessing Israel can receive is, therefore, the knowledge of the Messiah and a personal relationship with Him. Now we are ready to delve into some of the details of the blessing.

II. DETAILS OF THE BLESSING

A. What a Poem!

Let us first take note of the structure of this blessing, both in Hebrew and in English:

"May the Lord bless you and keep you."

Yevarekhekha Adonai v'yishmerekha.

יברכך יהוה וישמרך.

"May the Lord shine His countenance upon you and be gracious to you."

Ya'er Adonai panav elekha vichunekha.

יאר יהוה פניו אליך ויחנך.

"May the Lord lift up His countenance to you and establish peace for you."

Yisa Adonai panav elekha v'yasem l'kha shalom.

ישא יהוה פניו אליך וישם לך שלום.

Even if one does not know any Hebrew, it is easy to see the physical structure of this blessing just by looking at it. We can see that the blessing is cast in poetic form. This format consists of three lines, each line building upon the other as they add an additional thought to the previous one. In addition, each line in the Hebrew builds on the previous one by adding a symmetrical number of words: first 3, then 5, then finishing with 7 — the number for perfection and completion. This may suggest that the fulfilment of these blessings would contribute to make one a whole and complete person. Note especially in this regard that the last word of the blessing is "peace", *shalom* (שלום), the word which signifies wholeness.

B. Scattered Thoughts

1. The Name of God

Before we analyse each line, we have a few more scattered observations. First, each line begins by invoking the sacred Name of God, יהוה. This is the Name that stresses God's covenant-keeping attributes. By repeating it three times, the text puts the proper emphasis where it belongs — on the Lord Himself, Who is the only source for any blessing.

Since this blessing has three parts, we note that יהוה appears three times. This might possibly indicate to us that the Godhead in its entirety — Father, Son, and Spirit is involved in granting the unconditional benefits to the people.

Moreover, for those who know Hebrew, we can easily observe that the pronoun at the end of the verbs is in the singular. This would seem to suggest that this blessing, although addressed to the children (plural) of Israel, speaks to them as if they are one.

2. Amar or Daver?

Two verbs in Hebrew are usually used when one is speaking. We can use the verb "to say," *amar* (אמר), or we can use the verb "to speak," *davar* (דבר). When this passage begins in Numbers 6:23, both words are used. When God spoke to Moshe the common word daver was used. But when God instructed the priests to speak these words to Israel, He told them to speak to Israel and used the word amar." Rabbi Munk indicates that in the introduction to the blessing in 6:23, the kohanim are told to "speak" to Israel. The word that the text used is from the word, *amar* (אמר), which means, "to say". His comments on this are beautiful. He says, "The root אמר , say, in contrast to [d-b-r, דבר] speak, often connotes speaking in a low or soft voice."[66] This insight may indicate that it was really the soft, gentle voice of the Bridegroom (the Messiah), which was intending to communicate blessing upon His beloved wife through the priests.

III. EXPOSITION

A. The God Who Keeps

> "May the Lord bless you and keep you."
> *Yevarekhekha Adonai v'yishmerekha/*
> .יברכך יהוה וישמרך

The first request for blessing is to ask the Holy One to keep Israel. This word "keep" is the usual word for "guard" or "protect", *yishmerekha* (ישמרך). We have seen this word before. It speaks of guarding or *protecting* something. The Scriptures teach that the Lord is the Keeper of Israel. Only He has the ability to preserve the nation from sin, war, and famine. While He planned difficult times of distress and trial, ultimately this blessing will come true. Israel, despite all of her sin and her enemies, will be kept secure by the Holy One (cf. Jeremiah 31:33–37).

How does He keep us? In addition to the strength of His might, God also uses His Word to guard and protect us. The Torah often refers to itself by the word "*mishmeret*" (משמרת). This term is based on the word for protection. This depicts the Torah like a hedge. If we live by it, it will be our protection. Hence, this first blessing is one where we can participate in by knowing and living by God's Word, the Torah.

This is also the same for all who rely on the Holy One. If we are part of the holy community, the redeemed community by faith in the finished work of Yeshua the Messiah, the Lord will also keep us, for "no one can snatch them out of My Father's hands," says Yeshua (John 10:29). Of course, this would include us. If there is no spiritual or physical force in the entire universe, according to Romans 8:37–39, that can cause us to fall out of God's love for us, what then makes us think that we ourselves have that ability? It neither matters where we walk nor what we get into. If we are truly His, if we have been born from above and have received new life from the Father in Heaven, then He promises that He will keep us, just as He promised to keep Israel.

---

66. Munk, *The Call of the Torah: Vayikra*, 66.

B. The God Who Shines His Face upon Us

"May the Lord shine His countenance upon you and be gracious to you."

Ya'er Adonai panav elekha vichunekha

יאר יהוה פניו אליך ויחנך

The words "May the Lord shine His countenance upon you" take us back to the experience of Moses on Mount Sinai. Exodus 34:29 says, "It came about when Moses was coming down from Mount Sinai (and the two tablets of the testimony were in Moses' hand as he was coming down from the mountain), that Moses did not know that the skin of his face shone because of his speaking with Him." Hence, when God shines His face on us it is for us to reflect that glory back to Him and let it be seen by all.

Furthermore, having God's face shine upon us is like the beaming face of a parent for his beloved. Another facet of this expression is that when we see God's face shining on us, we are to see an expression of God's personality shining upon us. The face of God is the personality of God as turned towards man.

C. The God Who is Gracious

… and be gracious to you.

How is it that God can keep and guard such a people who knowingly sin against Him? The answer lies in the second request, the second blessing, "The Lord be gracious unto you." The Hebrew word translated "gracious" is from the verb *chanan* (חנן). According to BDB it can be translated "to show favour" or "to be gracious". This word, in conjunction with its Greek counterpart in the Apostolic Scriptures just reeks with unconditional forgiveness.

One of the best illustrations of this word is in the story of Hosea and Gomer. Just as Hosea was instructed to relate to his estranged and unfaithful wife Gomer, so does God relate to his sometimes estranged and unfaithful people, Israel. Despite their sorry spiritual state, God always grants forgiveness freely.

This also is the same way He is toward us. Ephesians 1:7 teaches that God "lavished" His grace on us who believe in Yeshua, despite knowing how rebellious some of our flesh can be. Specifically, Ephesians 1:7–8 says that we have "forgiveness of our sins in accordance with the riches of God's grace". This can be compared to a beggar who approaches a millionaire for a gift of money. If the millionaire gives him 100 we can say that he gave **out of** his riches. However, if he gives the beggar 100,000 then we can say that he gave to the beggar **in accordance with** his riches. God's grace account in His bank is far more than in the millions. It is limitless. Accordingly, Ephesians tells us that He gave to us grace, "in accordance with" and not "out of" the riches of His grace. Beloved, that is a lot of grace! Hence, it is on the basis of His grace that He can keep us. An unlimited source of grace means an unlimited amount of keeping!

One expression of God's grace is that He makes His face or countenance to shine upon us.

Hertz informs us that, "To cause the face to shine upon one is the Biblical idiom for to be friendly towards him. When God's "face" and/or "countenance" is said to be toward man and to shine upon him, it implies the outpouring of divine love and salvation."[67]

D. God is the God Who Lifts His Countenance to Us

"May the Lord lift up His countenance to you and establish peace for you."

Yisa Adonai panav elekha v'yasem l'kha shalom.

ישא יהוה פניו אליך וישם לך שלום.

Whereas "shining" refers to the benevolent look on God's face, to lift up one's eyes or face could mean to pay attention. Furthermore, the idea of the fallen face is one of anger and the idea of the hidden face is that of withholding support, favour, or peace. Thus, if God lifts his face toward his people, it means he has given them peace.

Furthermore, the expression "turn his face" might suggest pleasure and affection. This terminology has the functional equivalent of the word "smile."[68] Here the people are led to pray that the Lord will turn his face toward them in a gracious smile! This is more emphatic than the previous statement about God's face and it asks that God might pay attention to Israel. It may reflect the fact that he had chosen them and not other nations. If God hid his face, Israel would suffer and perish.

E. The God Who Grants Peace

If God is our friend, as we just learned, if He also keeps us, and if He freely lavishes us with His grace, as this blessing requests, then one thing is certain: We will have His Peace. This is more literally, "and may God put peace upon you."

Peace certainly is one of the "pillars of the world", according to the Talmud. In seeking to bless the Israelites with peace, the Holy One undoubtedly meant wholeness of life, and freedom from war with their enemies. However, perhaps it goes much beyond that, as great as those blessings are. Yeshua, the Prince of Peace, said that He came to give us such peace (John 14), the "peace that passes all understanding, guarding our hearts and our minds" (Philippians 4:7). Hence, peace is more than the absence of war. Peace comes with completeness, health, safety, and general well-being.

F. Bearers of "My Name" Numbers 6:27

"So they shall invoke My name on the sons of Israel, and I then will bless them."

The Aaronic Blessing finishes, with the note that the Lord told Aaron to bless Israel with those words and to "place My Name upon the children of Israel" "By the use of the Aaronic

---

67. Hertz, *Pentateuch and Haftarahs*, 595.

68. This is also Rashi's suggestion. Rashi, *Numbers*, ArtScroll Edition, Vol. 4, 66.

Benediction, the priests will put the sacred Name of the Lord into the hearts and minds of His people, and this will result in a blessing upon the nation."[69]

Another commentator says, "The words of the conclusion…may be the most surprising of all; for here the Lord says that this prayer is the means of placing his name on his people. Since the name [Adonai] is itself a term of blessing whereby the eternal God states his relatedness to his people, these words of blessing could not be more appropriate.

The prayer is designed to help the people experience the reality of the blessing of the Lord whose delight is to bring that blessing near; his promise is that he will do just that very thing.[70] When God puts His Name upon us it is as if He wants us to fully identify with Him. It is also as if He wants everyone to know that we belong to Him. He is saying that He is not ashamed to have us, His People, bear His name through all the earth. What a solemn responsibility. What an awesome privilege! Dennis Prager writes,

> To this day this blessing plays an important role in Jewish life. During synagogue services priests go before the congregation and call out this blessing…Rabbis often recite this blessing at the end of the service, and many parents offer this blessing to the children at the beginning of the Shabbat. In fact, this blessing is invoked in the liturgy of all Bible-based faiths.[71]

ADDITIONAL NOTES

Chapter 5

Verse 3
"Where I dwell among them" — The Hebrew for this phrase "I dwell" is *shokhen* (שוכן), a derivative of the word for Mishkan. Undoubtedly, it was this word that gave rise to the rabbinic term "shekinah" — a word used to denote the special presence of God in the Holy of Holies. The Lord's consent to dwell in the Tabernacle must be matched by Israel's scrupulousness in keeping the camp pure. Implied is that any impurity in the camp threatens the purity of the Tabernacle. In Canaan the demand for purity is extended to all of God's Land (Numbers 35:34). It could be that one reason for this scrupulousness was that God wanted to protect the picture of the distinction between His realm of life and the realm of sin and death.

Verses 1–4
There does not seem to have been a special place outside the community, they could live in any location that did not compromise the holiness of the camp. After the Israelites were settled in the Promised Land, special houses were built outside the cities for the tam'ei people who were afflicted supernaturally by God, presumably for sin.

69. R. K. Harrison, *Numbers* (*Wycliffe Exegetical Commentaries*), 134.
70. Ronald B. Allen, *Numbers* (*Expositor's Bible Commentary*), comments on Numbers 6:27.
71. Dennis Prager, *Numbers: God and Man in the Wilderness* (*The Rational Bible*), 66.

Verse 5–10
"The removal of physical impurities must be accompanied by the removal of moral wrongs."[72]

Verse 6
"and so is unfaithful to the Lord" — A wrong against another was considered as if the wrong were against the Lord.

Verses 7–8
The word translated "restitution" in these verses is the same word used in Leviticus chapter 5 to speak of the sin offering: *asham* (אשם). In Leviticus it means the sacrifice for guilt itself, whereas in our passage here in Numbers it is used specifically to speak of the restitution paid to the victim. This may give impetus to the viewpoint that making restitution is like bringing a guilt offering. One is made to God, the other is made to the person who was wronged.

Verse 7
"confess" — In light of our comments in the main body of this commentary concerning the concept of confession, Milgrom offers this helpful note: "The Septuagint correctly translates Hebrew *ve-hitvadu* (והתודו), as declare; the penitent's remorse must be articulated.[73]" Indeed, it must be declared to be just as God sees it!

Verse 7
"one fifth" — The penalty for apprehended theft is double the value of the article (Exodus 22:3) or more (Exodus 21:37). The intent of the sharp reduction of this penalty here to 20 percent is to encourage the voluntary surrender of the theft. It is found in ancient Near Eastern practice and in rabbinic law, where it is called *takkanat ha-shavim*, "a dispensation for the repentant." [74]

Verse 12
"unfaithful" — The Hebrew word here is *ma'alah*. (מעלה). This is the only time that this term is used to describe unfaithfulness outside of a vow, which one would make unto the Lord, and for idolatry. Straying after other gods is just like straying after another sexual partner outside of marriage and visa-versa. Milgrom also notes that the use of ma'alah for both idolatry and oath violation as well as marital unfaithfulness provides a common link connecting the passages in this context of Numbers 5:6–8 and 5:11–31.[75]

Verse 13
"carnal relations" — The Hebrew word translated carnal relations is the word for semen *shikhvat zera'* (שכבת-זרע). This would tell us specifically what "carnal relations" mean.

Verse 13
"no witness" — This verse seems to imply that adultery may be an exception to the rule, that for a death penalty to happen there must be two witnesses. However, the rabbis have circumvented

72. Hertz, *Pentateuch and Haftarahs*, 588.
73. Jacob Milgrom, *The JPS Torah Commentary: Numbers*, 35.
74. *Ibid.*, 35.
75. *Ibid.*, 37.

this and have traditionally required that her husband in the presence of two witnesses warn a potentially wayward wife against secluding herself with someone who is suspected of pursuing her.

Verse 17
"**holy water**" — The Rabbis, following Rashi, think this water is from the laver, making it especially set apart (holy).

Verse 18
That the removal of the head covering symbolized shame to the ancients is illustrated in the Mishnah where it says, "And a priest takes hold of her garments — if they be torn they be torn, if they be rent to tatters they be rent to tatters — so that he bares her bosom, and he loosens her hair."[76] It seems from this Mishnah, and Sotah 1.4, 1.6 that by the Second Temple Period, the woman was assumed guilty and shamed quite heavily during this Law of Jealousies. The text in Bamidbar, however, does not suggest this shameful treatment.

Verse 19
The Mishnah tells us that the kohen wrote the following on the scroll: "The Eternal made you an execration and an oath, and this water that indicates the curse shall go into your bowels, to make your belly to swell and your thigh to waste away."[77]

Verse 21
"**a curse among your people**" — According to Milgrom, this implies: "All of the women will use you in their imprecations, and when they curse each other, they will say, "If you have done such a thing may your end be like that of so-and-so." Such was the case in Jeremiah 29:22."[78]

Chapter 6
Verse 2
The term for "Nazarite", *nazir* (נזיר), can mean two things. It can be translated "consecrate", "dedicate", or it could refer to "a crown", such as hair.[79] It seems wisest to combine both renderings. If so, then we can define the Nazarite as one who dedicated himself to the Lord and one of the most distinguishing features was that he did not shave his *nazir*, his crown of hair. At the end of the Second Temple period, many women took the vow, which may account for the many laws regulating it in the Mishnah. Some examples of Nazarite women are Helena, a queen who was a convert (Mishnah Naz. 3.6) and Bernice, sister of King Agrippa II (Josephus, Wars 2.15.1).

---

76. B. Sotah 1.5
77. B. Sotah 2.3
78. Milgrom, *Numbers, JPS,* 41.
79. BDB, 634.

Verse 3

"**other fermented drink**"— This phrase is represented by the Hebrew word *shekhar* (שכר). It is "a comprehensive term for intoxicating liquors other than wine."[80] In the context of the Ancient Near East, however, this could mean beer as well as wine, but usually it means beer, because there was a different term for wine. Egypt and Mesopotamia were noted beer producers,[81] while from an early time in antiquity the inhabitants of Canaan were noted for producing and exporting wine. Milgrom notes that from archaeology we have evidence that the Philistines, particularly, were noted beer drinkers, judging from the beer jugs that have been found. He writes, "It is not difficult to infer from the ubiquity of these... beer jugs that the Philistines were mighty carousers... In this respect, archaeology is in full agreement with biblical tradition, as we see from the story of Samson."[82] The word for vinegar in the NASB is *chomets yayin* (חומץ יין), which is wine turned sour and often used as food by the poor, such as we see in Ruth 2:14.

Verse 5

"**no razor upon the head**" — "The hair was regarded as the symbol of the vital power at its full natural development; and the free growth of the hair on the head of the Nazarite represented the dedication of the man with all his strength and powers to the service of God."[83]

Verse 12

"**dedicate**" — If a Nazarite accidentally became *tam'ei* before his committed period was over, there was a sacrifice he/she had to bring. After the purification process was over, the Nazarite was then committed to continue with the stated period of the vow he voluntarily took upon himself. However, the Nazarite was to rededicate himself before the last of the required sacrifices was offered, the asham offering. The reason for this was apparently, that the re-consecration of his hair, etc. must be done before God's forgiveness was sought. An historical example of such a case is found in Queen Helena. Just before her seven-year vow was completed, she accidentally became tam'ei and was required to go for another seven years![84] In regard to the offerings, see Acts 21:23–26 where Paul not only brought offerings himself but paid for some others who were apparently coming out of a Nazarite vow.

Verse 22

Rabbi Munk paints a helpful historical context for the Aaronic Benediction. He says, "The Priestly Blessing originated on a grand and historic day in the life of the Jewish nation. Now that the Tabernacle was in place, HaShem would surely grant His salvation to the people. The

---

80. Hertz, *Pentateuch and Haftarahs*, 592.
81. See, for example, the delightful yet informative book called *In the Land of Ninkasi; A History of Beer in Ancient Mesopotamia*, by Professor Tate Paulette of North Caroline State University, which provides a full treatment of Mesopotamian beer in particular and beer in general in the Ancient Near East. ("Ninkasi" was the name for an ancient Mesopotamian beer goddess).
82. Milgrom, *Numbers, JPS*, 45.
83. Hertz, *Pentateuch and Haftarahs*, 592.
84. Milgrom, *Numbers, JPS*, 47.

promise of salvation was expressed in the words of the Priestly Blessing, "and establish peace for you" (6:26).[85]

Verses 22–27

Hebraic Roots teacher, Dwight Pryor ז"ל , keenly notes that this blessing is referred to five times in the Tanakh: Leviticus 9:22, Deuteronomy 10:8, Deuteronomy 21:5, Joshua 8:33 and 2 Chronicles 20:27. *Briteinu* editor Peter Styles notes that this five-fold reference possibly communicates an expression of the grace of God (5 is usually considered a symbolic number for grace).

A few years ago in burial caves located behind the Menachem Begin Museum in Jerusalem, Israeli archaeologist Gavriel Barkay, found the oldest known biblical inscription. It is on a small copper amulet from the 6th century BCE and it happens to be this priestly found in Numbers chapter 6.

Chapter 7

In this chapter we see the offerings and gifts that the heads of the tribes brought to the Levites for their use in the new Mishkan, including carts and animals with which to transport the parts of the Mishkan. The chapter only records the names of the heads, but it is reasonable to assume that these heads were merely representing the whole of their tribes. In other words, the riches were not just personal riches brought out of the "pockets" of the heads of the tribes.

There was a large number of objects brought by these tribal heads over the seven-day period, but it was all very much needed. One of the best ways that we can think of illustrating the need for so many bowls, etc., is to recount the scene that took place in the Second Temple when the Pesach lambs were slaughtered there. Josephus informs us that one year there were as many as 250,000 lambs slaughtered for Pesach. Rabbinic tradition required a minimum of one lamb for every 10 people! How was the slaughtering of 250,000 accomplished? The Mishnah informs us that the priests divided the huge crowd into three groups on the day before Pesach. When it was time to slaughter the lambs, one group was permitted to enter at a time to the sound of trumpets and the fully accompanied Levitical choir singing Psalms 113–118. When the people entered into the Temple courtyard, they were greeted by row upon row of priests dressed in scarlet, each holding silver or gold bowls, each row alternating silver and gold. The bowls were all used to catch the blood of the slain Passover lamb from this crowd of worshippers.[86] That is a lot of bowls!

Granted, this is an illustration from the Second Temple Period and a more advanced Temple system. Nonetheless, it furnishes us with a reality of how many implements were used by the priests who worked in the Mishkan/Temple to facilitate Israel sacrificing to the Lord.

---

85. Munk, *The Call of the Torah: Bamidbar*, 64.
86. B. Pesahim 5.6–10

STUDY QUESTIONS

1.   How would you describe the common thread connecting the contents in this parasha?

2.   Why do you think that the Lord required(s) someone to make restitution? Do you think that the principle of restitution can be applied to other areas of life? Explain!

3.   How is the sin(s) which required restitution sins against the Lord, as well as against man?

4.   What do you think about the ritual for a sotah in the law of Jealousies?

5.   Why was the woman's head uncovered?

6.   Why was an oath written on a scroll then erased in the bitter water?

7.   What affect do you think this ritual would have had on the rest of the community? What effect do you think it may have had on the woman in question?

8   Why do you think that the Law of Jealousies did not apply if a man was unfaithful in the marriage? Or did it? Explain.

9   Why do you think a person would become a Nazir?

10.   Why was one of the main characteristics of a Nazirite the growth of his hair?

11.   Why do you think that the Lord required a Nazir to abstain from the specified things in Bamidbar 6?

12.   Why do you think a Nazir was required to bring a sin offering upon the conclusion of his Vow?

13.   What does it mean to have the Lord's Name upon His people, as stated at the end of the Aaronic Benediction?

14.   Why do you think that the kohanim were to say the Blessing to the people? What purpose did it serve?

15.   Why were so many implements brought as gifts to the kohanim?

16.   Why were there animals and carts brought to the kohanim?

17.   Why do you think that we are given such details about the offerings that the heads of the tribes brought at the inauguration of the Mishkan in Numbers 7?

PARASHAT BEHA'ALOTEKHA בהעלותך

TORAH: NUMBERS 8:1–12:16
HAFTARAH: ZECHARIAH 2:14– 4:7

Parashat Beha'alotekha בהעלותך

The Holy One, blessed be He, said to Moses, I gave you spirit and intelligence to govern My children. I sought no other so that you might be unique in the enjoyment of that greatness. Yet you ask for the assistance of others! I want you to realize that they will receive nothing of Mine, but that I will take of the spirit which is upon you (Numbers 11:17). This notwithstanding, Moses lost nothing. [Bamidbar Rabbah 15.25]

This week's parasha begins with final instructions before the Mishkan begins its daily service. It also contains historical narrative, as will be true for several succeeding parashiyot. Consequently, we have decided to adopt this simple approach for this week:

I. Instructional Section
II. Historical Section
III. Moshe

I. INSTRUCTIONAL SECTION: FINAL MISHKAN PREPARATIONS

Our parasha opens with Moshe hearing instructions from the Lord from a new location. The last verse of last week's parasha told us that when the Mishkan was completely set up the Lord called Moshe into the innermost chamber. "From between the two cherubim above the atonement cover on the ark of Testimony. And He spoke with him…" (7:89).

A. To Comfort a Sulking Aaron?

One of the first instructions God spoke from His "new home" was for Moshe to teach Aaron how to kindle the Mishkan's golden menorah. Both the context and the wording however are rather curious. Rashi, following a midrash, notes that the section on the menorah comes immediately after the dedicatory offerings brought by the twelve tribes. He suggests that Aaron was feeling left out of this dedication service, so God comforted him by permitting him to be the one to light the menorah. Rashi writes,

> Why is the section, talking about the candelabrum, put in a section dealing with the offerings of the princes? Because when Aaron saw the dedication offerings of the princes, he then became uneasy in mind because neither he nor his tribe was with them in the dedication, whereupon the Holy One, blessed be He, said to him, "By thy life! Thy part is of greater importance than theirs, for thou wilt kindle and set in order the lamps."[87]

Rambam, among others, disagrees with this distinguished sage. We also humbly take issue with Rashi on this point. Among other things, it seems like rather an insult to Aaron to suggest that he was sulking! It seems to us that all we have here are just the finishing touches to a great dedication service, with everyone, including Aaron and his sons, doing their God-appointed tasks. To state it in everyday terms: When the lights are turned on, the house is ready to start functioning!

B. Let the Light Shine!

The text makes an issue of the way in which Aaron was to light the separate candles. The idiomatic Hebrew could perhaps best be translated to read, "When you light the lamps, the

---

87. Rashi: *Bamidbar*, ArtScroll Edition, 88.

seven lamps shall give light in front of the menorah." They were to illuminate the entire holy place where the golden table for the bread was also located.

The Torah does not tell us specifically what, if anything, the golden menorah may symbolize. Thus, we need to guard against any dogmatism in our interpretations of it. Notwithstanding, we might be able to see several pictures in it. For one it was shaped like a tree with blossoms on it. Perhaps this may remind us of the Tree of Life. Its light surely pictured the light of God. Seven lamps produced the light. Seven is almost universally accepted as the number of perfection. The gold, being the purest of all natural metals, stands for purity. Putting all of this together, can we suggest that the golden Menorah might be said to symbolize God's perfect presence and life, illuminating His sanctuary and through Moses, His people. Moreover, Israel was to have this menorah shine continually, "that [they] may perpetuate the light which I conferred on you as an example to the nations of the world."[88]

If one desires a more complete description of the golden menorah used during the Second Temple period, read the Babylonian Talmud, Tractate Menachot beginning at 28a.

C. The Great Wave!

The last part of the dedication of the Mishkan is in 8:5–26. Here we have a huge gathering of all the Levites at the Mishkan for consecration and final dedication to the work in the Mishkan. These verses again repeat the teaching about the replacement of Israel's firstborn by the Levites. One of the most impressive parts of this ceremony was the huge wave offering Aaron made of the Levites. It was as if they were all saying, "Here we are, Lord, at your service, ready to go!"

D. The Apprentices

Of special interest in this section is the teaching concerning the training of the new Levites for their work. We are told in 4:3 that a Levite could not begin his job until he was 30 years old. However apparently according to 8:23 new ones began their service when they were 25 years old. How can we reconcile this difference in ages? A common solution that has been offered is to suggest that at the age of 25 they began their apprenticeship and at the age of 30 they took up their priestly duties.

Who was to do the training? The older ones! It says in 8:25 that when they turned 50, their regular Levitical work was completed. However, 8:26 tells us, "He shall remain with his brethren in the Tent of Meeting to safeguard the charge (our translation)." Though we are not told specifically, it is reasonable to suggest that what he was doing was training the new recruits.

This pattern for training was to characterize God's people throughout the centuries. Paul, in *Titus* chapter two, taught that in the body of Messiah, as among the children of Israel, the older ones were to train the younger ones in spiritual and practical things. If God's people would but practise these instructions it would provide much needed meaning and purpose for the older members of our communities, rather than just letting them finish their lives feeling

---

88.   J. H. Hertz, *The Pentateuch and Haftarahs*, 605.

unproductive and ignored.

E. For Those Who Missed Pesach

The final instructional matter we will cover is in 9:1–14. The issue is Pesach. The context is that when Israel was about to celebrate their second Pesach since leaving Egypt, a practical problem arose. Some came to Moshe and asked him what they should do about offering the Pesach sacrifice if they were in a tam'ei condition from touching a dead body.

Moshe, not knowing exactly how to answer their question, took the matter directly to the Lord who taught this precept: Anyone who could not celebrate Pesach because of touching a dead body or because they were on a journey, were permitted to do so exactly one month after the others did. On the 14th of the second month, they were to celebrate Pesach.

This is a helpful and gracious response from the Lord. It represents His mercy and shows that He can sympathize with the imperfect conditions in which we live on planet earth. Pesach must still be kept but if circumstances absolutely prohibit it, we may do it on the same day of the following month. It should be noted however that our lives today are very different from theirs at the time of the offerings in God's House. The two conditions for exemption are a tam'ei condition and travel, i.e., they could not reach the House (or Mishkan) on the specified day. Both exemptions preclude the existence of the House or the national centre of worship. However, such a national centre no longer exists. Yeshua, The Pesach Lamb has already been slain once for all. Hence, there are few excuses for not keeping the Pesach in our day and age. Note especially the consequences outlined in 9:13–14 for failure to do so.

II. HISTORICAL SECTION

A. The Movements of the Camp

Leading nearly three million people through the wilderness was no easy task. It took enormous organization. The situation was further complicated with the construction of the Mishkan and the institution of the sacrificial system. There had to be strict adherence to God's regulations in such a system. All of this made any and every camp movement very difficult. However, God, whose idea it was to undertake such a complicated feat of transporting a whole nation from Egypt to the land of Canaan, made special provisions for camp organization in order to help facilitate easier movement. Our parasha reveals to us some of these specific provisions. We have already studied the camp organization in Bamidbar. Here in 9:15–10:36 we see some more specific organizational devices from the Holy One.

1. The Cloud and Fire

The first provision was the combined cloud and fire display of chapter 9. The text, expanding Exodus 34:5, explains that the camp would move or rest according to how a certain cloud or pillar of fire would move. Wherever and whenever the cloud (or fire) would move, so would the children of Israel. They were to faithfully follow the cloud.

The Torah connects the cloud with some aspect of the Lord Himself. When the cloud moved 9:18 tells us it was the same as saying, "At the commandment of the Lord the children of Israel journeyed…" Some commentators equate this Cloud with the Shekinah whose glorious light filled the Holy of Holies. We however think that they are two different phenomena. The Shekinah dwelt permanently in the Mishkan. The cloud dwelt outside of the Mishkan and moved. In either case however, both phenomena are a supernatural expression of God.

The use of the cloud and the pillar of fire to direct the movements of the camp must have been very strange to our forefathers. Yet where else could they have turned for direction in such a wilderness? The trust they would have learned was a lesson which would have implications for centuries. "This quiet, serene trust in God was the virtue that the people would need most for their journeys in the Diaspora, through the wilderness of the nations."[89]

The cloud and fire had an even more practical function. During the daytime the cloud provided essential protection from the dangerous, brilliant desert sun beating down upon the fragile elderly and the vulnerable young. At night the fire would provide much needed heat from the cold chill that characterizes such arid climates. The Gracious One thinks of everything!

2. Sound the Trumpets!

The second practical step in organizing the camp was the institution of the blasting of trumpets to either call meetings or to announce the beginning of a journey. This is found at the beginning of chapter 10.

The trumpets were not rams' horns (*shofarim*) but were two silver trumpets (*chatzotzerot*, חצוצרות). The text tells us that upon the sounding of given signals, certain things would take place. When there was a long blast with both of them the entire assembly of Israel would meet at the Mishkan. When only one trumpet blasted, only the leaders would meet. When the trumpets were sounded with short blasts, it signalled that it was time to follow the cloud and move the entire camp. Furthermore, a series of short blasts of both trumpets was to be sounded during times of war. In addition, the trumpets were also to be blown during the festivals.

For interest's sake, Josephus (writing in the 1st century ce) furnishes us with a verbal description of what he thought Moshe's trumpet looked like. "In length it was a little less than a cubit. It was composed of a narrow tube, somewhat thicker than a flute, but with so much breadth as was sufficient for admission of the breath of a man's mouth. It ended in the form of a bell, like common trumpets."[90]

The Hebrew words used in our text to describe the kinds of sounds that were to be made with the trumpets are also some of the same words used to describe the kind of sounds the modern shofar blower is to make on Rosh Hashanah. When 10:3 says in the NASB that the trumpet is to be "blown," the Hebrew is called a *teki'a*, associated with the verb, *tak'a* (תקע). Traditionally, this

89. Elie Munk, *The Call of the Torah: Bamidbar*, 102.
90. Flavius Josephus, *Antiquities of the Jews*, III.12.6.

sounds like a long blast. In 10:5, the word translated "alarm in the NASB: is *tru'ah* (תרועה). This traditionally sounds like a series (nine to eleven) of short, staccato notes. The remaining sound on Rosh Hashanah is called *shevarim* (שברים). This word is not in this passage of Torah. Though we are not certain, it appears to be from a Hebrew verb, *shavar* (שבר), that means, "to break", or "to shatter".[91] Accordingly, it traditionally consists of a series of three short, slurred soundings, breaking the teki'a up into three equal lengths. Thus, on Rosh Hashanah, the main pattern for the sounding of the shofar is as follows:

Tekiah: ▬▬▬▬
Shevarim: ‑ ‑ ‑
T'ruah: ▪▪▪▪▪▪▪
Tekiah: ▬▬▬▬

Now everyone knows what to do with the new shofar just purchased on the recent trip to Israel! However, practise hard because these sounds are repeated on Rosh Hashanah from at least 30 to 100 times!

Numbers 10:8 states that the use of the silver trumpets was to be a permanent practice among the Israelites but to our knowledge, we do not use them today. Why not? Why do we only sound the shofar and not the silver trumpets for their specified uses? Rashi provides the most common explanation accepted by many commentators. According to him, the answer seems to be that 10:2 teaches that Moshe himself was to make two trumpets, which were for his own possession. They were to be blown in his presence as if to a king.[92] Elie Munk elaborates on this by adding, "[Moshe] had been elevated to the position of king over Israel (see Deuteronomy 33:5). The trumpets were marks of honour and prestige for him. Moses had no equal in Israel. The trumpets were put away just before his death and never used again.[93]

We know that silver trumpets were used in the Second Temple Period. (Were they the original ones?) We can see them carved on the famous arch of Titus in Rome, built to commemorate Titus' victory in Jerusalem and the destruction of the Temple in 70 CE. Moreover, the Mishnah speaks of the use of the trumpets on Pesach to announce when the Pesach offerings were to begin.[94] Apart from this, we are not aware of any further use of silver trumpets in Jewish liturgy **since** the Second Temple Period. The reason apparently is that their use has always been closely tied to the Temple service. No Temple, no trumpet! Whenever a sound is needed, it is from the shofar.

3. A Question for the Rabbis

We have one final note about the trumpets. The *ArtScroll Chumash* tells us that the trumpets "were sounded by the kohanim in conjunction with the communal elevation and peace offerings

---

91. BDB, 990–991.
92. Rashi, *ArtScroll Edition.*, 105.
93. Munk, *The Call of the Torah: Bamidbar,* 103.
94. B. Peshchim 5.3

of the Sabbath and festival days."[95] We have already seen an example of this in regard to Pesach. We read this note in the *ArtScroll Chumash* with a sense of protest. According to Orthodox Jewish *halakhah*, it is not permitted to sound the shofar on Rosh Hashanah (biblically, the Festival of Trumpets) if it happens to fall on a Shabbat. We ask why not? If the silver trumpets were sounded for some of the Shabbat sacrificial services, then it would seem that even more so should the shofar be sounded on a festival which is specifically designated for that purpose!

Rabbi Munk, himself quite Orthodox, explains the traditional answer when he comments, "The practice of not blowing the shofar on the Sabbath is actually based only on a Rabbinical restriction that was established to prevent the possibility of someone carrying the shofar through the street to an expert for lessons in its use."[96] After citing this practice, Munk continues by pointing out the rabbinic principle used to create such a tradition. He says, "This points to a unique principle in that a commandment of the Torah to blow the shofar on a certain day must yield to a restriction of the Sages, ... aimed at preventing the transformation of that commandment into a possible sin.[97]

We protest! We protest all the more when we read of the reasoning of the sages for such a flagrant violation of the Torah; that they are prohibiting the Torah from being carried out only to avoid a *possible* violation of one of their own Shabbat restrictions!

B. "Arise, O Lord!"

We are examining some of the organizational provisions that our text reveals which helped to facilitate the mass-movement of Israel through the wilderness. We have looked at the cloud/fire, and we have discussed the trumpets. The next feature is another special one.

The sequence of movement was that first the cloud rose from the Mishkan and then the trumpets were sounded. However, immediately before the first tribal group led by Judah was to take the first step, Moshe was to shout, "Rise up, O Lord! May your enemies be scattered; may your foes flee before you." When the journey was finished, after the cloud rested, Moshe would shout again saying, "Return O Lord to the countless thousands of Israel." Reside in tranquillity, O Lord, among the myriad thousands of Israel (10:35–36)".

1. A War Cry

The cry by Moshe was, in essence, a war cry. It was as if he were the general shouting on behalf of the Commander-in-Chief (the Lord) to all of His enemies, "Here we come, you better flee!" Then when the "battle" was finished, the general was telling the Commander-in-Chief that because of His brilliantly orchestrated victory, He may now rest peacefully in the victorious camp of His army. Rabbi Hertz also sees this picture. He adds, "The ark going forward at the head of Israel's tribes, typified God in front of His people protecting and helping them and

---

95. *The Artscroll Chumash*, 783.
96. Elie Munk, *The Call of the Torah: Vayikra*, 282.
97. *Ibid.*

leading them on to final victory; when God arises against the hosts of Israel's enemies, they scatter as the darkness before the Sunlight."[98]

2. The Marks in the Text

The Rabbis of old recognized that this was, indeed, a most special part of the Torah. In order to indicate this, the ancient scribes maintained a set of special marks in the Hebrew text to show that 10:35–36 (the "war cry") was to be set apart from the rest of the text. The question is — was the insertion of these marks a product of the ancient Masoretes, the sages who preserved and copied the text of the Torah? Or, were they put in earlier, perhaps by Moshe? For those who read Hebrew, we reproduce here the text with the special marks highlighted and made larger:

Numbers 10:34 וַעֲנַן יְהוָה עֲלֵיהֶם יוֹמָם בְּנָסְעָם מִן־הַמַּחֲנֶה: **ן**

Numbers 10:35 וַיְהִי בִּנְסֹעַ הָאָרֹן וַיֹּאמֶר מֹשֶׁה קוּמָה ׀ יְהוָה וְיָפֻצוּ אֹיְבֶיךָ וְיָנֻסוּ מְשַׂנְאֶיךָ מִפָּנֶיךָ:

Numbers 10:36 וּבְנֻחֹה יֹאמַר שׁוּבָה יְהוָה רִבְבוֹת אַלְפֵי יִשְׂרָאֵל: **ן**

The Talmud denies that scribes placed them there and asserts, "The Holy One, blessed be He, provided signs above and below." According to the Talmudic sages, therefore, God Himself inserted these marks. Why do they think that He did so? The sages suggest two possibilities. The first one was that these marks served as separating marks, "to provide a break between the first (account of) punishment and the second (account of) punishment." We however do not see how they say the text speaks of punishment! However, another proposal is also set forth. The Talmud states that God placed these marks in the text, "to teach that this is not its (the passages, 10:35–36), place. (But) Rabbi said, 'No, it is not on that account, but because it ranks as a separate book'." [99]

In other words, the sages were suggesting that because of these marks, Numbers is divided into three books, therefore making it so that we have seven and not five books of Moses! To confirm their assertion, they state, "She (wisdom) has hewed out seven pillars (Proverbs 9:1); this refers to the seven books of the Torah."[100] Very interesting! However, we do not think that the rabbis were really insisting that there were supposed to be seven books of Torah. It seems that all they were trying to do is to emphasize the beauty and uniqueness of these words by Moshe. In other words that might be a rabbinic hyperbole.

Even in our day and age, this war cry from Moshe has become a much celebrated saying among Israel. For example, just before the Torah is taken from the ark in the synagogue service, we say the first line. When it is replaced, we say the second line. We do this realizing that the

---

98. Hertz, *Pentateuch and Haftarahs*, 613.
99. B. Shabbat 115b and 116a
100. B. Shabbat 116a

real source of all of our strength and victories is God and His Word. Our trusted commentator, J. H. Hertz, expounding on these words, quotes Alexander Maclaren, an evangelical thinker, "We too may take up the immortal through ancient words, and, at the beginnings and endings of all our efforts, offer this old prayer — the prayer that asked for a Divine Presence in the incipiency of our efforts, and the prayer which asked for a Divine Presence on the completion of our work."[101]

3. The Leaders

The last special provision God gave to Israel for the journey was more leadership. In truth, we think that it was not just to help make their journey easier, but it was also to help govern them while in the Land. This is found in 11:16–17, but as the context tells us, there is more to the story than just the appointment of 70 spirit-filled leaders. Let us examine it.

C. "You Can't Get There from Here!"

When we lived in New Hampshire, USA, we often heard a local adage used when we asked someone for directions. If the way was rather complicated, the direction-giver would often say, "You can't get there from here!" This meant that you had to take a rather roundabout way to get to where you were going. This seems to adequately describe what the Holy One was doing in these verses. Not only was He working some spiritual growth among the Israelites, but He was also maturing Moshe as well.

It was apparently God's intention all along to have a leadership of 70 wise, spirit-filled elders, shepherding and leading His people. At one point, in Exodus 18, He even instituted this concept. However, when the golden calf incident occurred, it seemed that this eldership was decimated because of sin. Hence, we find that Moshe is essentially the sole leader of Israel. How was God going to get Moshe to realize that he needed help again and how was God going to get Israel to realize that they could no longer depend solely on Moshe to lead them?

God's method of convincing Moshe was to use the "you can't get there from here" method. Because of the complexities of human behaviour, He could not just say, "Now appoint 70 men to be your elders." God had to thoroughly teach Israel the need, and at the same time thoroughly work in Moshe's life to get him to the point of desperation where he would realize that he simply could not get along any further without help. In Exodus 18 Moshe did not come to that conclusion by his own accord; Jethro helped him to see the need. Now, Moshe himself would be driven to come to that conclusion.

How did God do it? He accomplished it by letting His people complain. However, their complaining did not have the justification it had before, when as newly freed slaves they could not see how food and water would be provided in an arid wilderness. That was, in some ways, justified but this time when they complained about food, it was not out of desperation in fear of starvation. Instead, it was out of being spoiled! They simply wanted more variety of foods! They

---

101. Hertz, *Pentateuch and Haftyarahs*, 614.

wanted to eat some meat instead of just manna.

Please do not misunderstand. Even though we believe God orchestrated this revolt, it nonetheless was very real. The ones who complained were very guilty and deserved to be disciplined, as our text states. Notice how God handled them. He is like a typical parent in disciplining a child! He states in 11:20 that He, indeed, would give them what they think they wanted (as opposed to what they really needed!). In fact, they would eat meat "until it comes out of your nose!"

The tragedy in this episode was not really asking for meat to eat. They went beyond that and started to ask to go back to Egypt. In short, they were rebelling against God again. To be sure, not all were doing so, but a rebellion was to begin by a group referred to in the Hebrew in 11:4 as *ha'asafuf* (האספסף). This word is set in contrast to the children of Israel in the same verse. Its basic meaning is that of a "collection", or "gathering".[102] Hertz believes, "the Hebrew form is a contemptuous term denoting a number of people gathered together from all quarters, a rabble, or riffraff. It is identical with the mixed multitude of aliens who had attached themselves to the Israelites and accompanied them out of Egypt."[103]

Because of the strong influence of the group, many in Israel also rebelled and were subsequently disciplined by the Lord. Paul has this principle in mind in 1 Corinthians 5:6–11, where he warns us concerning our relationships in the body of Messiah and our connections with those who do not know our God: "Do you not know that a little leaven leavens the whole lump? I wrote to you not to associate with any so-called brother if he should be an immoral person, or covetous, or an idolater or a reveller or a drunkard, or a swindler-not even to eat with one" (Author's paraphrase). Such people can have as devastating an effect on life in the body of Messiah as the *asafuf* had in Israel.

This rebellion had its God-desired effect on Moshe. It proved too much for him to handle alone. He said in 11:14–15, "I cannot carry all these people by myself; the burden is too heavy for me." Here Moshe's protest was private, between him and the Holy One. The Lord responded in mercy. Moshe was now at the place spiritually where the Lord wanted him to be. He was ready for his next step of growth. For his own good, and for the good of Israel, the leadership needed to be shared.

This is a critical lesson many spiritual leaders, rabbis and pastors need to learn. Sharing the spiritual leadership not only enhances the well-being of the sheep, it also protects the leader. That is what Paul seems to imply in 1 Timothy 3–5, when he teaches that the leadership of God's people should not be one man but a plurality of godly elders.

---

102. BDB, 63.
103. Hertz, *Pentateuch and Haftarahs*, 614.

D. The Seventy and Two?

God's response to Moshe was to instruct him to select 70 elders from among the rest of the elders of Israel (11:16–17). The text indicates that there seemingly were two men left over: Eldad and Medad, "Two men remained in camp" (11:26). The wording is ambiguous and has provoked some speculation about whether or not they were among the 70. The Midrash offers this explanation:

> What did he [Moshe] do? He took seventy-two ballots and wrote on them elder, and another two ballots he left blank. Then he mixed them up in an urn and proclaimed, "Come and draw your ballots" A man who drew out a ballot inscribed with the word 'elder' knew that he had been appointed an elder and one who drew out a blank knew that he had not been appointed, and the superintendent would say to him, "There is still a ballot in the urn inscribed with the word elder, and had you been worthy of being appointed, you would have drawn it." The procedure having been adopted, the elders were duly appointed. Eldad and Medad who were there withdrew into the background saying: "We are unworthy of being among the appointed elders." In return for their self-effacement they proved to be superior to the elders.[104]

Some may say that this could never be. Men just do not act in such a godly, humble way. We object! In fact, we know a real Eldad (that is his Hebrew name). He was an elder in a congregation we led in Massachusetts before we made *aliyah*. He would have done exactly what the Midrash said the biblical Eldad did! It is amazing how beautiful the new creation can look when the Spirit of God controls him/her.

Speaking of God's Spirit . . .

1. "Charismatic" Elders

The choosing of these 70 elders is accompanied by an unusual phenomenon — they were endowed with the Spirit of God and prophesied (11:25). Some read into the text an ecstatic experience (Hertz and others), but it need not be interpreted that way. What seems to have happened is that God's Spirit, given to Moshe at Mount Sinai to equip him for the task God had for him, was passed on through Moshe to the seventy, so that they also could be sufficiently equipped. Moshe's share of the Spirit did not decrease. Instead, "The men, who now shared in his spiritual vision to a wider degree than they had done previously, would be all the more enabled to support him in the task of leadership to which he had been called."[105]

We do not know the exact nature of their prophecies. The Midrash suggests that it be about future things. Most likely it was as Hertz suggests, "the power of instructing and admonishing the people with an authority that was recognized as having its source in God."[106] This interpretation is perfectly compatible with what Paul teaches in 1 Corinthians 14:3. He says that "everyone who prophesies speaks to men for their strengthening, encouragement and comfort." Assuming this also described the words of these men, it would have been a great aid and help to

---

104. Bamidbar Rabbah 15.19–20
105. R.K. Harrison, *Numbers* (TOTC), 188.
106. Hertz, *Pentateuch and Haftarahs,* 616.

Moshe, as well as going a long way to building up the spiritual welfare of the camp.

Commentators differ in their opinions about how long they "prophesied". The Hebrew is ambiguous enough to yield several possibilities. Some, like Rashi, suggest, "They prophesied that day alone."[107] On the other hand, *Targum Onkelos* translates this verse to mean that the gift of prophecy did not leave them.

2. "Let Them All Prophesy!"

As for the two separate ones, Eldad and Medad, we are told that they kept themselves separate from the seventy and went through the camp prophesying, also under the power and control of the Spirit of God. Again, we assume that the same definition of prophecy held true for them as well as for the seventy.

Jewish literature is rich in ideas concerning the content of *their* prophecies. The student can read some suggestions in *Targum Jerushalmi;* the *Talmud* (Sanhedrin 17a); and *Midrash Tanchuma*, Korach 12. In contrast to the seventy however, the Hebrew verb "to prophesy" of 11:26 tells us that Eldad and Medad "continually prophesied" throughout the camp. In fact, they prophesied so much that Joshua, thinking that something was out of order, reported them to Moshe.

However, Moshe's response was significant. Instead of stopping them, he said, "wish that all the Lord's people were prophets and that the Lord would put his Spirit on them!" (11:29). Here "Moses expresses the conviction, which is true for all time, that the possession of the Spirit is not confined to particular persons or classes,"[108] but rather to all those who belong to the Lord through a personal relationship with Him.

III. Moshe

We come now to the final section of commentary for this week's Parasha. The text in chapter 12 focuses attention on Moshe's life, especially on those things that made him a great leader. Let us do the same. Let us see how many godly characteristics of Moshe the leader we can discover. When we do so, we can assume safely, that just as God moulded this man of God to walk after Him, so He does the same with us. Those things that characterized this leader also characterize the new creation leader, for he also was one of us! Because of time and space, we cannot amplify these points. We will just list them with a few brief comments. Notice that we are presenting this material in an outline format so that it easily is taught to others.

---

107. Rashi, *ArtScroll Edition,* 131.
108. Hertz, *Pentateuch and Haftarahs,* 617.

WHY WAS MOSHE SUCH A GREAT LEADER?

A. He Took His Problems to God

When one leads almost three million people there is surely hardly ever a moment when one is not facing a problem. Our text relates that some of the habitual problems of the Israelites happened to have been rebellion, both against God and against Moshe, God's appointed leader.

Such problems could be the end of most leaders if they are not handled properly. Moshe was not one of those kinds of people. We read continually that when problems arose Moshe took all of them directly to the Lord, sometimes in the privacy of the innermost sanctuary where fellowship between them was most intimate.

A leader cannot afford to handle his problems in any other way. He may choose to share them with others but ultimately, they must be shared openly and honestly with the only One Who is full of wisdom and truth.

B. He Was Honest With God

When confronted with the new rebellion about food in chapter 10, Moshe had had enough. (Not of food but of complaints!) He was ready to quit. He said that he would rather die than continue in such a leadership position. It is not recorded that he expressed any of this to some of his close aides. Instead, the text tells us that he went right to God with how he felt and thought. When he did so, while not being disrespectful, he nevertheless was completely honest with his feelings and thoughts to the Holy One. He knew and trusted God well enough to know that even if he did sin, "God is faithful and just to forgive that sin and to cleanse him from all unrighteousness" (1 John 1:9).

C. He Was Willing to Sacrifice for the Good of the People.

God endowed Moshe with two special gifts which most spiritual leaders would covet. He gifted Moshe with an outstanding leadership ability, which included wisdom, strength, charisma, and popularity. He also gifted Moshe with an acute gift of prophecy. The Rambam also recognized this in his famous Principle # 7: "I believe with perfect faith the prophecy of Moshe, our teacher, peace be unto him, was true, and that he was the chief of the prophets both those who preceded him and those who followed him." In fact, the Torah states that the prophetic office of Moshe would serve as a paradigm for the prophetic office Messiah Himself would walk (Deuteronomy 18 verse 15f).

A lesser leader would have done all he could to ensure that these gifts and abilities would not be shared with others. He would think perhaps, that if they were someone else may arise who may lead better or prophesy more, making it possible for the people to follow that new person instead of him. He would be afraid, envious and suspicious. These fleshly characteristics would hinder his thinking as well as his ability to adequately serve his people.

This was not the case with Moshe. He did not regard his precious gift of prophecy and the ensuing office as something for only himself. Chapter 11 tells us that he wanted to share this with others. For example, look at the Eldad and Medad incident. When they were freely prophesying around the camp, Moshe's chief aide, Joshua, tried to stop them. In essence Moshe said to him, "Joshua, why? Are you jealous for me and my gift and office?" Then Moshe let it be known how he really thought and felt. He said in 11:29 "I wish that all the Lord's people were prophets!"

D. He Shared His Leadership

Chapter 11 tells us how Moshe not only willingly shared his leadership with the 70 elders, but he actually asked for this plurality of eldership to be put into place. We are given no hint of any jealousy from Moshe.

This is how a new creation believer really is inside of himself. He knows that any gift that God has given to him was given for the sake of the whole body, not for his own personal pleasure and glory. Imagine what it would be like to be the only one through whom the Lord spoke? Can you imagine the awe in which people would look upon you? Can you sense the air of importance you would be able to carry around about yourself? The only one!

Perhaps this is what it may have been like for Moshe, or so some people thought. At least, according to chapter 12 that is what Miriam and Aaron were apparently beginning to think! Moshe wanted to take a Cushite woman for a wife, and they objected. To try to make their protest felt, they expostulated, "Has the Lord spoken only through Moses"? (12:2). Perhaps others were thinking the same, maybe they thought, "Can no one else around here also prophesy?"

This leads us to the next characteristic of Moshe's leadership.

E. He Did Not Act Defensively

Many leaders, when challenged on any of their decisions or ideas, sometimes act in a defensive manner. They do so, perhaps, out of insecurity. If they are trying to derive personal worth and identity from what they do and say, they are easily prone to such fleshly behaviour. When it comes out it usually manifests itself in short, curt answers, haughty attitudes, judgment making against the one who challenges them, or just plain lack of kindness.

Moshe was not like this. Chapter 12 shows how he conducted himself when he was challenged. It was a most difficult challenge, too, because it was from his own family — those who were supposed to know him best. However, notice his response. The only time he said something is in 12:13 where he interceded for Miriam after the Lord had disciplined her for her rebellion. Instead of defensiveness or unkindness, Moshe's response was one of kindness and love.

The new creation leader has no reason to be defensive about anything. Like Moshe, he knows who he is in Messiah and has the ability to trust his lot in His hands. One clarifying note here: we are not saying that the new creation should never defend himself, but we *are* saying that he should never make room in his flesh for defensiveness. There is a big difference. Moshe defended himself on occasion, but he did not act defensively.

F. He Related to God in an Intimate Way

One thing that certainly characterized Moshe's leadership was his intimate relationship with God. In fact, we would submit that this was the one thing which caused the other positive characteristics to manifest themselves.

When Miriam and Aaron challenged him in chapter 12, God Himself came to Moshe's defence. In doing so, He said a most remarkable thing about His servant Moshe. He said in 12:6-8, "When a prophet of the Lord is among you, I reveal myself to him in visions; I speak to him in dreams. But this is not true of my servant Moses; he is faithful in all my house. With him I speak face to face, clearly and not in riddles; he sees the form of the Lord." God said that Moshe was the most trusted one in all Israel because they (Moshe and the Holy One) met each other in intimate ways.

The godly leader also develops his personal relationship with the Lord. He learns to study His Word and to hear His voice from its pages. He does not rely on others to develop this relationship for him. He does it himself. He makes that effort to be alone with God, just as Moshe did.

G. Summary: Moshe Was More Humble Than Anyone Else!

If there were one word that would characterize Moshe, both as a man and as a leader, it would be humility. This is what God Himself said about him in 12:3, "Now Moses was a very humble man, more humble than anyone else on the face of the earth." How else could Moshe have walked in the essential characteristics of leadership described above, if he were not a humble man?

A key to his humility was that Moshe was not self-serving; instead, he was the servant of God (12:7). If a leader has his mind on himself, his image, his well-being, his goals and aspirations, he will inevitably walk in the flesh and the sheep will not be able to feel safe around him. However, if he has his thoughts centred on serving God and His sheep, he will be a safe leader.

This is the new creation leader. This is how Yeshua the Messiah Himself walked. This is what Yeshua taught concerning leadership. He said on more than one occasion, that the real leader is a servant. Our strength comes from serving, not ourselves but others. This is real humility.

ADDITIONAL NOTES

Chapter 8
Verse 4

"**according to the pattern which the Lord had shown Moses**" — The word "pattern" in the Hebrew is a participle from the verb to see, *l'ireh* (לראה). This usage is in the hiphil verbal stem, which would carry a causative idea. In other words, the Lord instructed Moshe to make the menorah "according to that which He caused Moshe to see." The stress is on the fact that this was a vision which God gave to Moshe, not some dream that Moshe had on his own. This is how all the plans for the Mishkan were revealed to Moshe.

Verse 7

"**water of cleansing**" — The Hebrew says literally, "waters of sin" *mai hatta't* (מי חטאת). This was most likely fresh water mixed with the ashes of the red heifer (see chapter 19), which is also called a *hatta't*.[109]

Verses 10–11

The dedication of the Levites consisted first of all of the entire House of Israel laying their hands upon them. It was as if the people were laying their hands on them like one lays his hands on an offering. The Levites were, in a sense, an offering for the firstborn of Israel. The second part was the "waving" of the Levites. The waving was also reminiscent of the offerings as well. "Because the Levites were made, so to speak, an expiatory offering in their (the Israelites) stead."[110] "Three wave offerings are mentioned in this chapter, corresponding to the three major Levite families: Kohat, Gershon, and Merari."[111]

As to the actual procedure of waving, we can only guess. Hertz does a good job at this speculation. He suggests, "The Levites were probably led backwards and forwards by Aaron in the direction of the Holy of Holies, or he may only have waved his hand over them."[112] This waving carried the idea that the Levites, having been given as an offering by the Israelites are now being given back to them as their servants in the matters of the Mishkan.

Verses 23–26

The starting age for the service of the Levites varied according to the Tanakh. Here it is stated to be at age 25. In Numbers 4:3, 23 and 30 it is stated to be age 30, and in 1 Chronicles 23:21, 27 it is listed at age 20. Why the differences? According to Milgrom, "The answer lies in the changed work profile of the Levites." When the Temple was built and the need for a lot of strenuous carrying work was eliminated, the age could be extended from 20 until death. The rabbis harmonize the discrepancy [i.e., 25 or 30] by conjecturing that at age twenty-five the Levite entered into training and perhaps served as an assistant, but only at age thirty did he assume his full role in the ranks of Levite labourers. The Essenes sect also thought this way. [113]

Chapter 9
Verses 1–5

In keeping with this established tradition of dedicating the Mishkan near Pesach, later dedications of the Temple were also climaxed with a celebration of one of the major festivals.

---

109. Jacob Milgrom, *The JPS Torah Commentary: Numbers*, 61.
110. Rashi, *ArtScroll Edition*, 43.
111. Munk, *The Call of the Torah: Bamidbar*, 91 and Rashi.
112. Hertz, *Pentateuch and Haftarahs,* 606.
113. Milgrom, *JPS Torah Commentary*, 65–66.

Such festivals include: Solomon on Sukkot (1 Kings 8:65–66), Hezekiah on Pesach (2 Chronicles 29–30), Josiah on Pesach (2 Kings 23:21–23), the exiles on Sukkot (Ezra 3:4), and Nehemiah on Sukkot (Nehemiah 8:13–18).

Verse 10

"on a journey" — The Hebrew indicates that a long journey is meant by using the words *b'derekh rechoka* (בדרך רחוקה). What is considered a long journey? The ancient sages had many opinions. Actually, there are two questions involved in this issue. The first is, "A long distance from where?" To this the ancient rabbis suggested two answers: 1) From the authorized altar at the Tabernacle (later the Temple in Jerusalem) or 2) From the household, implying that the Pesach could be eaten only within the family circle but not elsewhere.[114]

The second question is, "How far is considered a long distance?" The answers are given in reference to the Temple. Rabbi Akiva said that it would be beyond a radius drawn from the Temple to the village of Modi'in. This would be approximately 20 miles. Rabbis Eliezer and Yose applied it to anyone who could not reach the Temple threshold.[115]

Verse 13

"cut off from his people" — It is difficult to determine precisely what is meant here. Usually three suggestions are given: 1) excommunicated from the community, 2) execution through a court order, 3) some supernatural judgment from God.

Verses 15 ff

the cloud — This is a difficult phenomenon to explain. Harrison,[116] I, and others, agree that it was different from the cloud that was over the Ark, the Shekinah. Milgrom seems to connect the two in this way:"God leads Israel in its wilderness march not by His voice commands but by His appointed sign, the cloud-encased fire. During the day only the cloud is visible, the fire, presumably, dimmed by sunlight. But night renders the cloud invisible, and the luminous fire can be clearly seen."[117]

This fire is called in other passages, *kavod* (כבוד),"glory". The ascending or descending of this fire-cloud determined the time when Israel was to move or to encamp. Then, "whenever the Lord seeks to speak with Moses or manifests Himself to Israel, the kavod-fire leaves the cloud and descends upon the Ark-throne in the Holy of Holies."[118] This sounds very plausible.

Verse 15

This verse contains the most complete name for the Mishkan. It is called "the tabernacle of the tent of meeting", *hamishkan l'ohel ha'edut* (המשכן לאוהל העדות).

---

114. Milgrom, *JPS Torah Commentary,* 69.
115. *Ibid.*
116. See Harrison, *Numbers* (TOTC), 162.
117. Milgrom, *JPS Torah Commentary,* 70.
118. *Ibid.,* 71.

Verse 23

"**hear the Lord's order**" — Based on the tense of this verb "observed," a simple past tense ("perfect" in Biblical Hebrew), Milgrom concludes, "The Israelites faithfully followed the directions of the fire-cloud."[119] Notice that here the word "obey" is a typical rendering of the common Hebrew word "to hear". Hence, we have translated it as "hear."

Chapter 10

Verse 2

"**the trumpets**" — Milgrom informs us that according to Josephus, the trumpets were about one foot in length. These would have been too long to fit the picture of them on the Arch of Titus.[120]

Verses 8–10

"**a lasting ordinance for you and the generations to come**"—This signifies the importance of this teaching. Some (like Hertz) see this as referring to the fact that only the kohanim were to blow the trumpets, not to the trumpet use itself. Others (like Abravanel) say that even the Israelites could blow the trumpets. There were other occasions which were stated to be "for generations to come." These were Pesach (Exodus 12), Yom Kippur (Leviticus 16), and the ritual of the red heifer (Numbers 19).

Verse 10

"**at your times of rejoicing**" — This has traditionally been interpreted to mean Shabbat. However, it could be broader than that, to include any significant joyful day for the nation, such as a day of victory in war.

Verse 11

The rest of the journey to the Promised Land finally began 10 months and 19 days after their arrival at Sinai.

Verse 12

"**set out**" — The Hebrew word translated "set out" is from the verb, *nas'a* (נסע) which simply meant in that context "to pull up stakes".

Verse 25

It has been speculated that the tribe of Dan may have been insulted by being placed as the rear guard, that is, last. However, in reality, they were the ones who took care of anyone who fell down or straggled and were the ones who may have found dropped items. Therefore, it was a position of great responsibility and trust.

Verse 29

Who is Hobab? It is extremely difficult to accurately answer this question because of some confusing data. He is mentioned here as a brother-in-law of Moses, being the son of Jethro and from the Midianites. He is also mentioned in Judges 1:16 and 4:11. There, he is described as

---

119. Milgrom, *JPS Torah Commentary*, 72.
120. *Ibid.*

being from the Kenites and the father-in-law of Moses. Many solutions to the problem have been proposed. Some of these solutions are really complicated. It seems that we can think through this issue considering the following data:

1) The word for "in law" in both cases (Numbers and Judges) is *choten* (חותן). Perhaps this word should be translated as "relative by marriage" instead of being so precise as a father or brother-in-law.

2) It is possible that some Kenites and Midianites may have intermarried, giving Hobab this mixed genealogy.

3) Jethro, often called Moshe's father-in-law, is also confused with Reuel. Here Hobab is also called the son of Reuel. The simple way of understanding this may be to think of Reuel as the father of Jethro. Jethro is another name for Hobab. Since it was Jethro/Hobab who gave Zipporah to Moshe as a wife, this would make Reuel Zipporah's grandfather. It is not uncommon for children in this culture to call their grandfathers as "father."[121] (Are you sorry you asked!?)

Verse 33

"the ark" — This verse seems to contradict Numbers 2:17 and 10:21 which appear to indicate that the Mishkan, especially the Ark, was not the first object in the Israelite march. Milgrom, agreeing with Ibn Ezra and Ramban, says, "Probably during the initial stage the Ark did precede the marchers because the people feared the dangers in the wilderness."[122] Thus, it appears that there were at one point three things which went before the Israelites: the fire-cloud (Numbers 9:15–23; 14:14), the Ark (Numbers 10:33), and the Angel (Exodus 14:19; 23:20–23).

Verse 35

Who are the enemies referred to in this verse? Professor Leibowitz says: "The enemies of Israel are synonymous with the enemies of God. Whether we are worthy or not of this title, those bent on our destruction regard us as the standard bearers of truth and justice and the representatives of the divine law. And it is for this reason that they persecute and hate us."[123]

Chapter 11
Verse 1-3

This short section of three verses contains all of the essential elements of all the subsequent narratives describing Israel's complaints:[124]

- Complaint: 11:4–5; 12:1–2; 14:1–4; 17:6–7; 20:3–5; and 21:5
- Divine Discipline: 11:33; 12:9–10; 14:20–37; 16:32; 17:11; and 21:7

---

121. For a lengthier discussion see Hertz, 612; Harrison, 176–178; and Timothy R. Ashley, *The Book of Numbers* (NICOT), 194–197.
122. Milgrom, *op. cit.,* 80.
123. Nechama Leibowitz, *New Studies in Bamidbar*, 91.
124. *Ibid.,* 82.

- Immortalizing the incident by giving a name to the site: 11:34; 20:13; 21:3; Exodus 15:23; and 17:7

Verse 5

"**at no cost**" — Leibowitz has an interesting discussion about this phrase. Her point is that it was not that the people were able to purchase fish without money from the Egyptians but that they had food, but no responsibility to the Torah.[125]

Verse 10

"**The Lord became exceedingly angry**" — It was too much for the Lord to suffer this rejection of all that He had done for the people just because they wanted a variety of foods as well as desiring to return to Egypt.

Verses 16–17

The Talmud (Sanhedrin 2a) regards these seventy men as constituting the Great Sanhedrin. Rambam (*Hilchot Sanhedrin* 4:1) states that "Moshe ordained the seventy sages, and the Divine Presence then rested upon them."[126] The Sanhedrin or the 70 + 1 would govern Israel. We read about it also in the Apostolic Scriptures. This group was not needed for judicial functions; there was already a system set up for that. Rather it was the function of this body to help provide guidance and leadership.

Verse 18

"**consecrate yourselves**" — The Hebrew verb *hitkaddshu* (התקדשו) is from a word which means "to make yourselves holy", or "sanctify yourselves". Milgrom, with much insight, remarks that this entailed a ritual bath, the kind that precedes a sacrifice. "However, this notion may be double-edged: It also intimates that the coming sacrifice will be Israel" (11:34).[127]

Verse 25

"**prophesied**" — The Hebrew is from the verb *nava* (נבא). This Semitic root is very ancient, having been found in cuneiform tablets at Ebla, dating from about the 3rd millennium BCE. It is different from the word for "seer", which tells us that they most likely were not predicting the future. The word has something to do with speaking forth for someone. Thus, the new leaders spoke forth God's messages of comfort and encouragement to Moshe, and exhortation and encouragement to the people.

Chapter 12

Verse 1

the Cushite wife of Moshe — Scholars disagree about her identity. The Hebrew and biblical evidence also can lead to differences of opinion. Here are some of the suggestions and a little of their reasoning:

---

125. Leibowitz, *New Studies in Bamidbar*, 94–103.
126. *ArtScroll, Chumash*, 791.
127. Milgrom, *JPS Torah Commentary: Numbers*, 88.

1) Zipporah died, Moshe remarried. However, no evidence of her death yet in the text.

2) Moshe married a second wife. Nothing in Torah is against it except, perhaps for Genesis chapters 1 and 2.

3) The Cushite woman: The Hebrew *hakushit* (הכושית) could refer to an area called "Cushan", "the home of the North Arabian people called Kusi."[128] The Midianites were among these people or close by them.

4) This Cushite woman was from "Cush" or Ethiopia.

5) The description of her as a Cushite was a euphemistic reference to her great beauty.[129] Perhaps Miriam and Aaron were jealous!

Regardless of whether Moses' wife was Ethiopian or Midianite, the objection to her, it is implied, was ethnic (cf. Leviticus. 24:10). Strikingly, the rabbis raise no objection to her Cushite origin but, to the contrary, defend her.[130]

Verse 3

Humble — Harrison suggests that the Hebrew *anu* (ענו) should be better translated as "more tolerant" or "more long-suffering."[131] Milgrom notes, "its meaning is clarified by its synonymous parallel 'who seek the Lord'."[132] halot says that it means, "bowed, but in the sense of humble, or pious."[133]

Verses 6–8

Milgrom observes that these verses are poetry (and probably originate from an ancient epic about Moses). "This is apparent when they are typographically reset. They reveal an introverted structure." Then he offers the structure of these verses in poetic format.[134]

Verse 10

Miriam was leprous — The Hebrew for "leprous" is *metzorah* (מצורעה). This is one of the words in Leviticus 12–15 that speak of a supernatural, divine affliction sent to someone for un-confessed sin. Miriam, after being confronted by the Lord Himself apparently did not change her ways. God accordingly disciplined her. Moshe had to intercede for his sister.

128. Hertz, *Pentateuch and Haftarahs*, 618.
129. Rashi, *ArtScroll Edition*, 136–137.
130. Milgrom, *JPS Torah Commentary: Numbers*, 93.
131. Harrison, *Numbers,* 195.
132. Milgrom, *JPS Torah Commentary: Numbers*, 94.
133. HALOT, 855.
134. Milgrom, *JPS Torah Commentary: Numbers*, 95.

STUDY QUESTIONS

1. What symbolism do you see in the menorah?

2. Why do you think that God waited until this point in the narrative to instruct Aaron to light the menorah?

3. What does it mean to have the Israelites lay their hands on the Levites in their dedication service?

4. What does the waving of the Levites picture or symbolize?

5. What provision does God give for the training of Levites who are new to the Mishkan service?

6. What can we learn about God from His legislation about the second Pesach in chapter 9?

7. Why do you think God provided the cloud and the fire? Is there a connection between the cloud and the Shekinah? Why or why not?

8. What are the different occasions that called for the blowing of the silver trumpets?

9. What does it mean for Moshe to say "Arise, Oh Lord" and "Reside in tranquillity" in 10:35–36?

10. What was the real nature of the Israelite complaint in chapter 11? Why did it offend God?

11. Why did God raise up 70 new elders?

12. Why did they start to prophesy when the spirit came upon them? Whose spirit was it? What was the content of their prophecy?

13. Why do you think the story of Eldad and Medad is included?

14. What was Joshua upset about?

15. Who was the Cushite woman? Why did Moshe's marriage to her upset Miriam and Aaron?

16. Why do you think Miriam was disciplined and not Aaron?

17. What does it mean when it says that Moshe was the humblest man?

Parashat Shelakh שלח

Torah: Numbers 13:1–15:41
Haftarah: Joshua 2:1–24

Parashat Shelakh שלח

THE GREAT SPY DISASTER

Israel's history has several turning points. The parasha before us gives an account of one of those. It is one of the most famous stories in the Torah. It is also one of the most tragic. In this parasha, we find Israel on the threshold of the Promised Land. God had seemingly completed all the necessary preparations for them to enter. It was all going to be so great! Spies were sent to help make the necessary military preparations and to get the people excited about taking possession of their Land. Then disaster strikes. Sin! Unbelief! Rebellion! The result: 40 years of wandering in the wilderness, watching their parents and grandparents die alongside of them. This is *Parashat Shelach*. We will approach our study of this parasha using the following outline:

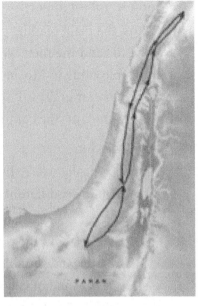

Map 2: Numbers 13 - Route of the Explorers

- I.   The Caper
- II. The Culprits
- III. The Conclusions
- IV. The Consequences
- V.   The Cure

I. THE CAPER

A. The Command

The text tells us that the Holy One told Moshe to send out people to spy out or explore the Land as they were encamped at Kedesh Barnea. However, was this really a command from the Lord? Whose caper was this anyway? We are raising this question because there are some differences among commentators about the validity of the very act of sending spies.

Rashi, following the sages of the Talmud, maintains that Israel sinned through the very act of sending spies. Rashi's reasoning is based on his understanding of Deuteronomy 1:22 where it states, "Then all of you came to me and said, 'Let us send men ahead to spy out the land for us and bring back a report about the route we are to take and the towns we will come to'." From this, Rashi reasons that the spies were sent, "by His permission, not by His command."[135] The part of the text which prompts this kind of reasoning is the words in 13:1 in the Hebrew, "Send for yourself," *shelakh lekhah* (שלח לך). In other words, the decision, it is suggested, was up to Moshe. Since rebellious people were pressuring him, he decided to send the spies. (By the way, this expression, *shelakh lekhah* also serves as the name of this parasha.)

However, it is possible to understand 13:1 in a different way. Perhaps when God said to

---

135. Rashi: *Bamidbar*, ArtScroll Edition, 148.

Moshe, "send for yourself," He did not mean that the decision was up to him. Rather He meant that instead of sending Moshe himself to search out the land, God was commanding him to send out qualified men *in his place*. In addition, this gives the imperative mood of the verb, "send", its fullest import.

Thus, the plain reading of the text seems to support the thought that it was God commanding Moshe to send the men. What about the passage in Deuteronomy? There, the text only tells us that people came to Moshe asking him to send spies. We can only assume that Moshe acted (as was his custom to do so) by going to the Lord to seek His wisdom. The answer to his request to the Holy One was the command in Numbers 13:1.

B. The Mission

What specifically were the spies to do in the Land? Moshe instructed them to gather information in six different categories:

1) What does the land look like?
2) What about the people in the land?
3) Is the land suitable for agriculture?
4) What kind of vegetation is in the land?
5) What about the cities?
6) Bring back some samples of the produce.

Based on these instructions we can assume that the spy mission was not merely for military purposes. Otherwise, why would Moshe want to know about the vegetation, for example? Conquering the Land was only one aspect of their goal. The Israelites had to know if, after defeating the enemy, they could realistically survive there.

Because of this, we can now suggest an alternative meaning to the term usually translated "to spy" in 13:2, *yaturu* (יתורו). It is from a verb that can easily be translated "to seek out" or "discover" rather than "to spy."[136] If we adopt this translation, then we can better explain why other information was sought than exclusively military intelligence.

C. The Territory

Note: In the following paragraphs we will not use a standard Bible translation. For the most part unless we indicate otherwise, we will work from the Hebrew text and offer our own translation.

The explorers searched out the land "from the Wilderness of Zin to the expanse at the approach to Hamat" (13:21). Instead of the phrase "approach to Hamat", the NIV says "Lebo Hamath". They also went to Hebron, to the Valley of Eshcol, to the Negev (13:22–24), to the seacoast, as well as to the Jordan Valley (13:29).

Most scholars agree that the Wilderness of Zin is the area southwest of the Dead Sea. This was in the south of Israel. They also went north. The place in the north that they went to is

---

136. HALOT, 1707.

described in Hebrew in 13:21 "the expanse at the approach to Hamat." In Hebrew it reads: *ad rehov levo chmat* (עד-רחוב לבא חמת). Scholars debate about whether these words should be translated or transliterated. If they are to be transliterated, they would signify place names. Thus, the spies went to Rehov, near Lebo Hamat. If they are to be translated, they could mean that the spies went from the Wilderness of Zin, in the south to "the expanse at the approach to Hamat" in the north.

No matter which way we choose to render this Hebrew phrase, the text seems to be talking about a Canaanite location in the north, not far from modern Syria and modern Lebanon. This would put it north of the "pan-handle" region of modern Israel.

The text says in 13:22–24 that they went to Hebron. Hebron is located about 18 miles south of Jerusalem. Actually, all one had to do was to follow the ridge road that travelled along the "spine" of Israel, the central mountain ridge, that goes from near Shechem in the centre, to past Hebron in the south, even to Be'er Sheva in the Negev. The Valley of Eschol is *nahal eschol* (נחל אשכל), or "valley of a cluster". The Hebrew word *nahal* (נחל) is really a wadi or a small valley where a seasonal stream flows. Harrison suggests that it could be identified as the modern Arab village of Burj Haskeh, about two miles north of Hebron.[137]

Finally, the mission began in "the season for the first ripe grapes" (13:20). In Israel, this meant that the time period was about late July to mid-August.

II. The Culprits

A. Special Men

The names of the explorers are specifically given to us in 13:4–15. The text notes a few noteworthy comments about these people that draws our attention.

First, the spies are called "heads or leaders among them". This meant that they were not tribal heads, but rather "men of importance, capable of grappling with so trying a task."[138] They are also called "men", *anashim* (אנשים). This sounds rather obvious, but do not be fooled by this detail. There might be more to it than we realize. Rashi, for example, interjects that, "Whenever the term [*anashim*] is used in Scripture, it is a term denoting worthiness".[139] Rashi's commentator, Rabbi Silbermann, attempts to qualify him by adding, "Rashi does not, of course, mean that the word אנשים [*anashim*] always designates "worthy men," but that it has this meaning in a passage where there is no particular reason why the sex of the people referred to should be emphasized.[140] The import of all of this is to suggest that these spies were not just ordinary men. Their peers regarded them as men who possessed special qualities and abilities that enabled them to be trusted to perform this critically important task of gathering necessary

---

137. R. K. Harrison, *Numbers* (TOTC), 206.
138. J. H. Hertz, *Pentateuch and Haftarahs*, 623.
139. Rashi, *ArtScroll Edition*, 62.
140. *Ibid.*

information.

B. Their Identity

We wish we knew more about each man. However, R. Isaac said, "It is a tradition in our possession from our forefathers that the spies were named after their actions."[141] The Talmud also continues by saying,

> But only with one has it survived with us: Sethur, the son of Michael. He was named Sethur because he undermined the works of the Holy One, blessed be He … R. Jochanan said, "We can also explain the name Nahbi the son of Vophsi. He was named Nahbi because he said the words of the Holy One, blessed be He."[142]

This argument carries more weight when we realize that often a Semitic name was intended to tell us something about the person. We might be able to take educated guesses at some of the names. [143] Perhaps it looks like this:

The Names of Infamy

Shammua (שמוע) — Associated with the word, שמטעה, meaning "a report".

Shaphat (שפט) — Associated with the word שפט, meaning "to judge."

Caleb (כלב) —Associated with the words: לב and כ, meaning, "according to the mind."

Yigal (יגאל) — Associated with the word גאל and in the form that means, "he redeems".

Hoshea (Later, Joshua) (הושיע) — Associated with the word ישע and means, salvation.

Palti (פלטי) — Associated with the word פלט, meaning "my escape" or "my deliverance".

Gaddiel (גדיאל) — Associated with the words אל and גדי meaning, "my fortune is God"

Gadi (גדי) — from the word גדי, meaning, "my fortune".

Ammiel (עמיאל) — Associated with the words אל and עמי, meaning, "my kinsman is God."

Setur (סתור) — Associated with the word סתר, meaning, "to hide" or "to conceal."

Nakhvi (נחבי) — Associated with the word חבה, meaning "faint-hearted."

Geuel (גאואל) — Associated with the words גאוה + אל, meaning" the majesty of God."

We leave it to the students to put this all together in a meaningful way to see what lessons there might be in this list for us.

C. The Two Heroes

The most famous names in the list are Joshua and Caleb. We know them because they turn out to be the two heroes of the group. Please see the "Additional Notes" for more comments on Caleb. As for Joshua, we are told in 13:16, "Moshe gave Hoshea son of Nun the name Joshua."

Hertz, perhaps, best explains the nature of this name change when he writes, "The change had already been made at the time of the victory over Amalek .... Hoshea signifies, 'He has

---

141. Babylonian Talmud Sotah 34b
142. *Ibid.*
143. Naturally, we cannot be dogmatic about these meanings. All of the translations of the names are based on information gleaned from BDB and HALOT.

helped.' Moses, by prefixing to it a letter of the Divine Name, changed it to Joshua, Hebrew: 'Yehoshua,' i.e. 'He [the Lord] will help,' at the same time indicating the Source of salvation."[144] The addition of the Hebrew letter (י) to the front of his name also changes the tense to the future tense. Hence, we can say that his name means, "The Lord will save/help/deliver". The Talmud says that this, in essence, reflects a prayer from Moshe. "As for Joshua, Moses had already prayed on his behalf as it is said, 'And Moses called Hoshea the son of Nun Joshea, may Jah save thee from the plan of the spies'."[145]

Another Joshua

Because of the difficulty of rendering Hebrew words into English, we often overlook an important feature of the name "Jesus". Jesus is from the Greek word *Iasous* (Ihsouς). This is the usual way to render the name Joshua into Greek. Over the period of time, the Hebrew "Joshua," *Yehoshua* (יהושע), was sometimes shortened to *Yeshua* (ישוע). Most of the examples of this appear in writings from the Second Temple Period. An exception of this is in 1 Chronicles 24:11 where we learn that Yeshua was the name of the head of one the classes of priests. Other examples from Second Temple Period writings are found in Ezra 2:40; 3:9; Nehemiah 3:19; and Nehemiah 7:11, among others. [146]

As we have seen, Joshua means, "The Lord will save/rescue/help/deliver". Hence, by calling the incarnated Messiah "Joshua", God was teaching us that it would be by this "Joshua" that He will save His people. Matthew (1:21) explicitly indicates that the salvation He came to affect was one from sin. Accordingly, His name was a prophecy of what He would accomplish and in whose power and strength He would accomplish it.

Today many simply refer to Him by His given Hebrew name, Yeshua (remember, this is a form of Joshua or Yehoshua). His parents would have called Him Yeshua, not Yehoshua and not Jesus.

Even though we do not know much about the personal qualities of these spies, we do know one thing: we know that they were highly qualified for this mission, and that they were in the company of extremely spiritual men (Joshua and Caleb). The names of these spies will forever go down into history as the men who "gave a bad report" about the Land of Promise and were, therefore, instrumental in leading Israel in rebellion against the command of God to go in and take possession of His Land. What a reputation!

---

144. Hertz, *Pentateuch and HJaftarahs*, 624.
145. B Sotah 34b
146. BDB, 221.

III. THE CONCLUSIONS

A. Subtlety to Moshe

Israeli commentator Nechama Leibowitz notes "The spies unburdened themselves on three occasions." Each, she contends, "combine to culminate in sin and rebellion against the Lord."[147] The first occasion was with Moshe. Here they superficially seem to give only a factual report, as good spies ought. For the most part, they described what they saw. However, after their initial description in 13:27, the text uses the Hebrew words in 13:28, *efes ki-'az* (עז-כי אפס). According to BDB, this phrase is spoken to, "qualify a previous statement." The words can therefore be rendered "save that", or "howbeit".[148] A strong "but" would also do. In other words, by inserting this little phrase, the spies turned their faithful objective report into a slightly subjective analysis. This subtle denunciation was done in the presence of their sage, Moshe.

B. Protest to Caleb

The second report was in response to Caleb. This time their negative feelings in their report was not so subtle. In 13:30, Caleb publicly and forthrightly takes issue with the negative analysis of the rest of the spies.

We are told that as he spoke, he had to "silence" the people. The word "silence" usually is used as an interjection, e.g., "Silence!" Here it is a verb used in the Hebrew imperfect tense. This tells us at least two things. First, the spies' report that was given to Moshe was also in earshot of the people. It was negative enough to cause a verbal stir among them. Hence, this is the need for Caleb to attempt to silence the spies. Secondly, it tells us that the report evoked such a response that Caleb had to attempt to keep them quiet enough for him to speak. Interestingly enough, it says that Caleb had to silence the people "toward Moshe". This indicates that already there was another rebellion brewing against Moshe.

Caleb tried hard to encourage the people to go into the Land, but the spies responded even more strongly to him. To Caleb, they were not as subtle as they pretended to be to Moshe. Their response to Caleb is in 13:31. On the surface, it is merely a repudiation of what he had just said. However, Leibowitz sees, in their retort to Caleb, a deeper and far more serious argument, one that was specifically fashioned against this man of God, Caleb.

Leibowitz hints that, perhaps, the most serious of the spies' response was to Caleb's encouraging words. She talks about the last Hebrew word in verse 31, *mimenu* (ממנו). She says rightly that this can be translated either as "than us" or "than him". On the one hand, it seems that the plain meaning of the text is obviously "they are stronger than we". However, the Midrash, cited by Rashi states: "they meant it in reference to Him that is Above".[149] In other words, they implied that the people of the Land were stronger than Him, than God, interpreting

---

147. Leibowitz, *New Studies in Bamidbar*, 137–138.
148. BDB, 67.
149. Rashi, *ArtScroll Edition*, 157.

mimenu in the third person.[150] Whether or not they actually meant "mimenu" literally to refer to God, the fact is that in the end that is really what they were saying.

C. An Evil Report to the People

The final occasion in which they gave their report was in the next verse, 13:32. Here they turn from Moshe and Caleb and speak directly to the people. "On the third occasion, the spies make no bones about the matter, and unrestrainedly reveal their feelings, casting to the winds all pretence of objectivity![151] Let us see what they say.

The text in 13:32 describes their report as a "bad report". Professor Ashley attempts to clarify what this means when he states "It is called an evil report (*davah*, דבה). This term contains within it the idea of negativity, falsehood, and strife. When 14:27 adds the word evil (רע) , it is merely clarifying what is already implicit."[152]

Their report was therefore false, negative, and designed to produce strife. A good example of a falsehood in their report is in 13:32 when they related that the "land devours its inhabitants". It is hard to know exactly what this means. Those of us living here, in Israel, today can testify to a certain aspect of this in that survival here is difficult at every point. However, whatever it means, the spies tell us that there were at least some people whom the Land did not devour — the giants! So, their report is not entirely correct. The truth of the matter is that if the giants were able to survive, how much more could those who were made powerful by the strength of the Lord! This, the spies (except for Joshua and Caleb) did not say. (See Additional Notes for more information.)

It seems that from the start the whole intent of the spies was to present a negative picture and a false report to the people of Israel. The text does not tell us why they brought back such a negative report. We can only guess. The Talmud suggests, "as the coming back was with an evil design, so the going was with an evil design." Thus, the sages assert that they were negative from the start. If so, then they had a good plan to discourage the people. The same Talmudic passage also relates some of their strategy: "Any piece of slander which has not some truth in the beginning, will not endure in the end."[153] In other words, if they intended giving a false report of their mission, the best way was to have it based at least partly on some piece of true information, which they tried to do. This is the worst kind of slander, and, as the Talmud indicates, its poison will frequently endure.

---

150. Leibowitz, *New Studies in Bamidbar*, 140.

151. *Ibid.,* 140.

152. Timothy R. Ashley, *The Book of Numbers* (*New International Commentary on the Old Testament – "NICOT"*), 242.

153. B Sotah 35a

IV. THE CONSEQUENCES

What a drama that unfolds before us in chapter 14! This is the chapter of consequences. The strategy of discouragement from the spies had its desired effect upon all present. First, we will examine the consequences the report had on the people. Next, we will see the effects it had on the godly leaders, and lastly, we will explore what effect the evil report had on the Lord Himself.

A. The People

The children of Israel gave an uncontrollable emotional response to the report. It had fallen upon ears ripe for a mutiny. We can see a three-fold progression to their reaction.

1. Bitter Emotion

The first stage of their response was one of bitter and intense emotion: "That night all the people of the community raised their voices and wept aloud" (14:1). A case of national hysteria began to set in. The spies' report induced fear. They began to reject the Land, the gift that God was giving them.

2. The Seeds of Rebellion

The second stage in their reaction was based on the first and came from it. Acting solely on their emotions, the narrative tells us that they immediately "grumbled against Moshe and Aaron .... Wouldn't it be better for us to go back to Egypt?" (14:1–3) Then, still in a highly charged emotional state, they plotted with one another and concluded, "We should choose a leader and go back to Egypt!" (14:4). A lie stirred fragile emotions that fanned a smouldering fire of rebellion. For whatever reason, the continual cry of the Israelites for a return to Egypt had now reached its highest pitch.

3. Violence!

The last stage of the people's reaction is outright violence. After Joshua and Caleb made a reasoned plea for their compliance to the Lord's will, 14:10 says, "But the whole assembly talked about stoning them." Apparently, this time, if the leaders would not step down, the people were willing to kill them because of a lie the spies had told them.

Can we share a very pointed application here? We are told in the Apostolic Scriptures (2 Corinthians 10:5) to "take every thought captive". If we let ungodly thoughts slip into our brains and dwell on them — thoughts which are not from the kingdom of God, but of that other kingdom, then it will always result in some kind of disaster. This is what happened in the camp of the Israelites. The spies told lies to the Children of Israel. It ended with disaster. Just as they should have taken the lies "captive" in order to not make room for these lies to fester in their brains, so should we. Our enemy wants to try in every possible way to get us to rebel against God and His Word. The new creation takes those thoughts captive.

"Weeping throughout the Generations"

This event had such a profound effect on Israel that even the Psalm writer in Psalm 106 alludes to it. Based on the attitude that caused this rejection of the Land, the Psalmist speaks of a future dispersion from the Land. He writes:

> Then they despised the pleasant Land; they did not believe His promise. They grumbled in their tents and did not obey the Lord. So, He swore to them with uplifted hand that He would make them fall in the desert, make their descendants fall among the nations and scatter them throughout the lands. among the nations and disperse them throughout the world. (Psalm 106:24–27)

The Torah says that the people cried upon hearing the false report. As a result, they rejected the Land. It would not be the last time they would cry. The sages say that the destruction of the First and Second Temples, as well as the "Great Spy Disaster" all happened on the same date in history — the 9th of Av (late July to early August). Their comments on this are sonorous: "The Holy One, blessed be He, said to them, 'You have wept without a cause; therefore I will set this day aside for a weeping throughout the generations to come'."[154]

B. The Godly Leaders

Needless to say, this episode must have had a devastating effect on Moshe, Aaron, Caleb, and Joshua. All of them would suffer persecution from the frenzied, rebellious people, but they kept their cool and reacted in two specific ways which were God's ways.

1. The Rip

Their first reaction was to humble themselves before the people. Led by Joshua in 14:6–9, the leaders "tore their clothes" out of mourning for such a wicked response from the people.

2. The Cluster

Their second reaction was to attempt to encourage the people by speaking the truth to them. However, one might wonder how were the people to decide whom to believe? What evidence can be brought to verify the story?

Sometimes in a trial, one piece of evidence, if it is critical enough, can be sufficient to convince the jurors to render their decision. This is true for our story in this parasha. What was the evidence that Joshua and Caleb brought forth? It was the cluster of grapes! God's sovereign hand was in this event. He had the explorers bring back with them concrete evidence from the Land which would shoot holes all through their story, although their minds were too bent on lying to notice it.

What did the cluster of grapes prove? It showed, first, the magnificent produce the Land was capable of growing. They cut the grapes in July, in the dead heat of the summer. For the grapes to be as large as the story hints at, large enough to need two men to carry them on poles, it would have meant that there were sufficient rains in the winter and abundant dew in the rainless

---

154. B Ta'anit 29a.

season to produce them. They also brought back pomegranates and figs in addition to the grapes (13:23–24). The Land, indeed, was a land that would have been good to live in. It was a land flowing with milk and honey.

Something else about the grapes stands out. The text seems to centre on the cluster, mentioning it twice. Was the Lord trying to speak something to them through the grapes besides how conducive the land was to produce fruit? Consider this: The Jewish people have always looked upon grapes and grape products as a symbol of joy. We do not know how ancient this attitude was, but we do know from Numbers 6, that grape products were one of the things from which people drew earthly pleasures, or joy. If so, then we are suggesting God was communicating an important message to them through the cluster of grapes. He was telling them that this was not only a land which would give them lots of food, but it was also one that would give them an abundance of joy and happiness — if, and only if — they would enter into it, possess it, live by the Torah, and devote themselves wholly to the Lord their God.

The explorers, then, may have intended to use the evidence of the grapes for their own devious purposes (See Rashi), but the Lord would use it to stand as a perpetual testimony against them.

C. God's Response

Not only did the spies' lies affect the people and the leaders, whom they almost killed, but also it had consequences from the Holy One.

1. A Test for Moshe

God's first response, in 14:11–12, is rather tricky to analyse. He threatened to wipe out the present population and build the nation again through Moshe. Moshe then responded by protesting that He cannot do so, because such an action would not look good in the eyes of the nations around them, not to mention the fact that God had made promises to the entire house of Israel that He was obligated to keep. God apparently heeded the argument and proceeded with a different course of action.

Was God's eternal plan changed through a human request? God forbid! How could a mere human be invested with so much authority? Our position is that God did not really intend to do as He said in 14:13–14! Instead, we think that He was merely *testing* Moshe. He wanted to test him in his faithfulness to follow God's Word. He wanted to test him in his commitment to defend God's name and reputation. He wanted also to test Moshe in his ability to love his people despite how they treated him or his God. Moshe passed all of these tests with flying colours.

Some people get their theology confused here. They are thrown by the plea of Moshe, thinking that it was his intercession that changed God's mind. In reality, however, we need to remember that God does many things at the same time. In the previous parasha, we observed how God was growing Moshe in his leadership abilities. The lesson continues here in chapter 14. It is inconceivable to think that the Sovereign of the universe could change His mind.

2. Discipline, Not Wrath

We are all familiar with the action that God took regarding the rebellious nation. Everyone of that generation who left Egypt would die in the wilderness. The exceptions were their children under 20 years old, as well as Joshua, and Caleb. As severe as this discipline was, Israel still sought to test God to see if He meant it. So, chapter 14 relates the story of how some of the Israelites decided on their own to do battle against the Amalekites and Canaanites under the pretence that they repented of their rebellion. The result was severe defeat. God meant what He said — they would not possess the Land until 40 years later.

It is important to remember that God's actions, although motivated by His justified and holy anger, were not necessarily expressions of His wrath, but rather of His *discipline*. God's wrath will be unleashed against all who are not His in the world to come. It is punitive. However, His discipline is directed against those who are called by His name when they need correction as children. It is corrective.

The Lord, therefore, levelled severe discipline upon the children of Israel. At the same time, He took Moshe to new heights in his ability to lead. The correction God gave Israel for their sin hurt them. It was a sore spanking with His rod of correction. However, the Holy One also took two more steps to "cure" Israel of their sin of rebellion and unbelief. We will treat these under a separate heading.

V. THE CURE

We have been speaking of the rebellion and unbelief of the people. The rabbis, however, also speak of the sin of idolatry. How was Israel ever going to learn to follow the Holy One? The text in chapter 15 provides some of the keys necessary in order for His children to walk in His ways.

A. Forgiveness

The first key is mentioned at the beginning of chapter 15. It is the instruction about bringing offerings. Why would God bring up the subject of sacrifices at this point in the Torah? Surely one of the most important reasons for doing so is to remind Israel of some of the most important spiritual gifts that He had provided for them — repentance and forgiveness.

As severe as God's disciplines are, the Holy One nevertheless, true to His character and Name, offers forgiveness through repentance, expressed through offering the appropriate sacrifice. The instructions about the sacrifices in chapter 15 were reminders to them that there was/is only one way out of their mess. It was as if the Lord were saying to them, "Come back to Me! Come close to Me! When you do, I will forgive and change you."

B. Visible Reminders

The habitual sin of rebellion and unbelief that had plagued Israel, almost from the inception of the nation, needed some definitive prevention measures. The Holy One, therefore, gave two visible reminders, which can be seen as teaching tools designed to help them in their struggle against these sins.

To many from today's believing world, these visible reminders may seem rather odd. However, in reality, they represent the heart and mind of a God who knows the frailty of our flesh and weakness of the human brain that is prone to forget His ways. Therefore, because of these weaknesses, God provided outward visible reminders for His people to utilize.

1. The Challah

The first of these teaching symbols, or visible reminders, is found in 15:17–21. God told them that when they "eat of the bread of the Land … you shall lift up an offering to the Lord" (author's translation). Bread is a staple. It was, and is, the most common everyday food. In ancient times it was freshly made each day. The Torah was teaching that when they entered the Land, they were to set apart from each batch of new dough, one loaf to be given to the Lord, i.e., to the kohanim. (Usually when the text says that something is to be offered to the Lord it means to Him through the priests who customarily consumed it.) It was the first loaf to be made of that batch of dough, a kind of first fruits offering. The text in 15:20 calls this loaf *challah* (חלה).

When they set challah aside from the rest of the batch of dough, the Israelites would take time to acknowledge daily Who their source of life was and how much He had provided. Moreover, by giving the challah to the Lord (the kohanim), it reminded them to give their best and first constantly to Him.

This practice is done today with a slight variation. We do not give a portion to the kohen. (Some observant Jews do make a loaf and burn it as the offering.) Instead, we call the special braided bread that we have on erev Shabbat "challah". We say a special blessing and acknowledge in a special way that He is the only source of life and sustenance. Practising the torah of the challah will help to constantly remind us of our Lord and Provider.

2. The Tsitsit

The second teaching symbol is found in 15:37–41. It is the teaching about the *tsitsit* (ציצת), or the fringes on the four corners of our garments. Like the challah, this also was designed to help prevent the Israelites from straying from the Lord.

The fringes are sewn onto the four corners of our garments. In today's world where four-cornered garments are not usually worn, so our sages have developed small four-cornered garments worn usually under our outer clothes so that only the fringes may show. They function like a string tied onto a finger — they are visible reminders. They remind us to, 1) guard all the commandments (15:39) and 2) to keep our minds and eyes on the Holy One (15:39). In other words, the fringes are outward visible reminders to walk as redeemed people (15:41).

The fringes also have another important feature. All tsitsit are to have a cord of blue. This is the same colour as the High Priest's robe. It is the colour, *tekhelet* (תחלת). Accordingly, wearing this in some way connects us to the High Priest. 1 Peter 2:9, alluding to Exodus 19:6, reminds us that we are, indeed, royal priests. In short, the blue also reminds us of who we are in Messiah — royal priests unto Him.

In addition, as we have written elsewhere, the colour tekhelet is the blue that reflects the heavens (Psalm 97:1–6). It is the blue that one sees when high up above the clouds in a jet plane. It is also the blue that the seas reflect from the sky. The blue of the heavens reminds us of the One who is above the heavens, the Holy One. Wearing tekhelet reflects the fact that we are new creations, with the Holy One living inside of us enabling us to reflect His righteousness on earth as it is in Heaven.

The fringes, therefore, remind us not only of the Lord, but also of who we are by faith in Him. If we can remember both, we will not fall into the sins that the Israelites fell into in this parasha, rebellion, unbelief, and idolatry.

Finally, it is noteworthy that the Hebrew word used to help describe the purpose of the fringes in 15:39 is from the same word that describes the mission of the spies/explorers in 13:2: *tur* (תור). (It is translated "follow after" in the NASB and "go after" in the NIV.) In 13:2 the eyes of the spies were to explore thoroughly the Promised Land and bring information back to God's people. However, here in 15:39 the eyes of God's people are *not* to "explore" things that are not taught in God's Word. The fringes are a visible reminder to watch how our eyes and minds go exploring.

IN EVERY GENERATION

The amazing thing about both the challah and the tsitsit is that after both teachings, the Holy One informs us that they are to be practised in every generation. That means that we have a wonderfully gracious God who cares enough about us to provide us with eating habits and clothing designed to help us to remember Him, His Word, and our identity in Him as new creations. Shall we then not take advantage of these wonderful provisions of grace? If that is not enough motivation to practise these parts of Torah, is it enough to know that our Messiah Himself, Yeshua, wore the fringes — and He did not even need the reminders? However, He knew that it was the teaching of His Father, and He knew that they were an opportunity to express who He was as One who belonged to God. How about us?

ADDITIONAL NOTES

Chapter 13
Verse 1
"to explore" (some translations use the word "spy") — Just a little point of interest here. The Hebrew word translated "spy" has come down to Modern Hebrew to mean, among other things, "to tour". It is the common word for "tourists". In fact, the logo for the Ministry of Tourism in Israel is two men carrying the cluster of grapes! The question is, were the spies tourists, or are modern tourists, spies?!

Verse 2
"a leader" — The Hebrew word is *nasi* (נשיא). This word is the Modern Hebrew word for "president". It has also been translated "prince", such as in R. Yehudah haNasi (Rabbi Judah the Prince, ca 200± ce). It is still difficult to determine from this word the specific nature of their position within the tribes, except that they were some kind of respected leaders.

Verses 4–15
Note that in the listing of the spies, no one from the tribe of Levi is represented.

Verse 17
Some translations here use the term "south" in this verse. — The Hebrew word translated "south" is the word *negev* (נגב). "The Negev" is the Modern Hebrew title for the southernmost part of Israel. In this passage, as with the other place names, it is difficult to know whether to translate the words or just transliterate them. Today's Negev extends from around Beersheba and Arad to form a triangle with the point ending at Eilat on the Red Sea. However, the Biblical Negev ended at the Beersheba–Arad basin, north of the modern border at Eilat.

Verse 21
"they went up" — The Hebrew word here is the same word from where we get the term "*aliyah*," or going up to live in the Land of Israel. Going to the Land is always a step up! However, in this case, it meant literally going higher in elevation. Did the spies make "aliyah" at this point?!

Verse 22
"Hebron" — The Hebrew verb changes from plural to singular where it says, "they came". It should read, "he came". This change speaks volumes. Most commentators, including myself, think that it was Caleb who went to Hebron. This interpretation is strengthened by Judges 1:20, where it says that Hebron was given to Caleb. Why is this significant? It is important perhaps because Hebron was the tomb of the Patriarchs, their forefathers. Caleb, in other words, went home!

Being in the Land was home to him. He would be willing to claim it no matter what the cost, whereas the others (except Joshua) did not go "home" to Hebron. Perhaps if they had thought like Caleb, and had done what he had, they might not have rebelled against the gift the Lord was giving to them — the Land, their home.

Verse 22

"**Hebron was built seven years before Zoan in Egypt.**" — This statement seems unnecessary in the context. The narrative would flow naturally without it. Why, therefore, did the Lord insert this into the Torah at this point?

Perhaps we can think of it in this way. The mention of Hebron was a way to remind the Israelites of the place of their origin, the home of their father, Abraham, the receiver of the Covenant that made them into a chosen people of God. Zoan, on the other hand was, according to Psalm 78:12 and 43, the place where God performed the miracles before Pharaoh through Moshe. Consequently, it was also one of the places where the Israelites dwelt when they were slaves in Egypt. (Most Bible maps place it in Goshen, as is seen in map 3.)

Hence, this verse may have been somewhat of a reminder to the Israelites that God was taking them to their home He promised through covenant. That home was, in fact, even founded before Zoan, the reminder of the Egypt to which they desired to return.

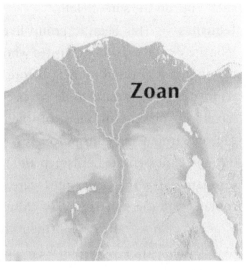

Map 3: *The eastern part of the Nile River Delta was called Goshen in the Bible.*

Verse 26

"**kadesh**" — The word Kadesh means "sanctuary." According to Milgrom, the modern name Ein Mishpat is another way of designating this place. Ein Mishpat means "spring of judgment". Milgrom notes that these are "names that are appropriate for a site in which Israel was settled for most of its wilderness sojourn ..."[155] We should note that Kadesh Barnea (The same as Kadesh) had more springs than any other parts of the Negev.

Verse 28

"**fortified**" — Cities in the Ancient Near East were fortified in at least two ways. First, they had walls. The walls of ancient Canaanite cities were sometimes about 30–50 feet high and about 15 feet thick and filled with debris. These are called "Casemate" Walls. Secondly, they built ramparts. Ramparts were artificial hills leading up to the walls that tended to make it more difficult for attackers to siege a city that had a wall. It is more difficult to fight uphill. When a city had a rampart, the walls were built on top of it. Sometimes, as was the case with Jericho and others, there were double walls where there was a wall at the base of the rampart, then the rampart, and finally a wall at the top of that.

Verse 29

"**Amalekites, Hittites, Jebusites, Amorites, and Canaanites**"

Amalekites — These were always considered strong foes of Israel. They lived in the Negev.

---

155. Milgrom *JPS: Numbers,* 104.

Hittites — The Hittites had a powerful empire, but it was mainly in the north. They seem to have vied with Egypt much of the time during the second millennia BCE for control of Canaan. However, sometimes the English word "Hittite" is a mistranslation for Hetitie. This is the family name for a Canaanite family living near ancient Hebron. Abraham bought the burial cave from such Ephron the son of Heth.

Jebusites — This Semitic group lived in the environs of Jerusalem, which was considered a Jebusite city. It was the Jebusites who brought the Gihon Spring within the city of Jerusalem by digging underground tunnels, before the spies were there.

Amorites — It is hard to be precise in our definition and analysis of the Amorites, "which is hardly surprising in view of their nomadic heritage."[156] This was a term used in the Mesopotamian cuneiform sources as early as the second half of the third millennium, to designate the Semitic herdsmen and their territory in the Syrian steppe west of the Euphrates.[157]

Canaanites — The Canaanites were a very loose collection of tribes, who were not Semitic but spoke a Semitic language very close to Hebrew. They lived mostly in the lowland regions of Israel. We know much about them through the discovery of Ugarit in present day Ras Shamra in Lebanon. They were not very united but dwelt in city-states and united to fight common enemies.

Verse 29

The four main geographical points of the Promised Land were designated in this verse:

South: the Negev
North and Central: the hill country
East: east bank of the Jordan River (Transjordan)
West: the Sea (the Mediterranean Sea).

Verse 33

"**Nephalim**" — The word *nephalim* (נפלים) in Hebrew actually means "fallen ones". They were first mentioned in Genesis 6:4, but this Genesis reference was before the flood. Were they the same kind of people group? In Genesis they were "mighty men" resulting from the union between the "sons of God" and the "daughters of men" (whoever these groups were). The text and background of Genesis 6 to suggest that this might have been a union involving pagan temple prostitutes.[158] At any rate, the text emphasizes their great size. To a short Semite, even a person 6-7 foot (2+ metres) tall may have been considered a "giant".

---

156. Harrison, *Numbers* (TOTC), 208.
157. Milgrom, *JPS: Numbers,* 105.
158. A suggestion provided by our son, Yoel, himself an accomplished Torah teacher.

Chapter 14

Verses 1–5

These verses use three different names for the people of Israel: the whole congregation, the people, and all the children of Israel. "By the use of these designations he (the author) emphasizes that all the people were, indeed, involved in the rebellion that is to follow."[159]

Verse 9

"**our prey**" (NASB) — This term signifies how easy it would be to destroy them. Their defence — the Hebrew reads "their shadow" — was "a common metaphor of great significance in a hot country."[160] This shows the extreme amount of faith and trust Joshua and Caleb had in the Lord to see this clearly into the spiritual realm. In this story, Joshua and Caleb rise in spiritual stature almost as high as Moshe himself. They are truly some of the greatest of our Biblical heroes.

Verses 13–19

In Moshe's first argument, "he poses the following theological problem: How is God to punish Israel and yet maintain the reputation of His power in the world? Ezekiel saw the same problem in Israel's exile and, hence, predicted Israel's restoration, even though undeserved."[161]

Verse 18

Like Exodus 34:6–8, Numbers 14:18 is also an example of prepositional revelation of God. The rabbis often consider Exodus 34 as a revelation of God's "Thirteen Attributes". In Numbers 14, they are summarized and only those which apply to this situation are mentioned. These are Patience, literally, "long nosed" — "an ancient literary image signifying 'compassion',"[162] and loving-kindness. Unlike its Exodus counterpart, "truth" is missing. "There are occasions when loving-kindness is important."[163] This is one of those occasions! However, it should be noted that both the LXX and the Samaritan Pentateuch add the words "and truth".[164]

Verses 33–34

Note that the number of years of wandering in the wilderness corresponds to the number of days the Land was spied out. God often did that in our history. For example, the number of years in Babylonian exile corresponded to the number of Shabbat years they did not keep. God is fair and just, as well as merciful.

Verse 44

"**in their presumption**" — The Hebrew verb here *ya'pilu* (יעפלו), has the causative force. It could mean, "to act defiantly", or "be arrogant", or "act presumptuously". It is from a root that means, "to swell", as when one's head swells up with pride.[165]

---

159. Ashley, *Numbers,* 245.
160. Hertz, *Pentateuch and Haftarahs,* 627.
161. Milgrom, *JPS: Numbers,* 110.
162. Harrison, *Numbers,* 214.
163. Hertz, *Pentateuch and Haftarahs,* 628.
164. Harrison, *Numbers,* 220.
165. BDB, 179.

Chapter 15

Verses 14–16

These verses are critical for those who live in the Promised Land. The Holy One states that while living in Israel, the *ger,* גר ("sojourner") is to live the same way as the native-born Israelite. This has important ramifications for believers today who are not Jews, but who also live in Israel. The laws for life in Israel differ from the regulations for life in the Diaspora. If a non-Jewish believer wants to live in Israel, he must abide by the Torah, as a Jewish person does.

Verse 32

Gathering wood on Shabbat — the man who did this was found guilty of breaking Shabbat and put to death. To understand this severe penalty, we must remember the important spiritual picture Shabbat paints. It pictures what it is like to be spiritually right with God, trusting in His work and ceasing from our own labours as the means we relied upon to "earn" His approval. If a person tries in any way, shape, or form, to add even the slightest measure of effort or merit of his own, to his salvation, he shows that he does not understand what the grace of God means, because he has not stopped working and rested in what Messiah did for him. The result can only be spiritual death, because he has spurned the all sufficient work of Yeshua in His atonement. Hence, work such as described in this passage is prohibited because it destroys the Torah picture that God intended to paint through the Shabbat.

Verses 37–40

"**tzitzit**" (ציצת) The nature of the tzitzit is illuminated by the literature and art of the Ancient Near East, which shows that the hem was ornate in comparison with the rest of the outer robe. The more important the individual, the more elaborate the embroidery of his hem. Its significance lies not in its artistry, but in its symbolism as an outward extension of the owner's person and authority.[166] Milgrom continues to explain that tzitzit are merely an extension of the hem, as illustrated in Ancient Near Eastern art.

---

166. Milgrom, *op. cit.*, 410.

STUDY QUESTIONS

1. Did God want the spies sent out, or was this an act of the "flesh"? Explain your answer.

2. Why do you think the Torah names the spies for us?

3. Why did Moshe re-name Hosea to Joshua?

4. What does Caleb's name mean in English? What, if anything, would it signify?

5. What seems to be the purposes of the spy mission?

6. What may have been the importance of bringing back such a huge cluster of grapes to the people, to God, and to the spies?

7. What seems to be the significance of the term *efes ki-az* (אפס כי-עז) at the beginning of 13:28?

8. How did Caleb attempt to silence the people? Why?

9. In their desire to return to Egypt, what were the people really expressing?

10. Why did Joshua and Caleb rip their clothes in 14:6?

11. What was the significance of the Shekinah appearing in 14:10?

12. What was Moshe's main argument against the Lord? Why was it such a good argument?

13. What was the "different spirit" that was upon Caleb in 14:24?

14. Why did the people attempt to go into battle against the Amalekites in 14:39-45?

15. If they "repented," why did God not grant them victory?

16. Why is the teaching on the sacrifices inserted right after this story, in chapter 15?

17. Why do you think the teaching about the sojourner is put here? Why do you think that the same laws that apply to the Jews also apply to non-Jews in the land of Israel? Or don't they? Explain.

18. What is the importance of setting aside the challah in chapter 15?

19. What do the fringes help us with? What does the colour blue signify? How can the fringes be worn today? Should they, or should they not be worn? Explain.

PARASHAT KORACH קורח

TORAH: NUMBERS 16:1–18:32
HAFTARAH: 1 SAMUEL 11: 14–12:22

Parashat Korach קורח

Scripture does not say, "Now Korach contented," or "assembled," or "spoke," or "commanded," but Korach "took." What did he take? He took nothing! It was his heart that carried him away! (Bamidbar Rabbah 18.16)

The Lord had issued a death sentence to the generation of people who had rejected the Land. The disciplines carried out as a result of Korach's rebellion culminating in 16:31–35 were some of the ways this death sentence was executed. Were they too sweeping? After all, not everyone 20 years old or older accepted the spies' report, did they? They could not all have been as rebellious as it seemed. Or were they?

This week's parasha begins to illustrate just how far the seeds of rebellion had spread in the camp of the Israelites. In reality, the problem was more serious than many would imagine. In this parasha, we will see how one incident of mutiny multiplied itself and resulted in the deaths of nearly 15,000 Israelites — and the 40 years of wandering had only just begun! Let us, therefore, examine *Parashat Korach* and learn what we can from this rebellion. As we do so, we will use this outline:

I.   The Challengers
II.   Their Contention
III. Moshe's Counter
IV.   God's Choice
V.   God's Confirmations

I. THE CHALLENGERS

Three sets of people set out to challenge the leadership of Moshe and Aaron according to 16:1-3. First, we have Korach, the leader of the rebellion. Being a Levite, he was a close relative of Moshe and Aaron. This fact comes into play when we examine his challenge. Next, were some people from the tribe of Reuben. What is significant in this? Reuben was the first born of the sons of Jacob. As such, he was normally entitled to the inheritance and family leadership, but, according to Genesis 49, he was by-passed in favour of Joseph and Judah. The effect of this detail is magnified when we remember that Korach was from the Kohathite clan. According to the camp arrangements, they encamped next to each other, on the south side of the Mishkan, and even journeyed very close to the Reubenites.

Let the midrash make the point: With Dathan and Abiram (16:1) … "From this text the saying is derived: 'Woe to the wicked and to his neighbour!' It applies to Dathan and to Abiram, neighbours of Korach … Datan and Abiram, however, were neighbours to a contentious man, were punished with him and were swept from the world."[167]

The third set of people who rebelled is the 250 who stood with Korach, Datan, and Abiram. We are told that the 250 people were "men, well known community leaders who had been appointed members of the council" (16:2). In some respects, this is the same description as that

---

167. Bamidbar Rabbah 17.5

of the spies. Both groups were considered leaders *anashim* (אנשים). Furthermore, they all had a name for themselves. The Hebrew text says literally, "men of a name". This means that many knew of them; they were popular in Israel. Finally, being men (*anashim*), they fell into the category of men whom Rashi in the last parasha defined as "worthy men".[168]

From this description, it seems that some of these 250 were chosen rulers of Israel whose purpose, according to Numbers 11:16, was to assist Moshe in ruling Israel. "The presence of such a respected delegation naturally lent credence to Korach's grievances."[169]

These then, are the leaders of this latest mutiny among the children of Israel. What was their problem?

II. THEIR CONTENTION

All three groups of discontents complained to Moshe and Aaron in 16:3 that Moshe and Aaron took too much power upon themselves. They may have thought: Here were two brothers, one was the spiritual leader, and the other was the prophet or lawgiver — the two highest positions in the nation. Our challengers accused them of "selfishly taking power and prestige for themselves at the expense of the rest of the nation which was just as qualified as they (for the entire assembly — all of them are holy)."[170]

A. What a Deal!

Let us state this challenge a little differently in order to try to get a grip on what seems to be the gripe of these troublemakers. From their perspective, it seemed like Moshe and Aaron had a real "racket" going on! One brother provided the laws, which enabled the other and his family to really rake it in! What a deal! Here is also a Midrash that describes the contention in this light. For its fullest impact, we will quote it at length:

> There was once a widow in my neighbourhood who had two daughters and one field. When she came to plough, Moshe said to her, "You shall not plough with an ox and an ass together" (Deuteronomy 22:10).
> When she came to sow, he said to her, "You shall not sow thy field with divers seeds" (Leviticus 19:19). When she came to reap and stack the corn, he said to her, "Leave gleanings, the forgotten sheaf, and the corner of the field for the poor." When she came to thresh, he said to her, "Give tithes, priestly dues, the first and second tithes." She justified heaven's pronouncement and gave him.
> What did this poor woman do? She went and sold her field and purchased with the proceeds two lambs, to clothe herself from its shearing and enjoy its products. As soon as they gave birth, Aaron came and said to her, "Give me the first-born since the Holy One blessed be He said, 'Every first-born that shall be born of thy herd and flock, the male one, thou shalt consecrate to the Lord thy God'." She justified heaven's pronouncement and gave him the offspring.
> The time came for the shearing, and she sheared them. Then came Aaron and said to her, "Give me the first of the shearing since the Holy One blessed be He said, 'And this shall be the priest's

---

168. Rashi: *Bamidbar*, ArtScroll Edition, 148.
169. *The ArtScroll Chumash*, 821.
170. *Ibid.*

due from the people, from those who offer a sacrifice'..." (Deuteronomy 18:3). Thereupon she said, "Since I have no more strength to withstand the man, I shall slaughter them and eat them." As soon as she had slaughtered them, Aaron came and said to her, "Give me the shoulder, two cheeks and maw" (Deuteronomy 18:3). Whereupon she said, "Even after I have slaughtered them, I am not delivered from his hand. Let them be forbidden my use." Said Aaron to her, "In that case it is all mine since the Holy One said, 'Every devoted thing ... in Israel shall be Mine'" (Numbers 18:14).

He took them, departed, and left her weeping with her two daughters. Such was the lot that befell this unfortunate woman! So much they do in the name of the Holy One blessed be He.[171]

This is quite possibly how Korach and his conspirators may have felt and thought regarding the leadership of Moshe and Aaron. They posed a challenge to what was perceived to be by the rebels, a monopoly in the national leadership.

B. Green with Envy?

Their challenge has another possible angel to it. The text is very careful to point out the family names of the leaders of this rebellion. If these people wanted to rebel, the fires of jealousy and envy could very easily have spurred them on from their families.

Remember that some were from the tribe of Reuben. They may have thought that their tribe should have been the national leaders instead of Judah, or especially instead of Moshe, who was from Levi. It seems reasonable that when the Reubenites saw the honoured position of Judah in the camp formation, jealousy could easily have taken root. However, this jealousy would naturally have been against Judah, not against the descendants of Levi. How did this envy toward Moshe and Aaron get a foothold among the conspirators?

It came in through Korach, who himself was a Levite. Also remember that Korach's family encamped in very close proximity to the Reubenites. This undoubtedly helped to spread the fires of contention. Accordingly, Korach may have been thinking, "Why was Aaron chosen to be the spiritual leader when others may also qualify?" Thus, Korach could have been jealous of both his cousin Aaron who had received the position of High Priest, and of his other cousin, Elizaphan, son of Uzziel, who had been chosen to lead the family of Kohat" (3:30).

Moreover, note that the text tells us in 16:1, "Korach took ...", but the direct object for the verb "took" is missing. Rabbi Munk helps us to understand the importance of this grammatical detail when he writes, "The interpretation given by Rashi is that he "took" himself, that is, he separated himself from the community. Other commentators explain that he took on feelings of envy and took it upon himself to change his path in life."[172]

> Indeed, Korach took. He took what was not his to have while Moshe and Aaron gave what had been given to them. In the end, Korach was responsible for taking the lives of many of his countryman. In the process he blamed Moshe for it. But it was really he who simply took.

---

171. Nechama Leibowitz, *New Studies in Bamidbar*, 188–189.
172. Elie Munk, *The Call of the Torah: Bamidbar*, 186.

C. Same Tune, Different Words

Korach's cronies had more to say. It was not enough that Korach would inspire them to challenge the right of Moshe and Aaron to lead Israel. They also had to revert to the same tune that the rebellious have sung since leaving Egypt. Only this tune has a slightly different variation.

Datan and Abiram had two problems with Moshe. They felt that he "dominated" them, making himself the ruler over them. They stated the second problem like this; "You haven't brought us into a land flowing with milk and honey or given us an inheritance of fields and vineyards. (16:14). Instead, "You have brought us up out of a land flowing with milk and honey to kill us in the desert...." (16:13).

In each of Israel's rebellions, there are similarities, but also differences in the way they are expressed. The first rebellions came out of a fear of hunger or starvation and as their perception of the reality of their freedom and seemingly insecure life in the wilderness gradually worsened. When it did, the children of Israel made pleas to go back to Egypt, lest they die in the wilderness. Then their rebellion progressed to an even worse state. In Numbers 11, they cried out for the "free" Egyptian fish. They seem to have forgotten that although they did not have to pay over the counter for the fish, nevertheless, they paid with their freedom, and in some cases, their very lives.

Now, in this parasha, the complainers take their obstinacy to even greater depths. Here, we see them referring to Egypt in the same way the Lord referred to the Promised Land. It is a complete reversal. It represents the horrible depth into which the mutiny had sunk. Leibowitz draws a sobering application from all of this. She compares this attitude to the contemporary descendants of Jacob who find complacency in the Diaspora equivalent to being in their "Jerusalem". She remarks,

> But here is something new and unprecedented — a complete reversal of values, calling black white and white, black. What was slavery is termed freedom; the land of uncleanness is given the title exclusively applied to the holy land. It is a symbol for all time to those who in the lands of their dispersion proclaim: "Here is our Jerusalem!"[173]

D. Please Discard the Label

Let us take the application we learn from this rebellion of the Israelites even a step further, for this lesson is critical for life in the Body of Messiah.

Just as Datan and Abiram distorted reality and made false judgment calls regarding the Promised Land, so also do some in the body of Messiah today. Our judgments and labelling are not concerning the Land, necessarily, but concerning people — other brothers and sisters in Messiah. New Creations avoid making judgments and unfairly labelling people. This distorts the truth of who they are in Messiah. Our new man desires to look at that other believer whom some may call "irksome" and know him after the Spirit instead of the flesh. This is what Paul

---

173. Leibowitz, *op. cit.,* 210.

was describing in 2 Corinthians 5:16 when he said, "So from now on, we regard no one from a worldly point of view, though we once regarded Messiah in this way, we do so no longer. Therefore, if anyone is in Messiah, he is a new creation ..."

It may be true that some believers may walk in their flesh much of the time, but we need to remember that their flesh is not their real identity. They, like us, are truly new people. In Messiah, we are saints and not sinners! Judging and labelling someone falsely may actually contribute to that believer walking in the flesh. For, he may be walking in the flesh because of a false perception of himself based on the feedback he gets from other brothers and sisters. However, we can really help him/her, and give due glory to God, by referring to him in truthful, biblical terms, using God's description of him such as "child of God" "justified one", or "forgiven one", rather than with words that merely describe his flesh. In other words, we must not describe a believer according to his flesh, because that is his flesh — it is not the real him!

III. MOSHE'S COUNTER

A. The Firepans

Moshe's response to Korach and his group was two-fold. His first action was to propose a test. This test suggested by Moshe was very shrewd. He told them to gather firepans for the burning of incense, an important act of worship within the Mishkan. By doing so, in essence, Moshe offered the challengers to play priest for a moment and see if their service in the Mishkan would be acceptable to the Holy One. "He challenges them to test their claims to equality with Aaron by undergoing a species of ordeal. They are to assume, for once, the functions of priesthood, and God would show whether or not He approved of such assumptions."[174]

This was a life-or-death test. If their incense was acceptable, they would live. If, not, then they would follow the fate of some previous fellow countrymen who also attempted to burn incense which was unacceptable to the Holy One, Nadav and Avihu (Leviticus 10:1ff.). By putting the test off to the next morning, Moshe was granting them time to contemplate seriously the consequences of their rebellion. Would they be willing to stake their life on their claims? Moreover, this test also put the burden of proof on the Lord Himself and not upon Moshe, Aaron, or Korach. Moshe was completely trusting God to either vindicate him or show that Korach was correct.

B. An Angry Moshe

Nevertheless, Moshe also had another response. After he had formally announced the "test", he then appealed to Korach and his followers to reason with him and talk things out. This, of course was a failure, only because he was attempting to reason with people who were very unreasonable and completely bent on impeaching him. It was in this appeal that the other

---

174. J. H. Hertz, *The Pentateuch and Haftarahs*, 639.

leaders, Datan and Abiram, were afforded an opportunity to vent their sentiments about the present situation of the nation in the wilderness and irrationally plead to be taken back to Egypt.

This was enough for Moshe. At first, he humbled himself (16:4), becoming totally frustrated with trying to communicate rationally with his detractors. Then, some translations say that Moshe became "distressed". The Hebrew word here in 16:15 would be better translated as "angry". Indeed, the verse tells us that Moshe got "very angry"!

IV. GOD'S CHOICE

It now became time for the Holy One to intervene. God would show everyone, without a doubt, who His choice was for leading the nation. There were several steps in God's plan.

A. Separate Yourselves

The first step, in 16:20–23, was to command everyone to stand clear of the dwelling places of Korach, Datan, and Abiram. Interestingly enough, this command came even before the firepan test began. Apparently, the situation was getting too critical to wait until the incense started burning. Every time such rebellion breaks out in the camp of God, the instructions are always the same — stand clear of the rebels!

B. The Terrible Sound

The second step was to create an unforgettable scene. In 16:31–34 God caused the earth to open and swallow the three leaders along with their households, burying them alive in the pit.

This naturally had a terrorizing effect on the Israelites. The text states that, "all Israel that was around them fled at their sound, for they said, 'Lest the earth swallow us'!" (16:34, author's translation). The Hebrew for sound *kol* (קוֹל) also be translated "voice". If so, then the whole camp heard the gruesome sound of their shrieking voices as they plummeted into the earth's opening. Targum Yonathan adds to the drama by saying, "The Lord is in the right, and true are His judgments, and true are the words of Moses His servant, but we are the evil ones who have rebelled against Him."

It is unfortunate that many Jewish commentators make a mistake at this point. Basing their ideas on the Talmud (Sanhedrin 110a), many suggest that Korach's death is not accounted for in this story. For example, Munk flatly states, "Korach's punishment is not explicitly mentioned."[175] However, all they need to do is to read Numbers 26:10–11 where the Torah specifically tells us that Korach was swallowed up by the earth with Datan and Abiram.

C. The Consuming fire

Are we ready for the next part of God's reaction? It is in 16:35. God's fire came and consumed the 250 who were holding the firepans in the Mishkan. The event was quick and startling. To comment further would only take away from its full impact.

---

175. Munk, *The Call of the Torah: Bamidbar*, 202.

D. Plating the Altar

God's final step in reacting to the rebellion was to instruct Eleazer to throw away the remaining incense flame but save the 250 copper firepans. With them, the Israelites were to make a hammered-out plate covering for the altar.

We can see a valuable lesson here. How could something, which was used to effectuate God's judgment, be used for such a holy object as the Altar? We suggest that the Lord is painting another of His brilliant teaching pictures. The Altar was the place where the horrors of sin were vividly portrayed through the bloody sacrifices that were continually offered there. By having the Altar covered with the metal of the firepans, God was demonstrating how horrible the sin of *rebellion* is. In fact, a case could be made to assert that rebellion against God is at the root of all sin. Hence, no matter which sin was being atoned for at the Altar, the blood was also "covering" the copper covers. In other words, the atoning blood also covered the rebellion that was at the core of that sin.

E. The Aftermath

We would think that upon witnessing all of these supernatural phenomena, each and every child of Jacob would have walked closely with the Lord for the rest of his life. However, as Nechama Leibowitz suggests,

> They were simply not moved by the miracles! A miracle cannot serve either to accredit the emissary or his mission. Whoever is consumed by doubts and scepticism will always find an explanation of the miracles. Just the same as he does not acknowledge the Almighty as the guiding power behind his servants and prophets, so he will not detect the workings of providence behind the wonders of the creation, both in its natural and supernatural aspects.[176]

We need to remember this fact when we are working with those who do not follow the Lord. There seems to be a craze in today's believing world for the miraculous. We need to remember that if the Lord is already softening the soil of their nephesh, then perhaps, seeing a miracle is not going to contribute to their journey to the Lord. However, if God has not been preparing that person, then our task is purely to share the message and let God perform whatever miracles He chooses or not chooses to perform.

Having this in mind, we can now begin to understand what happened in 16:41ff. where the children of Israel complained on the next day, accusing Moshe and Aaron saying, "You have killed the people of the Lord." Instantly, the Lord sent a supernatural plague throughout the camp because of their un-confessed and un-repented sin.

So it happened that a rebellion begun by three men, spread to 250, and was now responsible for contributing to the deaths of nearly 15,000 people of Israel. As was the case with other disciplinary plagues sent by the Lord, this one, being supernatural, would need a supernatural cure! Rashi provides an insightful explanation concerning the cure that the Lord provided, as Aaron anointed the sinners with incense. He comments,

---

176. Leibowitz, *New Studies in Bamidbar,* 216.

Why did Moses have Aaron stop the plague with incense? Because Israel was jeering and complaining about the incense saying, "It is deadly poison. Nadav and Avihu died through it and two hundred and fifty people died through it." The Holy One blessed is He, said, "You shall see that it is a plague stopper, and sin is what kills."[177]

V. GOD'S CONFIRMATION

The rest of the parasha centres on God confirming and re-affirming Aaron and the Levites to the ministry.

A. The Buds

God confirms Aaron as the High Priest. To do this, He initiates another test, (17:1f). Each tribe was to put a rod/stick with the leader's name written on it into the Mishkan before the Ark. The staff that blossomed was the one whom the Holy One had chosen to be the leader. Rabbi Hertz suggests that these rods were those that were "ordinarily carried by the princes as the symbol of tribal authority."[178]

We all know the results. The next day not only had Aaron's rod budded, but it even had almonds on it! It is difficult to determine exactly why Aaron's rod was of almond wood. Understanding the nature of the Hebrew word may shed some more light on the question.

The Hebrew word for almond is *shaked* (שקד). However, in addition to it meaning "almond", the verbal form of this noun could also mean "to watch" or "to be awake".[179] These renderings may have been derived from the fact that in Israel, the almond tree is one of the first trees to blossom in late winter. To many, its fragrant pink-white blossoms are an encouragement that the cold, rainy winter will soon pass. Its blossoms would, therefore, "awaken" people to watch for the coming of spring. It would appear from all of this that the Lord might have been demonstrating to all Israel that Aaron and the Levites were the spiritual watchmen over Israel. Perhaps this was how the test confirmed God's choice.

B. A Permanent Reminder

The presence of the almond branch in the Ark reminded the people of the failed rebellion and served "as a sign to the rebellious. This will put an end to their grumbling against me, so that they will not die (17:10)". It also reminded them that God had *His* appointed leadership to watch over the nation.

Rabbi Munk sees another purpose for the almond branch in the Ark. He says that its presence also reminded Israel that there was to be a careful distinction between the three divisions of Israelites. He says that it seems clear that some sort of "spiritual hierarchy was now being introduced to the Jewish nation, and there was a need to have it take root in the hearts and minds of the people. The division of the people into categories of kohanim, Levites, and

---

177. Rashi, *ArtScroll; Edition*, 210.
178. Hertz, *Pentateuch and Haftarahs*, 644.
179. BDB, 1052.

Israelites would now become fixed for all time, as a part of the everyday life of the Jew."[180]

C. Where Is It?

Aaron's rod functioning as a permanent sign to Israel is slightly problematic. The problem is that no one today knows where it is! The location of the Ark and its contents is one of the greatest of the world's unsolved mysteries and the subject of many a fable, legend and movie!

The best we can do is to point students to Yoma 52b. Here we read, "Surely it has been taught: When the Ark was hidden, there was hidden with it the bottle containing the manna, and that containing the sprinkling water, the staff of Aaron with its almonds and blossoms, and the chest which the Philistines had sent as a gift to the God of Israel...." Then we are told, "Who hid it? Josiah hid it."

There you have it! Here is the information you needed to begin your search for Aaron's blossomed rod and the lost Ark!

As for the rest of the Torah portion, chapter 18 is merely a recapitulation of the duties, responsibilities, and calling of the Levites. The significance of this chapter lies in its context. It follows the Korach incident and serves as a reaffirmation of God's choice for the service of the Mishkan.

EXCURSUS: SPIRITUAL REBELLION

This parasha has often been used to provide a biblical basis to defend a certain kind of authority assumed by some spiritual leaders, especially those whose leadership responsibilities are in local congregations. The defence usually goes something like this: "Do not speak against God's anointed, do not act against God's anointed. For just like Korach rebelled against Moshe and was judged by God for doing so, so will anyone who questions, challenges, or does something contrary to their spiritual leader." We feel compelled to make a few remarks about this issue.

First, we would like to share some of our experience in the body of Messiah in this area. We have been believers in Yeshua for over 50 years. As young believers, we were active as budding leaders in a well-known organization for believers on our secular university campus. Eventually we graduated from both a Biblical University and an excellent seminary. From graduation in 1978 until our *aliyah* to Israel in 1992, Ariel served as a pastor for three congregations, including a Messianic Jewish one. From our experiences in the believing world, we are aware of what many spiritual leaders think about this issue, and we have also been sheep under the leadership of a pastor. From these experiences in the Body of Messiah we have some critical as well as (we hope) some helpful remarks to make.

The body of Messiah has a definite problem concerning the area of spiritual rebellion. Part of the problem is that we do not think that the Body of Messiah has succeeded in defining its authority structure. Oftentimes it thinks that it patterns itself after the authority structure of

180. Munk, *The Call of the Torah: Bamidbar*, 209.

ancient Israel. The pastor is usually perceived to be like Moshe or Aaron. He is given absolute authority, even over his "under shepherds", whether they are called deacons, elders, or just "the board".

This arrangement is totally unsatisfactory for several reasons. First, there is an immense cultural and vocational, gap between ancient Israel and the Body of Messiah. To be sure, there are also many similarities. In fact, in the case of Jewish believers in Yeshua, one can make a good argument that the two situations are, indeed, one! However, for the most part, the local expression of the Body of Messiah does not possess the specific calling of ancient Israel, and therefore, cannot share the same leadership structure.

A second reason is the usual result of such an unbiblical analogy. When a spiritual leader perceives himself as a Moshe or Aaron, too often those who disagree with him are considered rebels like Korach or, in the case of women, like "Jezebels". When this type of leadership structure is in force, it provides a fertile breeding ground for one of the most serious "unspoken" problems facing the body of Messiah today — spiritual abuse.

We have met with scores of people who have submitted themselves at one time or another to such authority minded leadership. We ourselves also have first-hand experience with such leadership. (Not in our current fellowship!)

We call it "unspoken" because of the chemistry between the "Moses" and the sheep. Armed with a mandate from on high, the leader pronounces dictate after dictate to manipulate and shame the sheep into blind obedience. When the sheep question such authority, they are labelled as rebellious, shamed, and embarrassed into compliance. If trouble or disunity occurs resulting from their challenging the leader's teaching or authority, the questioning sheep are usually silenced as the *cause* of the problem rather than considered the victim of the autocratic and insecure leader's problems.

In our opinion, it is unbiblical to use *Parashat Korach* as a biblical guide to defend the dictates of a power-hungry leader who claims to be God's anointed. If we are in such a situation, we need not fear the earth opening up when we challenge or even oppose such a leader! In truth, many such leaders need to be called into question and should be at the scrutiny of all of the sheep who depend upon them for spiritual food, comfort, encouragement, and direction. Let us not use this precious Torah as an aid to propagate any more spiritual abuse in the body of Messiah.

Yet, there is a proper biblical leadership and authority structure that all believers need to follow. Yeshua, the Chief Shepherd, teaches some of the basic guidelines for authority and submission in His Body in John 10. He says that the sheep follow the real shepherd because they know his voice. Yeshua says, "I am the good Shepherd. The good shepherd lays down his life for the sheep" (John 10:1–21).

From this passage, we learn that a leader's authority comes from his servanthood. It is empowered by his willingness to know the sheep personally enough to lay his life down for them. The sheep will gladly follow this kind of a leader. However, when a leader thinks that he has to exhort the sheep to follow him, to submit to him as God's anointed, he has already shown that he no longer has that anointing, assuming he had it from the start.

ADDITIONAL NOTES

Chapter 16

Verse 3
"The whole community is holy" — Although the people were technically "holy" or "set apart" from all nations, their actions such as in the previous parasha and this one revealed that they were not holy unto *God*. Hence, Korach's argument fails at the start.

Verse 3
They "**assembled**" themselves — The verb for "assembled" is *kahal* (קהל). The noun form of this is the same word used to denote a congregation. This was apparently a "congregational split"!

Verse 11
Hertz believes that as a result of Moshe defending Aaron's Divine appointment, some of the Levites left Korach's rebellion. His proof is in 1 Chronicles 6:22 where we find some of Korach's descendants leading in sacred song. We also know that there are some Psalms attributed to "The Sons of Korach".

Verse 14
"**gouge out those men's eyes**" — "This idiom also means 'hoodwink' and corresponds to the modern idioms, 'throw dust in the eyes' or 'pull the wool over the eyes'."[181]

Verse 33
"**the grave**" —The Hebrew word is *sheol*, שאל. "This word was the usual designation for the repository for the physically dead, both righteous and unrighteous. It was also a word used elsewhere in the Ancient Near East, where it meant the 'netherworld', located just below the ground level."[182] Harrison also stresses that the Torah expresses little, if any, concept of the afterlife. Hence, as used in this passage, "It is best to understand sheol as equivalent to 'the grave', without imposing upon the concept ideas that were apparently not [current] at the time in Israel."[183] Jacob Milgrom notes that eventually the word sheol became associated with where the wicked go whilst the righteous ascend heavenward. Moreover, he says that the rabbis later replaced the term sheol by *Gehinnom*.[184]

---

181. Milgrom, *JPS: Numbers*, 134.
182. R.K. Harrison, *Introduction to the Old Testament*, 238.
183. Harrison, *Introduction*, 239.
184. Milgrom, *JPS: Numbers*, 138.

Chapter 17
(English verses in parenthesis)
Jewish translations and other translations have a difference between verse enumeration. In most Jewish Bibles, chapter 16 finishes with verse 35, while other translations finish chapter 16 at 17:15, making the story of the rod begin chapter 17 in their Bibles. It really does not matter at all since the original Torah had no verse or chapter numbers.

Verse 2 (37)
"**Eleazar**" — Eleazar, and not Aaron the High Priest, was assigned with removing the fire pans, probably because as the High Priest, Aaron had to be more scrupulous over what he touched.

Verse 2 (37)
"**They have become holy**" — The firepans became holy unto the Lord because the 250 men who previously privately owned the firepans, now "had sanctified the censers for use in their ill-fated incense service."[185]

Verse 3 (38)
bronze plated sheets —This story and that of Exodus 27:2; 38:2 seems to have a discrepancy. In Exodus 26 it seems that the Altar was already bronze plated. However, we can see at least two possible solutions to this apparent contradiction. The first possibility is supported by the LXX translation, which indicates that this is the story of how the Altar got to be bronze plated as is indicated in the Exodus accounts. The second possibility is that this could be simply a second bronze plating.[186]

Verse 3 (38)
"**sign**" — The Hebrew word is *ote* (אות) This is the first of two special remembrance signs or symbols that the Lord created in this parasha, the second being the rod of Aaron. Both the rod and the copper plating from the firepans were to serve as reminders for all Israel because they were placed in specially designated spots in "The House". God wanted everyone to have as many reminders as necessary to the fact that His House was special and must be run only according to His orders.

Verse 6 (41)
The people of Israel did not learn from the supernatural death of the rebellious ones. Because they still carried bitterness and resentfulness against the Lord and Moshe in their hearts, God had to afflict them with a supernatural plague. The kind of plague is not specified. The text only tells us that they were "smitten".

Verse 11 (46)
"**firepan**" — "The same firepans that brought death to the unauthorized 250 averts death in the hands of the authorized."[187] It is the same also with the incense.

---

185. *ArtScroll Chumash*, 827.
186. Milgrom, *JPS: Numbers,* 140.
187. *Ibid.*

Verse 16 (17:2)

"**rod**" — The Hebrew word translated "rod" is *matteh* (מטה). It could also be rendered "staff", "branch", "shaft", or even "tribe".[188] This last sense lends credence to Hertz's idea that the "rod" was some kind of a staff which represented the tribe, some kind of a symbolic staff carried by the leader of the tribe. Milgrom words it all beautifully when he says, "The double meaning of matteh is significant: The dead matteh (staff) springs to life and represents the living matteh (tribe) that God blesses. Furthermore, only the matteh (staff/tribe) of Levi is qualified to be in the presence of God.[189]

Verse 22 (17:10–11)

The rabbis suggest that Moshe placed the staff in the Holy of Holies, not inside the Ark, but in front of it.[190]

Verses 27–28 (17:13)

These verses come in sharp contrast with the preceding ones where the Holy One goes out of His way to provide means for the survival of the nation, giving them a reminder against rebellion. It was totally out of irrational emotion that the people began to complain anew and express their fears of punishment.

Chapter 18

This chapter is very comprehensive in its summary of the duties, privileges, and responsibilities of the kohanim and Levites. The topics it covers are:

- The general Mishkan duties which they were to "safeguard", verses 1–7;
- the offerings they were to oversee, verses 8–19;
- their "heritage", verse 20;
- the "tax" or financial provision for the kohanim, verses 21–24; and
- their own "taxes" or giving responsibilities to the Lord, verses 25–32.

---

188. BDB, 641.
189. Milgrom, *JPS: Numbers,* 142.
190. *Ibid.,* 144.

STUDY QUESTIONS

1. What can we learn from the context of the story of Korach, especially coming immediately after the story of "The Great Spy Disaster"?

2. What is significant about knowing which tribe Korach, Dathan, and Abiram came from? List some of the things we can learn from these details.

3. What was the nature of the complaint against Moshe and Aaron?

4. What kind of reaction did Moshe show when he was first confronted with the complaints? What does this say about the kind of leader he was?

5. Whose idea was the fire-pan test? Do you think it should have been done? Why, or why not?

6. What was the nature of the fire-pan test?

7. What was Moshe trying to do with the leaders of the rebellion before the fire-pan test? Why?

8. Describe the response from Dathan and Abiram to Moshe's pleas. What were they accusing Moshe of doing?

9. Outline God's plan of action in dealing with the mutiny.

10. Why do you think God had the people separate themselves before the earth opened up?

11. Why do you think, "all Israel fled from the sound" in 16:34?

12. Why did God instruct that the firepans be placed as a cover for the altar?

13. Why did God send the plague in 16:6–15? What was its cure?

14. What was significant about the rods?

15. What happened to Aaron's rod and why was it important? Why do you think we cannot find the rod?

16. How did God reaffirm His choice of the Levites, kohanim, and Aaron?

17. What is significant about chapter 18? Discuss its place in the context of the story of Korach's rebellion.

18. What can we learn from this parasha about the nature of authority in the body of Messiah? What are some of the pitfalls of comparing the authority of Moshe to a pastor?

PARASHAT CHUKAT חקת

TORAH: NUMBERS 19:1–22:1
HAFTARAH: JUDGES 11:1–33

Parashat Chukat חקת

What reason did He see for punishing them by means of serpents? The Holy One, blessed be He, therefore said, "Let the serpent, who was the first to introduce slander, come and punish those who speak slander." (Bemidbar Rabbah 19.22)

MINI-MYSTERIES

Besides the opening parashiyot of Genesis, very few Torah portions have more important events in them than the one now before us. In this parasha we learn about the ashes of the red cow; the waters of Meribah; the death of Aaron and Miriam; the elevated snake; and the first battles of this new generation as they travel to the edge of the Promised Land and encamp across from Jericho on the plains of Moab.

Yet, for all of its action, are there any parashiyot that contain more mysteries than this one? What is the mystery of the red cow? How and why did it work? What specifically was the sin of Moshe that forfeited him the right to enter the Promised Land? How did looking at a bronze snake on a pole cure those who had been bitten by real serpents? For these reasons, we have chosen to call this week's commentary "Mini-Mysteries"!

As we embark on our study of some of these mini-mysteries, we need to keep in mind the larger context of the book of Numbers. Two strands of thought are behind every event or passage in Numbers: 1) preparations for life in the Promised Land, and 2) fulfilment of the promise of the Lord's discipline (except for Caleb and Joshua) resulting in the present generation of people twenty years old and older will not enter the land. Many events chronicled in Numbers are there for these reasons. Here, then is the list of mini mysteries that we will examine:

I.   The First Mini-Mystery — The Red Cow
II. The Second Mini-Mystery — The Sin of Moshe and Aaron
III. The Third Mini-Mystery — Death and Denial
IV. The Fourth Mini-Mystery — The Healing Snake
V.   The Fifth Mini-Mystery — The Secret Writings

I. THE FIRST MINI-MYSTERY — THE RED COW

The teaching of the ashes of the red heifer (Somehow calling it a "heifer" makes it sound more mysterious!) is found in chapter 19. A heifer is a cow that has never had a yoke on it. 19:1–10 teach the procedure for a strange ritual and 19:11–22 provide some examples of its application.

The text calls the teaching about the red cow a *chukat haTorah* (חוקת התורה). The word that appears in our text of Numbers 19:2, *chakah* (חקה), seems related to the word *chakak* (חקק).[191] This term carries the idea of hollowing out something or engraving something, hence to stipulate something in writing or to make something legally binding.[192] Accordingly, we are to think of the red cow ritual as a law, so important that it is considered to be written down to be

---

191. HALOT, 347.
192. *Ibid.*

legally binding upon all of God's people.

In addition, according to the rabbis, a *chukah* is usually considered to be a teaching in which there appears to be no rational explanation; it is to be received and followed by faith. If that is true, then we have an example *par excellence* here with the red cow ritual. It is a real stumper! Even Philip Blackman, the eminent Mishnaic commentator admits, "This ordinance has passed human comprehension and is the most mysterious rite in Scripture — none of the many attempts to explain it are convincingly satisfactory."[193] In other words, what we have here is a real mystery!

The mystery is not in the *details* of the ritual. They are clear. A perfect red cow, which was never under a yoke, was taken outside the camp where she was slain under the supervision of the High Priest. Some blood was sprinkled toward the Mishkan. Then the cow was burnt on the Altar and the ashes were mixed with water, hyssop, cedar wood, and a crimson thread. This mixture was carefully set aside to be used in the purification process of one who was *tam'ei*, especially from contact with a dead human. In addition, the Mishnah provides even more specific details about how the ritual was carried out, particularly during the Second Temple Period. In fact, one whole tractate, *Parah*, is devoted to the subject.

Unanswered Questions

While there is an abundance of information concerning the *procedure* of the ritual, there is little definitive knowledge concerning the *meaning* of it. Therein is the mystery! For instance, why is a cow chosen for this purpose and why must it be red? Furthermore, why, paradoxically, does the person who takes the ashes from the cow that are used to purify, become himself *tam'ei* (not ritually acceptable) and in need of the very ashes he has just prepared? Why are the other components added to the ashes of the red cow? Researching various suggestions on how these and other related questions could prove to be an education in itself!

One of the clearest interpretations we found is from JPS commentator, Jacob Milgrom. He says that a cow is chosen because 1) it is large and therefore provides the greatest number of ashes. 2) A bull, on the other hand, could not be chosen because it represents the sin offering of the high priest or the community (Leviticus 4:13–21). 3) The cow is intended for individual use and the female may be brought for a sin offering (Leviticus 4:22–23). 4) It is red because, "the association of red with blood is widely attested in primitive cultures. Thus, the red hide of the cow symbolically adds to the quantity of blood in the ash mixture (as does the crimson yarn and the [red] cedar; v. 7) and enhances its potency." [194]

Yet, for all of this, there is still an aura of mystery surrounding this ritual. What do all of the special ingredients mean and why were these particular things chosen? Is there symbolism to it all and, if so, what is that symbolism?

193. Philip Blackman, *The Mishnah*, vol. 6, 402.
194. Jacob Milgrom, *The JPS Torah Commentary: Numbers*, "Excursus #48," 440.

Non-Jewish commentators are even more silent on the meaning and symbolism of this peculiar ceremony. One thing, however, which they are quick to point out, is the fact that the ashes of the red cow are mentioned in Hebrews 9:11–13 in connection with the atonement of Yeshua. In this passage, the writer is speaking about two kinds of cleansing. He says that the ritual of the red heifer cleanses our body of ritual defilement while the cleansing wrought by Yeshua does the same for the unseen us. We can safely conclude that the physical cleansing might picture the other unseen or spiritual cleaning.

However, we must not fall into the trap of saying that what Yeshua did nullifies the ritual of the red heifer. I used to think that way. However, we no longer think that is true. Someday God will build His House again in Jerusalem. When that happens, the Torah for the red heifer will most definitely apply again. The sacrificial death of Yeshua does not contradict that. The ritual of the red cow affects the body. Yeshua's atonement affects the unseen parts of His people.

Midrash Rabbah tells a story to illustrate how complex the red cow ritual is to understand, thereby requiring mere adherence without understanding:

A heathen questioned Rabban Johanan ben Zakkai, saying: "The things you Jews do appear to be a kind of sorcery. A cow is brought, it is burned, is pounded into ash, and its ash is gathered up. Then when one of you gets defiled by contact with a corpse, two or three drops of the ash mixed with water are sprinkled upon him, and he is told, 'You are cleansed!'"

Rabban Johanan asked the heathen: "Has the spirit of madness ever possessed you?" He replied: "No." (He asked the heathen again): "Have you ever seen a man whom the spirit of madness has possessed?" The heathen replied: "Yes." "And what do you do for such a man?" (The heathen replied): "Roots are brought, the smoke of their burning is made to rise about him, and water is sprinkled upon him until the spirit of madness flees."

Rabban Johanan then said: "Do not your ears hear what your mouth is saying? It is the same with a man who is defiled by contact with a corpse — he, too, is possessed by a spirit, the spirit of uncleanness, and Scripture says, 'I will make [false] prophets as well as the unclean spirit vanish from the land'" (Zechariah 13:2).

Now when the heathen left, Rabban Johanan's disciples said: "Our master, you put off that heathen with a mere reed of an answer [lit. "you shoved aside that heathen with a reed"], but what answer will you give us?"

Rabban Johanan answered: "By your lives, I swear: The corpse does not have the power by itself to defile, nor does the mixture of ash and water have the power by itself to cleanse. The truth is that the purifying power of the red cow is a decree of the Holy One. The Holy One said: I have set it down as a statute, I have issued it as a decree. You are not permitted to transgress My decree. 'This is the ritual law'"[195]

Whatever the ritual of the red heifer means, it certainly causes us to focus on the importance that God places on the status of being either tahor or tam'ei. These things are difficult for us to fully comprehend, largely because of the faulty translations of impure or unclean. The bottom line is that God's holiness is such that those who have come into contact with either the realm of sin or the realm of death are at least temporarily prohibited from coming physically into the special presence of God in His House. Of course, one may come into the unseen presence of the

---

195. Bamidbar Rabbah 19.8

Holy One anytime. Yet to participate in His sacred House here on earth requires special regulations.

II. The Second Mini-Mystery — The Sin of Moshe and Aaron   20:1–13

Chapter 20 of Numbers contains another difficult riddle to solve. It centres on the story of yet another complaint from the children of Israel. They griped, as usual, that they did not have enough water. As a result, as usual, they began to demand to go back to Egypt. Moshe and Aaron took the matter directly to the Lord in the Tent of Meeting where God gave them their answer. God said, "Take the staff … gather the assembly together. Speak to that rock before their eyes and it will pour out its water. You will bring water out of the rock for the community so that they and their livestock can drink." (20:8)

Disaster for Moshe and Aaron

Up to that point, Moshe and Aaron did as the Lord commanded — at least so it appears. However, 20:12 tells us that they did not "trust in Me enough to honour Me as holy in the sight of the Israelites." Therefore, the Holy One informed them that they would not bring Israel into the Promised Land. The question is: What did Moshe and Aaron do wrong?

The text in our parasha is clear when the Lord describes their crime as mistrust. ("You did not trust Me," says 20:12–13). But the text does not get more specific than that. In 20:23–24, it says that their crime was rebellion. Then in Deuteronomy 32:48-51 we are told that they trespassed against the Lord. Finally, Psalm 106:33 mentions this incident and says that Moshe used "rash words." The term translated "rash words" means to "speak impetuously, thoughtlessly." [196] Except for Psalm 106, each time this incident is mentioned, the Scriptures says that whatever Moshe did he did not sanctify the Holy One in Israel. Thus, the Torah says, that Moshe did not trust God, he rebelled against God, trespassed against God, and spoke rashly. It is all summarized by saying that Moshe did not sanctify God in the midst of Israel. Yet we are not told any more details than that. The Torah does not get any more specific.

In what way did Moshe and Aaron not sanctify God in their midst? Naturally, this vagueness has intrigued the commentators, who have brought forth several possible explanations. They run the gamut from disobedience, to anger, to presumptuousness.

Nechama and Rashi

As usual, Israeli commentator, the late Professor Nechama Leibowitz, does her homework. She cites some famous and trusted Jewish sages on this matter, providing us with their opinions, interpretations, and their rebuttals to each other's views.[197] In addition, the eminent Jewish Torah scholar, Rashi, says, "keep it simple!" He reminds us that all of us are familiar with the

---

196. HALOT, 120.
197. Leibowitz, *New Studies in Bamidbar*, 236–247.

fact that Moshe struck the rock twice when all God told him to do was to "speak" to it. Should we dismiss this simple explanation?

Who is correct? Which crime did Moshe and Aaron, commit to warrant such a discipline from the Holy One? We cannot be certain, although personally we lean towards Rashi's simple explanation as described above. Leibowitz herself concludes her comments on this issue by citing Rambam who says, "See what we have said, against what has already been said about it, and let the truth have its way."[198] Perhaps we should settle the matter like evangelical commentator, Timothy Ashley who says: "The story has been transmitted in its current vague form in order to inform readers that Moses and Aaron were kept from the land of promise by their sin without incriminating these heroes of the faith with very specific crimes."[199]

III. THE THIRD MINI-MYSTERY — DEATH AND DENIAL

The bulk of the *parasha* is the story of "death and denial", as R. K. Harrison put it.[200] Both Aaron and Miriam die. One mystery is, why did not Israel mourn Miriam like they did Aaron, (or even apparently Moshe, c.f. Deuteronomy 34:5–8). Furthermore, we learn in this parasha about the refusal of Edom and Moab to let the children of Israel pass through them on their way to Canaan. The puzzle concerning this is, why was Israel refused passage through Edom and Moab? Or, for that matter, why did Israel enter the Promised Land from *that* direction instead of from the west or south? Let us elaborate more on these issues.

A. Great Mourning

Miriam's death in 20:1 happened almost without notice. The text hardly says anything about it, but this is not the case with Aaron's death. We are told in 20:29 that Moshe and Eleazar, Aaron's oldest son, descended Mount Hor after burying Aaron, "when the whole community learned that Aaron had died, the entire house of Israel mourned for him thirty days." The text emphasizes that the entire house of Israel mourned for Aaron. This Hebraic phrase does not mean that each and every last Israelite cried for thirty days! It merely suggests that people from every segment of Israeli society (men, women, and children) and the majority of the nation mourned.

Of course, it is not difficult to see why they would have mourned so extensively. Aaron was a great man. He was there from the beginning of the redemption, along with Moshe, pleading before Pharaoh to let Israel go. Moreover, being the first High Priest, Aaron would have become familiar with many of the individual Israelites on a personal basis, teaching or counselling them. It is interesting that in later Jewish thought, Aaron is considered a peacemaker. R. Hillel bids every man to be a "disciple of Aaron, loving peace and pursuing peace, loving his fellowmen and

---

198. Leibowitz, *New Studies in Bamidbar*, 247.
199. Timothy R. Ashley, *Numbers* (NICOT), 393.
200. R.K. Harrison, *Numbers* (TOTC), 269.

bringing them near to the Torah."[201]

Regarding Miriam — while she was a great woman in her own right, much of the nation would still remember the trouble she caused Moshe when she questioned his right to have the wife that he took for himself. This may have been a major reason why we do not read about such national mourning for her death as we do for Aaron and Moshe.

B. On the March

According to this parasha, the Israelites began to be on the move again, this time for the final leg of their journey. The Lord began to lead them to position them into the proper location from which to enter the Land. The entrance the Lord chose for them was from the east. However, coming up from Egypt, the most logical entrance would have been from the south and west. Apparently, the Lord may have felt that they were not yet ready to face a strong Philistine militia in the west.[202] Also, it appears that strategically, an entrance from the east would have served to help to divide the Land, making it more difficult for the Canaanites to defend it. Besides, three main possible routes into the populated central mountains all converged at Jericho. Indeed, this was very strategic.

This section of Numbers is a veritable gold mine for biblical geographers! In it we find names of routes, names of rivers, names of peoples and territories. Because of that, it is practically impossible to study this part of the parasha without some good maps.

1.   The Routes

The word *derekh* (דרך) is used frequently in the Tanakh to designate either the actual name of a road or to indicate in which direction a road or path went. We cannot say for every instance, but at least in the Torah and the older historical books, when the word derekh is preceded by a verb of travel and followed by a geographical name, it might be preserving the actual *name* of the road. However, derekh is also used to indicate in which *direction* the road went. In ancient Israel, roads were usually named according to their destination.[203] In our parasha we have a few examples of the names of actual roads.

---

201. J. H. Hertz, *The Pentateuch and Haftarahs*, 659.
202. The Philistines as a national group did not enter into the Promised Land until the Egyptians, following their attack on Egypt, around the year 1200 BCE rebuffed them. However, as indicated by the accounts of the Patriarchs in Genesis, there seems to have been a rather strong colony of Philistines already in Canaan before that time. The Philistines always seemed to have had a strong military. They also were the ones credited as having introduced the Iron Age into the Ancient Near East. Although the children of Israel were advancing into Canaan well before the major arrival of most of the Philistines, nevertheless, whatever number of Philistines that was already there would have posed a strong threat to them militarily.
203. David A. Dorsey, *The Roads and Highways of Ancient Israel*, 49, 217.

The King's Road (Derekh HaMelekh, דרך המלך) 20:17, 21:22 (#1 on Map)
This road ran north-south connecting Damascus with Eilat. This is the only case in the Tanakh where a road is not named after its direction. "It is possible, however, that the road was not actually named the "King's Road," but that it is called that in Numbers as a *descriptive* term to express the idea of "the main road," or "the public road." [204]

The Spies' Road (Derekh haAtarim, דרך האתרים)   21:1 (#2 on Map)
This is a route that went from Kadesh Barnea in the south Negev past Tel Arad to the north. However, a branch of this road came up from Eilat and joined it at Dimona. Was this road so-named because the explorers of chapter 13 travelled along the main section of it? It is possible.

The Reed Sea Road (Derekh Yam Suf Road, דרך ים סוף)   21:4 (#3 on Map)
Mentioning the Yom Suf Road here does not mean that the Israelites went back to the Reed Sea, which they crossed 40 years ago when they came out of Egypt. (The NASB translated it as the Red Sea. "Reed Sea" is more accurate to the Hebrew.) Rather, this is *the name* of a road that, if taken west, would have led people to the Reed Sea. However, they were heading east, not west.

The Bashan Road (Derekh HaBashan, דרך הבשן)   21:33 (#4 on Map)
This road could have been a section of the King's Road. By this time, Israel had the freedom to travel on this main highway. Or, this could have been a branch from the King's Road, heading to Bashan, whereas the king's Road headed to Damascus, to the northeast. It was on this road that Og, the King of Bashan met Israel at Edrei to do battle with them.

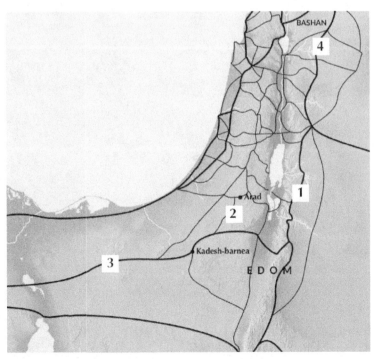

Map 4:   Routes

204. David A. Dorsey, *The Roads and Highways of Ancient Israel*, 50.

2. The Locations

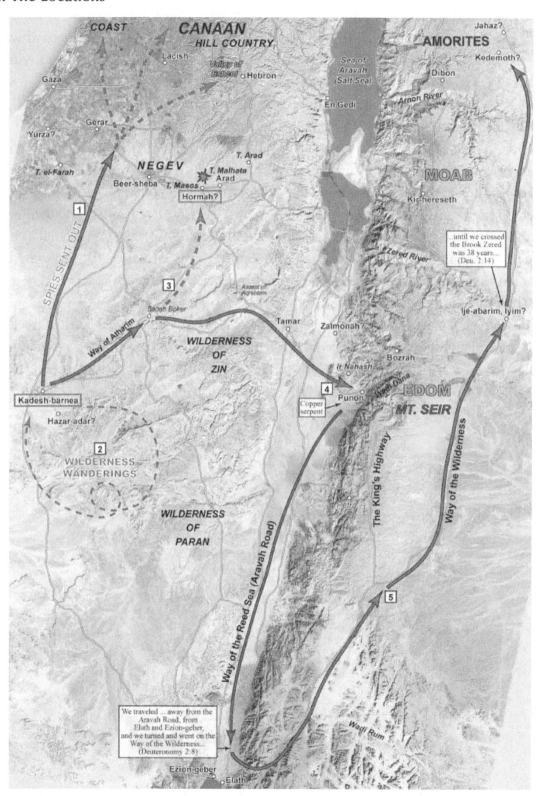

Map 5:   Locations in Parashat Chukat

Midbar Tzin (מדבר צן) at Kadesh 20:1

It seems that they came full circle in their wilderness wanderings. We find the Israelites back at Kadesh Barnea, the place where they began to wander after rejecting the Land back in Numbers 13. Midbar Tzin is in the Negev and seems to cover the territory from south-central Negev to the southwest of the Dead Sea. Essentially, popular Ein Avdat is part of it! Miriam dies in that area. See map 5.

Kadesh to Mt. Hor, near Edom 20:14; 22–23

Request is made to Edom for Israel to pass through their territory. Edom refuses. Aaron dies and is buried. Eleazar is the new High Priest. Sometimes Edom was strong and extended their territory from east of the Rift Valley to the eastern Negev. That seems to be the case here in Numbers.

The Battle with Arad 21:1–3

According to HALOT, the word "Arad" is from Arabic and it means "wild ass."[205] However, which Arad attacked Israel? The present Israéli city of Arad (where we live!) did not exist then. What is called Tel Arad, about 10 km to the west of modern Arad, was not occupied either at this time. Two other sites are possible candidates for this Arad in Numbers 21. The better possibility is called Tell Malchata, located on an Israeli military base, about 15 km (about 9.5 miles) south of modern Tel Arad. However, it is possible that Arad was the name of an *area*, rather than one city. We find it helpful to quote biblical historian Alfred J. Hoerth on the subject of Arad. He writes:

> Numbers 21:1–3 states that the King of Arad came out to fight Israel, but extensive excavation shows that the site of Arad in the northern Negev was not then occupied. Two solutions have been proposed to resolve this problem. On the basis of Judges 1:16–17 the king may have been ruler over an area rather than a specific city. Or, since Egyptian records speak of two Arads, the king in Numbers 21 could have been ruler over the other Arad. Tell Malhatah, less than eight miles from "Greater Arad," has been tentatively identified as the second Arad.[206]

We are told that these people were Canaanites. Perhaps Moshe is telling us that it is now beginning, that is, the beginning of Israel replacing the Canaanites in the Promised Land.

By-passing Edom 21:4

"The people became impatient because of the journey." Things are beginning to be set up for the incident with the snakes, which follows.

Ovot (אובות), ye-abarim (עיי העברים) 21:4

We do not know where Ovot is. But the location called Ye-avarim is range of mountains on the western edge of the Moabite plateau including Mount Nebo. The name Avarim is related to 'ever עבר, meaning "across." It is probably named from the perspective of one who is on the western side of the Jordan Valley, who to this day cannot but be impressed by the grandeur of

---

205. HALOT, 881.
206. Alfred J. Hoerth, *Archaeology of the Old Testament*, n. 2, 202.

the mountain range on his eastern horizon, on the other side ('*ever*) of the Jordan. The site Iyyim has not been identified. See map 6 on page 140.

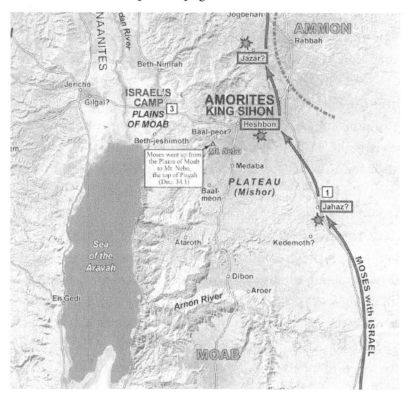

Map 6: Mt Nebo

Mattanah to Nahaliel, and from Nahaliel to Bamot, and from Bamot to the valley that is in the land of Moab, at the top of Pisgah which overlooks the wasteland.   21:19–20
We do not know where some of these places are. Pisgah, however, is mentioned. We will see more of Pisgah in the final parasha of Deuteronomy. Deuteronomy 34:1 tells us that "Moshe went up from the plains of Moab to Mount Nebo, to the top of Pisgah, which is opposite Jericho." Basically, Mount Nebo is situated amidst the Avarim range, located east, southeast of Jericho on the east side of the Jordan River. Mount Nebo, amidst this range, rises 2,631 feet (800 meters) above sea level. Then "the jumbled slopes of Pisgah (the "Cleft") form the particular section of the Avarim hills that have broken apart exactly below Mount Nebo."[207] The text indicates that Moshe made the ascent to Mount Pisgah alone, died there, and the Lord Himself buried Moshe.

Of special interest is the last Hebrew word of Numbers 21:20. It mentions a specific geographic feature called "*yeshimon* (ישימון)" Yeshimon is "always in combination or parallel with *midbar*, מדבר."[208] Deuteronomy 32:10 describes yeshimon as "the howling waste of a

207. Paul H. Wright, *The Holman Illustrated Guide to Biblical Geography: Reading the Land*, 374–375.
208. HALOT, 447.

wilderness." Yeshimon is a wasteland "beyond the limits of normal human lifestyle and endurance. In such a land God Himself intervened to keep His people alive …"[209] This is the type of territory Israel had to pass through. They were tough people!

Nahal Arnon to Nahal Yabbok 21:24

These two *nahalim* (wadis) form the natural boundaries for the Ammonites and the Moabites. The border for these people fluctuated from time to time. Basically, Moav was between these two Nahalim.

Israel's First Settlements   21:25–26; 31–35

Finally, Numbers records the very first permanent settlement of the Israelites. The wilderness wandering is just about over! Israel took several locations in present day western Jordan from the Arnon River to north of the Golan Heights today. This was capped by the Battle of Edrei. See map 5.

C. The Streams

Three waterways are mentioned in this parasha, besides the word "Reed Sea," which was just the name of a road that led one to the Reed Sea. Each of the waterways are called *nahalim*, נהלים.. A *nahal* is like a canyon carved by moving water. Sometimes the bed of the canyon has running water like a stream or small river, sometimes it does not. See Map 7 (Accordance).

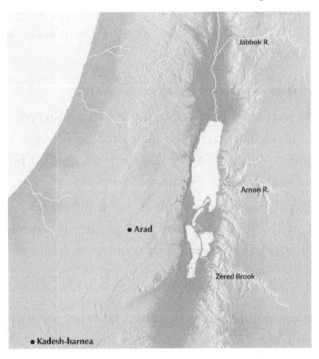

Map 7: Some streams

Nahal Zered   21:12

---

209. Wright, *Reading the Land*, 51.

This flows west from Edom into the southern end of the Dead Sea and marks the northern border of Edom.

Nahal Arnon   21:13

This flows west from Moav into the Dead Sea across from Ein Gedi. It marks, what was sometimes the border between Moav and Ammon. (21:13). When Moav was strong, the border went further north along the east bank of the Dead Sea and lower Jordan Valley.

Nahal Yabbok   21:34

This is about half-way between the Dead Sea and Lake Kinneret. Jacob followed it as it flowed into the Jordan River. Possibly Abraham did the same as they came to Canaan from Haran.

Summary

Professor James Monson says that the "Land of the Bible" is the playing board of biblical history. Studying this playing board makes the Bible come alive."[210] We know that sometimes maps can be tedious to some. However, these are not just any maps. These show us the features of Immanuel's Land (Isaiah 8:8) as well as where the Covenant People lived and travelled. As we study the geography mentioned to us in our parasha, we see that it must have been written by an eyewitness. Moreover, we perceive that what we are reading is truly an accurate historical record of how God fulfilled His promises to His people. Thus, knowing the routes, the dirt and rocks, and lay of the land will help the Bible student to get a more accurate picture of how God's people lived, thus helping the Bible to come alive.

IV. THE FOURTH MYSTERY — THE HEALING SNAKE

The ashes of the red heifer have already mystified us. We have also been stumped in ascertaining Moshe and Aaron's specific sin that warranted their prohibition from entering the Land. Now, in 21:4–9, we are confronted with yet another mystery: an uplifted bronze snake that has the ability to heal people from snakebites!

The context for this miracle-working serpent is one in which we find the children of Israel complaining, yet again, of the food that God had graciously supplied for them. As usual, following their complaint, they made their customary pleas to return to the delectable cuisine of Egypt, comparing it to the "worthless" or "contemptible" manna that the Lord had been supplying for them.

To make matters even worse, this time they were at odds not just with Moshe, as was the case in times past, but also with the Lord. We know this from the use of the plural suffix on the Hebrew verb "you (pl.) brought us up". (Although it might be possible to interpret that plural "you" with referring to both Moshe and Aaron). It was bad enough to reject the one whom God placed into leadership, but now, "they equated a slave with his Owner."[211]

---

210. James M. Monson, *Regions on the Run: Introductory Map Studies in the Land of the Bible*, 3.
211. Rashi: *Badmidbar*, ArtScroll Edition, 252.

1. Removal of Protection

In response to this disrespect shown to the Holy One and His choice servants, God sent fiery snakes which bit many of the Israelites. The NIV reads "venomous", but the Hebrew uses the adjective *seraphim* (שרפים) which means "fiery." Actually, this was somewhat of a miracle in disguise. For forty years they had lived in the wilderness — a place infested with snakes and scorpions. It is a real miracle that they had not, up to this point, been afflicted with these deadly pests. In reality, it seems that God merely let loose the snakes from which He had been protecting them, instead of sending them from nowhere. The miracle was in the protection of the past forty years, not in the sending of the snakes.

2. The Healing Snake

It is most appropriate that we are speaking of miracles in this passage. One miracle is that Israel genuinely repented by confessing their sin against the Lord in 21:7 and turning from it! However, another miracle followed. Reacting to their repentance, God instructed Moshe to make a bronze replica of one of the fiery serpents and to place it on a pole. All who looked upon it would be healed from their snakebite. Moshe listened and formed a such a snake. He then placed it on a pole.

It is fascinating that, according to BDB, the Hebrew word translated "pole" in 21:8 is also the same word for "miracle" *nes* (נס),[212] If it is not the same word, it certainly constituted a wordplay. Just as a pole is lifted up and used as a standard bearer for people to see, so is a miracle. It is lifted up for all to see something wonderful, magnificent, and awesome about God. In this case, the *nes* was the healing wrought by the act of looking up at the bronze serpent.

The question remains; how did it happen that people were healed from their snakebites by merely looking at a bronze serpent lifted up on a pole? Moreover, what was God teaching us through this? Naturally, the answer to these questions remains a great mystery to many commentators. For some, the Mishnah, perhaps comes the closest in explaining the meaning of this whole event. Here we are told that it was not the serpent itself that did the healing. Rather, "What it indicates is that when Israel turned their thoughts above and subjected their hearts to their Father in heaven, they were healed, but otherwise they pined away."[213]

3. That Other "Pole"

Actually, the Mishnah is not far from the truth. It unwittingly points to a reality about which the compilers of the Mishnah would strongly object! The complete answer to this mystery is found in John 3:12–15. Here the crucifixion of Yeshua is compared to the bronze serpent being lifted up on a pole. In fact, we might argue that this is the reason *why* God had the bronze serpent put up on a pole — in order to provide a picture of the work of Messiah.

The truth is that we need to keep "looking up"! Specifically, just as the bronze serpent healed

212. BDB, 652.
213. B. Rosh Hashanah 3:8

all who "looked" on it when they listened to God's Word, so also Yeshua was lifted up on the "pole" so that all who are bitten by the "Snake", being poisoned by the venom of sin, might be healed of that sin through Yeshua's sacrificial death. John 3:15 confirms that "everyone who believes (taking God at His Word) in Him may have eternal life."

Moreover, just as the "pole" was a "miracle" so also was the work of Yeshua on the tree. God accepted the blood of one perfect Man in the place of sinners. However, He did not keep the sacrifice dead. Three days later, Yeshua rose from the dead! This was indeed a great miracle! Hence, the "pole" — the cross — became a miracle as it helped to effectuate the perfect atonement accomplished by the Son of God for all who would but put their faith in Him. In addition, Colossians 2:15 says, "When He had disarmed the rulers and authorities, He made a public display of them, having triumphed over them through Him." Thus, Yeshua's death was a victory over The Snake, Satan himself and all of his other lesser snakes!

4. Where Is the Bronze Serpent?

The Scriptures indicate that Israel kept that bronze serpent for many years. However, as things usually go, it eventually became an object of idolatrous worship. Accordingly, 2 Kings 18:4 says that King Hezekiah destroyed it. It does not matter, though, whether Israel still kept the serpent. What matters most of all is that Israel looks to the real Healer, lifted up on a crucifixion stake, affecting healing for the most poisonous snakebite of them all — sin. Romans 11 tells us that while many among Israel are looking more and more to the Holy One, the Messiah, someday *all* Israel will look and be saved.

V. THE FIFTH MYSTERY — THE SECRET WRITINGS

This is a unique section of Torah because it quotes three peculiar poems: one from an extra-biblical writing, the second is a song which was composed by the Israelites, and the third is some proverbs composed by the Israelites.

A. Song of the Wars of the Lord (21:14–15)

The first poem is from a composition referred to in the text as, *The Book of the Wars of the Lord*. The purpose of this quotation is to support the claim in 21:13 that the Nahal Arnon was the border between the Moabites and the Amorites. The book, however, remains a mystery to us. We do not know its author, although Jewish tradition attributes it to Abraham. Yet, there is no proof of that, not even a hint! The quotation is also a puzzle because of the difficult Hebrew text, which attests to its antiquity.[214]

B. The Song of the Well (21:16f)

Another strange quotation is found in our text immediately after the citation of the *Wars of the Lord* book. This time it is a short Israelite poem sung to commemorate the delightful discovery of a well in Moav.

---

214. Harrison, *Numbers* (TOTC), 280.

The find of a well in this arid wilderness was always the occasion for song and dance. Harrison suggests "the various lines of the composition were sung antiphonally with perhaps three groups chanting a line each."[215] The song indicates that the nation's leaders also participated in the work of digging this well (21:18). The leadership example and the precious find of water provided great encouragement to Israel as they faced more journeying and further conquest.

The Midrash observes that the names of both Moshe and God are not mentioned in this jubilant song. That, indeed, is quite peculiar, especially since it was God who led Moshe to direct Israel to this location. The Midrash provides its own reasons for the absence of these names. The answer is fascinating, so we will quote it at length:

> Why is Moses not mentioned in this context? Because he owed his punishment to water, and no man praises his executioner. Why is not the name of the Holy One, blessed be He, mentioned? This may be illustrated by the case of a governor who made a feast for the king. The king asked, "Will my friend be there?" "No," he was told. Said he, "Then I also am not going there." In the same way the Holy One, blessed be He, said, "Since Moses is not mentioned there, I also will not be mentioned there."[216]

C. The Song of Heshbon (21:27–30)

The last peculiar citation is the quotation of a proverb that was apparently well known at the time. This quotation comes in the wake of the Israelite victory over Sihon, the stubborn king of Heshbon of the Amorites. Israel asked him for passage. He refused. So, the Lord directed Israel to take up swords against him. To commemorate their victory, Moshe cited some famous proverbs to compare the Israelite victory over the Amorites to the previous Amorite victory over the Moabites. According to 21:27 in the NIV, poets wrote about these wars. However, the Hebrew indicates by use of the word *moshalim* (משלים), that what was recorded was really written by those who compose proverbs.

Some people think that this song may, in fact, originally have been an Amorite song, celebrating their victory over the Moabites. If that is the case, then Israel took over this ballad and adopted it for their victory celebration over the composers, the Amorites.

The prophet Jeremiah, some 700 years later, again adopted this very same song as a prophecy of judgment against Moab (Jeremiah 48:46). Over the years, Moab gained more strength and proved to be a menace to Israel, especially by attempting to allure them to worship Chemosh, the national deity of the Moabites. Jeremiah, in his use of this song from Numbers predicts the final downfall of both Chemosh and the Moabites who honour him. Interestingly enough, however, Jeremiah also predicts the ultimate restoration of the Moabite nation in the "last days" by the Lord Himself, as He turns them toward Himself.

---

215. Harrison, *Numbers* (TOTC), 282.
216. Bamidbar Rabbah 19.26

D. Are They Inspired Writings?

One thing these writings teach us is that we see evidence of creative literary ability in ancient Israel. They were not entirely an oral culture. Reading and writing were not strange to them. In addition, we also see that Moshe apparently either had a collection of writings from which he drew material, or he had some works memorized, possibly from his days as a student in Egypt — or both!

Furthermore, we can also observe that Moshe used other material to compose the Torah, in addition to direct revelation from God. We saw some evidence of this in Genesis. The presence of the repeated phrase, "These are the family histories of …" could be evidence that Moshe drew material from a collection of clay tablets that was passed on to him.[217] That might be where he found material for the family stories in Genesis. Hence, we can see that there was "no absence of literary activity in the days of Moshe."[218]

Before we close this week's commentary, we need to make an important point regarding these "mysterious" writings we have just cited. Does the inclusion of the extra-biblical citations into the Word of God imply that these original sources are equally inspired words from the mouth of the Holy One?

The answer is simple, but important. To be sure, the original secular writings from which these have been borrowed by Moshe were/are not the inspired words of God. The doctrine of inspiration as it is usually taught in both traditional Jewish and Evangelical circles does not demand that they are divinely inspired. What is important is that whatever the Holy One instructed by His Spirit to His human writers to be written into the Scriptures had to be recorded with 100% accuracy, just as the Lord gave it. We assume that when Moshe was instructed by the Spirit of God to quote these secular songs, he did so with the perfect accuracy required by the Holy One. Hence, God did not inspire the original secular poems, but the perfect recording of them makes the particular quotation part of the infallible, inspired, authoritative Word of God.

---

217. R. K. Harrison in his *Introduction to the Old Testament* presents this possibility. An examination of his whole treatment is best. It is located on pages 543–553.

218. Hertz, *Pentateuch and Haftarahs*, 661.

ADDITIONAL NOTES

Chapter 19
Verses 11–22
Because there is no Temple today in which to carry out these directions, one way in which traditional Jews fulfil these directives is to ceremonially wash their hands before entering their homes upon returning from a funeral. Verse 17

The offering of the red cow is called here in Hebrew *serefat hachatta't* (שרפת החטאת). This would indicate that this was some kind sin offering. Yet, it bears little resemblance to a regular sin offering. For one, it is burnt entirely outside of the camp and, secondly its blood is not sprinkled upon the altar. Milgrom notes that the sin offering "absorbs the impurity it has purged. For that reason, it must be eliminated by incineration."[219]

Chapter 20
Verse 5
Figs and pomegranates were precisely the same things brought back by the spies from Canaan. The people apparently thought that they were being short changed.

Verse 10
Yet another opinion: According to Milgrom, "we" is the fatal pronoun designating the sin of Moshe, not hitting the rock twice. By using the word "we", "Moses ascribes the miracle to himself and to Aaron", and not to God.[220]

Verse 13
"Meribah" — In the Torah, two places are called Meribah. The first is in Exodus 17:7. The second is here. The Hebrew word *meribah* (מריבה), means "strife". Hence, on both occasions where this word is used, the situation was the same — Israel was at strife against Moshe and God over their water supply. Accordingly, both places were named the same. To distinguish each place, the Meribah in Numbers 20:13 is often called "Meribat-Kadesh".

Verse 14
"King of Edom" — Perhaps "chieftain" would have been a better title. Edom, Moab, the Midianites, Ammon, and the Canaanites at this point in history (13th to 15th centuries BCE) were not strongly unified kingdoms. They were consolidated, but loosely organized. In fact, the earliest archaeological reference to the people of Seir (a city of Edom) is in the 14th century BCE in the Amarna Tablets. These are texts from Tel el-Amarna in Egypt, and they mention incursions of Bedouin tribes from the "lands of Seir" but did not name any Edomite cities of leaders. This suggests a typically nomadic Bronze Age group that was not organized along any national lines.[221]

219. Hertz, *Pentateuch and Haftarahs*, 439.
220. Milgrom, *JPS: Numbers*, 165.
221. Harrison, *Numbers*, 270–271.

Verse 19

"**main road**" — The Hebrew word here is *m'salah* (מסלה). It is a designation for a highway and never a city street.[222] It is also closely connected to a cognitive (Akkadian) word meaning "infantry road". "In other words, Israel volunteers to leave behind wagons, that is, its water provisions (thence necessitating the purchase of water from the Edornites), and to march as "backpacking" infantry."[223]

Chapter 21

Verse 4

Read this verse carefully. It does not say that they went *back* to the Reed Sea again. It merely says that one of the roads the Israelites travelled upon was called the "The Way to (of) the Reed Sea," *derekh yam suph* (דרך ים-סוף). In other words, this road was known as "The Reed Sea Highway." It led to and from the Reed Sea. However, it does not necessitate that they went all the way back to the Reed Sea where they crossed in Exodus.

Verse 6

"**the fiery serpents**" (הנחשים השרפים) (See main body of text.) — Hertz suggests that this should be translated: "the serpents, the fiery ones". The exact identification of these snakes is hard to determine. Commentators have given many suggestions. Linguistically it is possible to relate the word "serpent" *nachash* (נחש) to the Hebrew word for copper or bronze (*nakhush*, נחוש). This would be a description of their colour. Furthermore, the Hebrew for "fiery", is the word, *saraph* (שרף) meanins "burning". This may refer to the kind of reaction the bite had on the human body. In the end, however, we just do not know for sure what kind of snakes they were. Perhaps it is as Harrison suggests: "Since the incident was a natural event actuated by supernatural considerations, the most poisonous desert reptile would be eminently suitable for inflicting divine punishment upon the rebellious Israelites."[224]

Verse 8

Milgrom cites a very interesting paraphrase of this verse in Targum Jonathan. The Targum reads, "If he [the victim] directed his heart to the name of the Memra of the Lord, he would live."[225] The use of the Aramaic word "Memra" (ממרא) is widely attested to throughout the Targumim. The most common translation of it is "Word". It has often been suggested that it is the word "memra" which lies behind the word "Word" of John 1:1. If so, then this Targum is attesting to the fact that God was directing the Israelites' hearts to Messiah! But we cannot prove this!

---

222. BDB, 700.
223. Harrison, *Numbers,* 270–271.
224. *Ibid.,* 276.
225. Milgrom, *JPS: Numbers,* 174.

Verse 9

The close connection between the Hebrew for "snake" and the Hebrew for "copper" (explained above) may explain why Moshe made the snake out of copper (or bronze). Another reason is that there were copper deposits in the general area of the south-eastern Negev and Aravah.

Verse 9

"**looked at**" — The Hebrew word is the verb *nabat* (נבט). This word can mean to look at something and consider it.[226] It was not merely the act of physically seeing the up-raised copper snake that caused the healing. It was that its presence caused (The Hebrew verb is in the *hiphil* form which has a causative thrust.) the people to think about their sin and God's remedy.

Verse 17

"According to the Talmud, this song was sung in the Temple in Jerusalem every third Shabbat afternoon and the Song of the Sea on the other two Shabbat afternoons."[227]

---

226. BDB, 613.
227. Milgrom, *JPS: Numbers*, 177.

STUDY QUESTIONS

1. How do you explain the "mystery" of the red cow? Why did the handling of its ashes render one tam'ei when those very ashes were produced to help change a tam'ei state into a tahor state?

2. Why were the three components mentioned in 19:6 added to the water and the red cow ashes?

3. Why were people who came into contact with dead humans, even though they needed to bury the corpse, called tam'ei?

4. Why did the Israelites complain again in 20:1–13?

5. What was the response of Moshe and Aaron to this complaint?

6. What did God tell them to do?

7. What was their sin?

8. Why was the sin of Aaron and Moshe severe enough to deny them the privilege of leading Israel into the Promised Land?

9. How did God, in the end, sanctify Himself through Aaron and Moshe (20:13)?

10. Why do you think that Edom would not let Israel pass through their territory?

11. Why did God prohibit Israel from engaging in battle with the Edomites?

12. Why was Aaron taken to a mountain in order to die?

13. Why was the Battle of Arad called "Hormah"?

14. Why did God send the snakes?

15. Why did the Lord have Moshe make a copper snake and place it upon a pole?

16. What significance, if any, is it that the word for "pole" and "miracle" are the same in Hebrew?

17. Explain the use of this story in John chapter 3.

18. Why do you think the Holy One had Israel enter the Promised Land from the east other than from the south or west?

19. Who presently occupies the land of the Amorites and the land of Bashan?

20. Why do you think there are so many unsolved mysteries in this parasha? Or, are they really unsolved!? Explain.

Parashat Balak בלק

Torah: Numbers 22:2–25:9
Haftarah: Micah 5:6–6:8

Parashat Balak בלק

And the Lord opened the mouth of the donkey—to teach him that the mouth and the tongue are in His power; that if he sought to curse—his mouth was in His power. (Bamidbar Rabbah 20.12).

WHILE ISRAEL PLAYED...

If the previous parasha was entitled "Mini-Mysteries", then the one this week should be entitled "Mega Mystery!" For, who could ever explain God speaking to and through a donkey? As tempting as it is to try to solve this enigma, we will, nevertheless, resist. Instead, for the sake of brevity, we will attempt to give a general overview of the whole parasha.

Perhaps a better title for this week's commentary could be something like, "While Israel Played ..." Indeed, Numbers 25:1 tells us that while Israel was at Shittim, they played the harlot with Moabite women. Meanwhile, the bulk of this parasha centres on what God was doing behind the scenes in order to make it possible for Israel to take possession of the Land.

Hence, what the Holy One was doing will be the topic of this week's commentary. Thus, while Israel played the harlot with the Moabite women on the plains of Moab opposite Jericho (25:1 ff.)...

    I.   God was spreading Israel's reputation among the nations.
    II.   God was stifling Israel's enemies.
    III. God was sanctioning the supernatural.
    IV. God was surrounding Israel with His Grace.
    V.   God was speaking.

I. GOD WAS SPREADING ISRAEL'S REPUTATION AMONG THE NATIONS

Israel may have been playing the harlot with the Moabite and the Midianite women and flirting with their gods (or was it the other way around?), but God certainly did not forget them. Indeed, the Scripture testifies that He neither slumbers nor sleeps (Psalm 121:4)! One thing God was busy doing was that He was making sure that the surrounding nations received a healthy dose of awe and respect for the might of Israel. Hence, 22:2–3 says, "Balak, son of Zippor, saw all that Israel had done to the Amorites, and Moab was terrified because there were so many people. Indeed Moab was filled with dread because of the Israelites."

Whatever sin Israel was engaging in down in the Jordan Valley on the Plains of Moab, up in the mountains God was making sure that their enemies were seeing Israel through different eyes. The Almighty was presenting the *real* Israel to them. They were viewing an Israel that God had created, a redeemed community, powerful with the strength of His might.

The application of this point is simple but powerful. We see here a demonstration of the grace of God. Israel certainly did not deserve the fear/respect of the nations. They were acting just as other godless people act. However, God had created a different Israel. He desired that the godless nations got a glimpse of the true Israel, the Israel of God's making, His precious, peculiar, holy community.

The truth of the matter is that for all believers in Messiah, even though we may act like Israel was acting in Shittim, the real us is completely different. Often, God grants us His mercy, in that, despite how our flesh behaves, people may still see us as we really are inside as new creations, and fear God because of what and who He made us to be.

II. GOD WAS STIFLING ISRAEL'S ENEMIES

This parasha presents a clear contrast between two kingdoms: the kingdom of light and the kingdom of darkness. We see them pitted against each other. On the one hand, there is the Almighty, the Lord, the King of the Universe, the Lord Most High, the Guardian and Keeper of Israel. On the other hand, there is the sorcerer, the diviner, one of the most skilful of all diviners, Balaam.

A. The Torah Testifies Against Balaam

How proficient was Balaam as a pagan sorcerer? We can examine three sources of evidence for his powers. The first piece of evidence is the text in Numbers itself. Balak, the leader of the Moabites was so confident in Balaam's ability to practise his evil craft that he said of Balaam, "For I know that whomever you bless is blessed and whomever you curse is accursed. (22:6)" Confident of his ability, Balak was willing to pay good money to have Balaam curse Israel. Thus, the Torah testifies concerning Balaam's dark ability to practise his ungodly curses.

B. The Sages Are Against Balaam

The second evidence of Balaam's reputation comes from the tradition of the ancient Jewish sages. Just how proficient Balaam was at his sorcery is amply illustrated for us in the Talmud. In fact, the Babylonian Talmud Sanhedrin 105 is devoted almost entirely to rabbinic comments and interpretations of this Torah Portion. These comments are extremely severe. They cast Balaam in the worst possible light.

Why do they do so? It is because the rabbis observed that the text in Numbers shows that Balaam knew much about the Lord, including His sacred Name. Yet, despite this intimate knowledge of God, Balaam still resorted to his own demonic, idolatrous practices. It is true that he refused to curse Israel upon the request of Balak. However, was that because of his love and awe of God, or was it because of his fear of God's power to overcome his own deities to which he still wanted to cling? "In light of this, the sages contend that 'Now only Balaam will not enter the future world, but other heathens will enter. On whose authority is the Mishnah taught? On R. Joshua's. For it has been taught, R. Eliezer said, 'The wicked shall be turned into hell'."[228]

The Talmud makes even worse comments. For example, the Sages said "Balaam committed bestiality with his ass."[229] Finally, after an assortment of other charges, the rabbis saw Balaam as

228. B. Sanhedrin 105a
229. *Ibid.*, 105a

such a wicked man that when he remarked in Numbers 24:5, "How goodly are your tents, O Jacob, your dwelling places, O Israel," they contend that in this apparent blessing Balaam "wished to curse them that they (the Israelites) should possess no synagogues or school houses."[230] That remark, of course, was a typical rabbinic hyperbole, for there were no such institutions in ancient Israel during the time of the Exodus and the Conquest.

C. The Apostolic Scriptures Are Against Balaam

At this point in our studies, we were almost getting angry with the Sages, for, in our cursory reading of the parasha we were fooled. We really did not think that Balaam was such a wicked man. On the contrary, it seems that the text paints him in a rather favourable light. For example, several times we find him refusing to curse Israel as Balak was requesting.

Moreover, Balaam makes some lofty statements that may be interpreted as representing a close relationship between him and the Lord. For example, in 23:26 Balaam seemingly rebukes Balak when he said, "Did I not tell you I must do whatever the Lord says?" Again, notice the platitudes Balaam expresses in 23:18–24. This sounds like one of the Psalms of praise from King David himself!

While there is real truth in Balaam's words, this truth hardly expresses the reality of his heart. For whatever reason, the weight of Scripture is against him. It was not just the rabbis who had a problem with his sincerity before the Lord, but the Apostolic Scriptures also expresses this condemnation. We can see at least two examples. The first is from 2 Peter 2:15 where Peter compares false prophets with men like Balaam. He says, "They have left the straight way and wandered off to follow the way of Balaam, son of Beor, who loved the wages of wickedness. But he was rebuked for his wrongdoing by a donkey — a beast without speech — who spoke with a man's voice and restrained the prophet's madness."

A second and even more remarkable passage is from Jude, who gives several examples of the worst types of godless people: Cain, Korach, and Balaam. He says that these godless people (one of whom was Balaam), "serve as an example of those who suffer the punishment of eternal fire" (verses 7–11).

Notice how close both Peter and Jude come to echoing the tradition of the rabbis recorded in the Talmud! This similarity suggests that the Apostles were more familiar with and educated in rabbinic tradition than we may have originally thought. Nonetheless, their characterization of Balaam is clearly the most definitive because they were writing under the inspiration of the Spirit of God. Because of this evidence, we were forced to change our whole theory regarding the goodness of Balaam and to agree with the sages, Peter, and Jude about the wickedness of Balaam.

---

230. B. Sanhedrin 105b

D. A Mixed Review

It seems that the main evidence that all of the biblical writers, as well as the Sages, have against Balaam is the testimony in Numbers 31:16 that it was Balaam who attempted to seduce Israel with the prostitutes and the false gods. He is also accused of spiritual blindness when his donkey saw the angel while he did not. However, Balaam also comes across in this parasha as somewhat of a hero. He is repeatedly portrayed as the one who consistently informs Balak that he would not curse Israel but, instead, do what God said and bless it.

We are not alone in the mixed reviews about Balaam. Other biblical passages also see him in a more favourable light. Such a one is Micah. Micah, an 8th century BCE prophet of God, almost defends Balaam's character when he says, "My people, remember what Balak the king of Moab counselled and what Balaam son of Beor answered" (Micah 6:5).

Some extra-biblical evidence even portrays Balaam in a favourable light. One example is found in *Pseudo-Philo. Pseudo-Philo* is from a late 2nd Temple Period (or early post destruction period). It is from a Jewish writing called *Biblical Antiquities.* This is a rather lengthy chronicle retelling biblical history from Adam to the death of Saul. "Lengthy portions of Scripture are briefly summarized or completely bypassed. Other sections are paraphrased, with occasional verbatim quotations. Still others are interpolated with prayers, speeches, or narrative expansions."[231] The most ancient copy in existence today is in Latin, "which is generally thought to be a translation from a Greek translation of a Hebrew original. The author is unknown, but the work came to be attributed to Philo of Alexandria because it was transmitted with genuine works of Philo."[232]

In this piece of Jewish writing, we find a passage that records a prayer Balaam supposedly offered to God where the writer of *Pseudo-Philo* pictures Balaam in a favourable light. Moreover, in one midrash Balaam is considered to be a man who was "greater in wisdom than Moses."[233] Another midrash says that "There were three features possessed by the prophecy of Balaam that were absent from that of Moses."[234] Thus, according to at least this one extra-Biblical writing, "Balaam was in some respects even superior to Moses."[235]

An extremely fascinating, ancient commentary was written about Balaam. This was found by a Dutch archaeologist digging in 1967 in an ancient delta formed by the juncture of the Jabbok and Jordan Rivers. Here he found inscriptions in what may have been a dialect of old Hebrew, on the walls of a Temple dating from the 8th century BCE. This inscription, which was not in the

---

231. Michael, E. Stone, ed., *Jewish Writings of the Second Temple Period: Apocrypha, Pseudepigrapha, Qumran Sectarian Writings, Philo, and Josephus.* 107

232. *Ibid.,* 110.

233. Milgrom, *The JPS Torah Commentary: Numbers,* 470 citing a midrash called "Seder Eliyahu Rabbah" 26:142.

234. Milgrom, *The JPS Torah Commentary: Numbers,* quoting Exodus Rabbah 3:1 and Numbers Rabbah 14:20. 470.

235. *Ibid.*

best of condition, mentioned Balaam. This is startling because it is the oldest extra-biblical confirmation of the story. Moreover, it was found in a geographical area just north of where the story took place. Balaam is not even introduced, hinting at the fact that he was well known to the people who wrote this inscription (Following the Study Questions is a description of this famous "Balaam Inscription.")[236] In addition, in this inscription

> Balaam is presented as a seer, not as a sorcerer, in keeping with the biblical narrative…Equally significant is that Balaam is presented in a positive light, again in agreement with the main biblical story…It has also been noted…that the prophet Micah, also of the eighth century, holds a favourable opinion of Balaam. However, the accusation that Balaam devised the scheme to have the Moabite women seduce Israel into worshipping Baal-peor may be traceable to Deir 'Alla's assertion that Balaam founded a pagan (fertility?) cult. This means that both views of Balaam, positive and negative, are contemporary.[237]

Thus, according to different sources of evidence, the study of Balaam's character is extremely complex. He is at once both a hero and a villain.

E. Balaam's Power Was Stopped

As far as Balak was concerned, however, Balaam had the reputation as one of the region's top sorcerers. Therefore, aware of what kind of person he was, Balak summoned him to curse Israel. However, much to the amazement — of even Balaam himself — Balaam could not utter one curse against Israel! The Sovereign of the Universe took control and forced him to utter only blessings upon Israel.

The rabbinic Sages also agree with this understanding. "'And the Lord put a word in Balaam's mouth'," Rabbi Eliezar said: "An angel", Rabbi Yohanan said: "a hook".[238] Moreover, according to Rabbi Yohanan, "He uttered the blessings in spite of himself, forced against his will, struggling and in distress like a fish that is hooked, to do the bidding of his master."[239]

III. GOD WAS SANCTIONING THE SUPERNATURAL

Israel was in Shittim, on the Plains of Moab, playing the harlot with both women and idols. However, the God of Israel was hard at work behind the scenes protecting Israel's very existence. Supernatural powers of darkness wanted Israel to be destroyed. The medium of their evil was through the potential curses of their servant, the sorcerer Balaam. In addition, human foes also sought their demise. While Israel was busy imbibing in the ways of the world, the Lord was astounding this world with His supernatural power. God demonstrated His supernatural power in at least three ways.

---

236. Todd Bolen and Bill Schlegel, *The Geography of Transjordan*, Field Study Notes from the course on Transjordan by the authors at IBEX, (the Israeli campus of The Master's University), 6.
237. Milgrom, *JPS: Numbers,* 476.
238. B. Sanhedrin 105b
239. Leibowitz, *New Studies in Bamidbar*, 284.

A. Turning Curses into Blessings

The first demonstration of God's magnificent power was to turn potential curses into blessings. Given the description above about Balaam's abilities and character, this was no mean task. However, to understand the importance of it we need to look for a moment at the nature of a blessing and the nature of a curse in order to understand what was going on.

A reasonable amount of material has been written about the subject of cursing and blessing, all expressing various viewpoints. Some suggest strongly that the power of blessing/cursing comes in the very words themselves. They say that it works itself out in that the words provide great impetus and encouragement for the Powers of Darkness (demons) or the Powers of Light (God's angels) to accomplish their assigned tasks.

Jewish commentator, Nechama Leibowitz, expresses another plausible outlook. She argues in favour of a slightly different approach. Citing various scholars to support her point, she suggests that "… it is not necessarily demons nor angels who were/are encouraged by the blessings/curses, but human powers." Given the extent of popular belief in the power of curses and blessings and what a sorcerer could accomplish in uttering them, Leibowitz cites Abravanel saying, "Had Balaam cursed Israel, the surrounding nations would have picked up courage and gone to battle with Israel on the strength of the curses. But when they heard how God had turned them into blessings, they would then realize who was Master … and would lose all desire to fight His people."[240]

However, Leibowitz also expresses another equally fascinating viewpoint about the blessings and curses. She says that the Lord.

> was concerned to protect all His creatures from error. He does not want to be instrumental in bolstering superstition. Had Balaam cursed Israel, the Moabites would certainly have assumed that the reason why the Israelites refrained from attacking them was due to their effect, and not because the Almighty had forbidden them…[241]

Despite how one views the matter of curses and blessings, at the very least, we can say that while Israel was playing in the plains of Moab, God was protecting them in ways beyond human comprehension. He was doing this by stifling the powers of the demons who wanted to consume Israel, and by stifling the idolatrous nations who wanted to devour them as well. It was a mighty, supernatural protection against attacks from the vicious and powerful forces of darkness whose sole intent was to destroy God's people, thereby foiling His plans.

B. The Angel

The second supernatural demonstration of God's protection was the sending of the angel in 22:22. Balaam was making a journey to play into the hands of Balak, the king who desired to curse Israel. God warned him not to go, but despite his assurance to the Lord that he would speak only that which God told him, 22:22 says, "God was very angry when he went." Balaam,

---

240. Leibowitz, *New Studies in Bamidbar*, 305.
241. *Ibid.*

his mind set on making the journey, was then confronted along the way by the appearance of an angel, sent by God "to oppose him" (22:22).

Anytime an angel appears in the realm of human existence, it is a supernatural event, but this one certainly stands out as one of the most memorable. For, while the angel was sent to deal with the human Balaam, nevertheless, it was not he who saw the angel, but his donkey! Moreover, it was not just a singular appearance; the angel manifested himself several times. On each occasion, the human was oblivious to him, but the animal wasn't! To put it rather crassly, one wonders who the real ass was!

The lesson here is profound. Here was a man bent on doing evil. He came into direct contact with the realm of the supernatural — and did not even notice it. Instead, his donkey saw it! In like manner, how many of us do not see what God is doing or hear what He is saying because we are set on acting according to our flesh, ignoring what the Spirit wants to do?

C. The Donkey

Perhaps the most famous supernatural demonstration by the Holy One in this parasha is the talking donkey. Of course, sceptics abound, who insist that it is foolish to assert that an animal can have dialogue with a human. Some suggest that it was a prophetic vision. Others, such as Luzatto, assert that, "The ass did not actually utter any words, but made a plaintive sound which implied protest…Balaam, in his anger, answered the ass much as any man might shout at his beast of burden."[242]

Despite all of the rationalizations, we must let this passage stand as it is. For one thing, although the text does not specify this, we must remember what an affect this would have had on a pagan sorcerer. His own awareness of his spiritual inability to see the angel would have been amplified by hearing the Most High speak through one of the lowliest of animals. Beyond that, however, any one sceptical about the reality of a talking animal needs simply to ask himself: Why not? If there is a Most High God Who made the heavens and the earth, including all that is in them, surely it must be within His capability to miraculously cause a donkey to speak.

The lesson to Balaam, as well as to us, is that the Holy One is the Sovereign of this universe. As such, only He has the power to determine what should be said and what should not be said. If He has decreed that only blessings should have come from the mouth of Balaam, or that a donkey may speak human words, it is His prerogative to do so, and no one may challenge Him or thwart His will. In short, it is as the Midrash says, "And the Lord opened the mouth of the donkey — to teach him that the mouth and the tongue are in His power; that if he sought to curse — his mouth was in His power."[243]

---

242. Leibowitz, *New Studies in Bamidbar,* 298.
243. Bamidbar Rabbah 20:12

IV. GOD WAS SURROUNDING ISRAEL WITH HIS GRACE

Such drama was going on in the mountains of Moab among people who cared not for the Holy One and His ways! The Holy One was pulling out all stops in revealing Himself to them. At the same time, He was also taking great pains to make sure that His peculiar people were protected and remained the objects of blessing from even the idolaters.

In this parasha, we see clearly the extent of the grace and mercy of God. Someone once defined the difference between grace and mercy in this way: "Grace is God giving us what we do not deserve. Mercy is God not giving us what we do deserve!" In chapter 25, Israel deserved wrath and annihilation for their immorality and idolatry.

To be sure, an unspecified number of Moabites and their allies, the Midianites, worked hard for Israel's destruction, hoping to accomplish it through their curses. To counter their efforts, the Lord stifled their chief sorcerer from doing that. Seeing that they could not accomplish Israel's demise through the curse, they attempted to do so through enticing them into idolatry and its accompanying immorality. "For the worship of Baal-Peor, (literally 'the lord of the mountain of Peor'), was associated with, and partly consisted in, the most licentious rites."[244]

This crime was enough to kindle the wrath of God (25:3). Although God dealt severely with those who were guilty, nevertheless, He spared the nation from being totally consumed by His anger. This was His mercy. He did not give them what they deserved!

Not only did the Lord grant mercy to Israel, He also abundantly poured out His grace to them. He gave them blessings, which they did not deserve. Look, for example, at the various gifts that He gave them, even when they were most undeserving: He protected them, He forgave them, He preserved them, He supplied their needs, He confounded the idolatrous on Israel's behalf, He spoke blessings to them, He stopped the plague, causing it to afflict only those who were guilty, and, much, much more. God did all of this for at least two reasons. First, He loved them. Secondly, He was determined to be faithful to His covenant that He made with them.

V. GOD WAS SPEAKING

Throughout most of the parashiyot we have heard God speaking. He spoke to Moshe. He spoke to Aaron. He spoke to others, but in this parasha, He is almost silent towards Israel as they were wandering away from Him and talking up a storm to the idolaters! One of the most amazing aspects of God speaking in this parasha is that He was not just commanding the idolatrous Balaam, as one might think the Sovereign of the universe has a right to do, but He was actually carrying on a negotiating dialogue with Balaam. Many people ask, "Does God hear the prayers of the unsaved?" In answering, we need to keep in mind how the Holy One conversed with this most unholy one!

---

244. J. H. Hertz, *Pentateuch and Haftarahs*, 681.

A. God Spoke to the Idolatrous

To whom was God speaking? He was speaking, first of all, to the idol worshipers and sorcerers, Balak and Balaam. He was revealing Himself to them, speaking through an angel — even through a donkey!

Another way God spoke was by means of what might be referred to as a "Torah Picture". We are referring to 24:1ff where Balaam looked out and saw the formation of the Camp of Israel on the plains beneath him. It must have been a powerful picture of the presence of the Holy One among the Israelites. What a portrait of beauty, orderliness, atonement, and fellowship with God he must have seen. God, indeed, spoke to Him from this gigantic picture. So much so that we read that when he saw the Camp, "the spirit of God was upon him" and then he began to speak a most beautiful blessing upon Israel.

Another way God spoke to Balaam, of course, was supernaturally through the donkey and through the angel. We have already discussed this. The fourth way God spoke to him was by direct revelation. In 24:2 the "spirit of God" was upon him. This phrase is reminiscent of the way the biblical prophets received their revelations. When God's Spirit came upon them, they spoke what God told them through His Spirit.

B. God Spoke to Israel

God also spoke to Israel, but His manner of speaking was very unusual. Most of the time, He spoke through His servants, the Prophets — from Moshe to Malachi. In this parasha, however, God spoke to Israel through the mouth of one who had the most power to curse them. He spoke through an idol worshiper. However, by the time Balaam spoke to Israel, he no longer had the spiritual blindness that prohibited him from even seeing the angel. Instead, he spoke as "the man with the open eye". This came after seeing the powerful Torah Picture of the encampment of Israel. Apparently, he was shocked into spiritual reality, even if for only a brief moment.

People everywhere who love the Lord and His people, Israel, have forever revered what God spoke through this man, once he had had his eyes opened. It has even found its way into the Siddur and chanted every Shabbat in the synagogue:

> How goodly are your tents, O Jacob, your dwelling places, O Israel stretching out like brooks, like gardens by a river, like aloes planted by the Lord, like cedars by water. Water shall flow from his wells, and his seed shall be by abundant waters, his king shall be exalted over Agag, and his kingdom shall be upraised (24:5–7).

C. God Spoke About the Messiah

God spoke to Israel yet in one more way. In 24:17, the Lord, through the mouth of Balaam says, "A star will come out of Jacob; a sceptre will rise out of Israel. He will crush the foreheads of Moab…" The prophecy continues to expand to include the descendants of Edom who will suffer destruction by this "Star" as well.

In the Ancient Near East, the term "star" was commonly used to refer to a royal figure.[245] During the Second Temple Period in Israel, the rabbis also thought of it in that way. Hence, The Targum interprets the word "star" here to refer to a "king". The writers of the Dead Sea Scrolls picked up on this theme and actually said that the "Star" in Numbers was a prediction of the Messiah![246]

Furthermore, during the days of the Bar Kochba revolt against Rome (132–135 ce), this verse was applied to Shimon Bar Kochba the "Son of a Star", the leader of the revolt whom the famous Rabbi Akiva declared to be the Messiah. To support his messiahship, his name was actually changed from "son of a Lar" (bar Kosiba) to "son of a Star" (bar Kochba). Numbers 24:17 was the biblical text which was used to support this claim.

All of this evidence points to the fact that from ancient days, this passage was understood by the people of God as a Messianic text, predicting something about the person and work of the Messiah. Even the medieval commentator Rashi says that this whole passage is both a reference to King David, who was the first to subject Moab, and to King Messiah.[247]

In this prophecy, Balaam was predicting the downfall of Moab and Edom, the two nemeses of Israel who sought to curse them and refused the right of passage to them. A certain strong and important ruler, the "Star", would ultimately accomplish this downfall. Ancient Jewish interpretation seems unanimous that while King David would fulfil some of it, King Messiah would be the one to ultimately subdue all of Israel's enemies.

This passage, interestingly enough, is never used in reference to the messiahship of Yeshua in the Apostolic Scriptures. However, when we examine His Person and Work, we can confidently say, as does Harrison, "Jesus fulfilled supremely the role predicted by Balaam of a divinely appointed King who far exceeded the work of His earthly ancestor David by ushering in God's kingdom upon the earth (Matthew 12:28; Luke 11:20)."[248]

God was doing all of these things while Israel played the harlot on the plains of Moab, as they were about to enter the Promised Land. For the most part, Israel was totally oblivious to all that the Holy One was accomplishing for them while they played. If only we could be aware of the unseen work our loving Father does for us, especially in the times when, like Israel, we too may walk in our flesh. This parasha, perhaps, more than any other one confirms to us the truth of Romans 8:28–39, which speaks of the unfathomable and unconditional love the Father has for all of us who have placed our faith in the "Star", King Messiah.

245. Timothy R. Ashley, *Numbers (NICOT)*, 500.
246. 1QM 11:6–7
247. Rashi: *Bamidbar*, ArtScroll Edition, 310–311.
248. R. K. Harrison, *Numbers*, 324.

ADDITIONAL NOTES

Chapter 22

"Rabbinic Tradition calls these chapters the 'Section of Balaam', a designation that accords with the view that the Torah was compiled from separate scrolls."[249] Do not be too alarmed at this viewpoint. It does not deny Mosaic authorship. It merely points to one of Moshe's sources. We saw something similar in our studies in Bereshit where we suggested the possibility that Genesis may have originally been a collection of clay tablets passed down through the family history. Moshe, the recipient of these tablets, added more information and put it all together.

Verse 5

"**Pethor**" — From several sources we can identify this location as Pitru, on one of the tributaries of the Euphrates River south of Carchemish in ancient Aram. This was about a 20-day journey from Moab. Since the Torah describes four such trips, then the entire time span of this story must have been about 3 months.[250]

Verse 5

"**Balaam**" — His name can mean several possible things:

   1) A mad people
   2) He went out of his mind because of the immensity of his knowledge
   3) He who swallows up the people
   4) Corrupter of the people
   5) His son is a beast.[251]

He is such an enigma. Hertz portrays his character well for us when he states,

> It seems probable that he had from the first, learned some elements of pure religion in his home in Mesopotamia, the cradle of the ancestors of Israel. But unlike these [his spiritual ancestors] he is represented in Scripture as at the same time heathen sorcerer, true prophet, and the perverter who suggested a peculiarly abhorrent means of bringing about the ruin of Israel.[252]

Thus, the character of this unique person confuses even the best of commentators! Hence, we agree with Wenham that, "It must be remembered that biblical writers rarely comment explicitly on the characters of the actors. The narrator's emotional and moral values are as a rule conveyed indirectly, by the implicit tenor of the stories."[253]

Verse 9

Balaam's first encounter with God — Typical of such biblical encounters, it came at night. Having been hired by Balak previously to this encounter with God, the drama of the rest of the story is now set when God comes into the picture.

249. Milgrom, *JPS: Numbers,* 185.
250. *Ibid.,* 186.
251. *Ibid.*
252. Hertz, *Pentateuch and Haftarahs,* 668.
253. Gordon J. Wenham, *Numbers (TOTC),* 167.

Verse 11

"**curse**" — Rashi notes that Balaam's word for "curse", **kavah** (קבה), is a stronger word than that which was used by Balak, the one who hired Balaam. Balak used the word **arah** (ארה).[254] Munk explains that Rashi was indicating that "the word which Balaam used is a stronger term because it refers to a curse based on the utterance of the Divine Name, whereas the word which Balak had used connotes a curse from magic and the occult. Hence, we see that Balak did not think of going as far as Balaam did in his rejection of Israel."[255]

Verse 18

"**The Lord My God**" — The Talmud (Sanhedrin 106b) declares that Balaam had first been a prophet and later defected to the practice of magic.[256] It is easy to see the conflict here between his loyalty to God and his bend toward the occult.

Verse 22

"**God's anger**" — At first glance this verse seems contradictory to what was previously said. God formerly gave Balaam permission to go, but here God is angry with him for going. However, it should be pointed out that God's permission to go was conditional, that is, He said Balaam may go to Balak but he may not speak against Israel. Quite possibly this verse might be indicating that God, the discerner of the intentions of man's minds, knew that Balaam went intent on not listening to God's condition. That is why God was angry according to this verse.

Verse 28

"**The Lord opened the donkey's mouth**" — Obviously this was quite a phenomenon. One way that some Jewish commentators have dealt with it is to suggest that "the speaking ass was ordained by God on the eve of the first Sabbath — that is, as part of the Creation — and therefore did not constitute an interruption of the natural order."[257]

On the other hand, historically, most commentators have seen a real miracle here. "Many commentators, both in ancient and modern times, take the account of the miracle in these verses literally. Nothing is impossible to Omnipotence, they hold; and a speaking ass is no more marvellous than a speaking serpent or any of the other miracles."[258]

Then, there is the rationalist view, rather typified by the Rambam who considered this story as enacted in a dream or vision of the night. Finally, "another explanation holds that the Text nowhere states that the ass gave utterance to human sounds. It's weird behaviour in the presence of the angel, and its wild cries at the cruel beatings, were understood by Balaam to mean the words given in the Text (Luzzatto)."[259]

Undoubtedly even more suggestions make their rounds in addition to those above. As for us,

254. Rashi, *Numbers: ArtScroll Edition*, 275–276.
255. Elie Munk, *The Call of the Torah: Bamidbar*, 269.
256. *Ibid.*, 270.
257. Milgrom, *JPS: Numbers*, 191.
258. Hertz, *Pentateuch and Haftarahs*, 671.
259. *Ibid.*

we understand the text in a literal way. It is up to the students to study and draw their own conclusions.

Verse 29

"**a sword**" — Notice the irony here. Balaam, without a sword, is desirous of using one upon a poor innocent donkey while the angel, whom Balaam cannot see yet, does have a sword, but refused to use it on Balaam who did deserve it.

Chapter 23

Verse 1

"**seven**" — Wenham cites a similar Babylonian practice.

> At dawn in the presence of Ea, Shamash, and Marduk [Babylonian deities], you must set up seven altars, place seven incense burners of cypress and pour out the blood of seven sheep... When this was done, the diviner presented himself before the deity and reminded him of the burnt offerings.[260]

In Israel seven was also a very important symbolic number. Many consider seven to be symbolic of completion.

Verses 7–10

Balaam's first utterance — This merely recalls the events leading up to the pact with Balak and Balaam. Note the parallelism in these utterances, which were given in poetry. It seems that almost all of God's prophecies were in poetry.

Verse 7

"**hills of the east**" — The Hebrew word for east here is *kedem* (קדם).

> From the Egyptian story of Sinuhe, Qedem seems to designate a specific territory in the Syrian desert east of the Phoenician coast...Genesis 29:1 actually identifies Qedem as the region from which the patriarchs stemmed. Elsewhere in Scripture, Qedem applies to the entire desert fringe, beginning in the north at the middle Euphrates and running south to the eastern border of present-day Syria and Jordan.[261]

The term "hills", however, limits the specific territory in reference here to a little north in the mountains of eastern Syria. Elsewhere the word qedem, does not necessarily have a geographical emphasis, but rather stresses time. Thus, qedem may refer to that which is from a long time ago. Such a possible use might be seen in Genesis 2:8.

Verse 9

"Through the Spirit, Balaam is able to appreciate Israel's peculiar character. Because God has chosen her, she is different from the other nations."[262]

Verses 13–26

Balaam's second utterance — In 23:13 Balak changes the place of the sacrificial ritual, hoping that it would influence a change in Balaam's prophecies. However, the Lord clearly spoke

260. Wenham, *Numbers*, 172.
261. Milgrom, *JPS: Numbers,* 196.
262. *Ibid.,* 173–174.

through Balaam in this second prophecy that He, God, does not change! When He designates a blessing for Israel, no one is able to or may change it into a curse. Like the beginning of the first utterance, this second one begins with a denouncement of Balak's theology and presents the true picture of God.

Verse 21

The first prophecy announced the difference between Israel and the nations. This second one provides some of the specific ways in which Israel differs. In this verse, we are told that Israel has no human king. Instead, the Lord is referred to as Israel's King.

Verse 23

Another difference between Israel and her neighbours is that Israel did not use divination. "This is the central point of the entire 'Book of Balaam:' because God has provided Israel with prophets, it has no need to resort to magical arts to determine His will."[263]

Chapter 24

Verses 1–17

Balaam's third prophecy — 24:2 indicates that this third utterance is different from the first two. Previously, God put words into his mouth. This time, the text says that "the Spirit of God came upon him," meaning that perhaps this time Balaam fell into an ecstatic trance as he saw the vision…"[264] Moreover, whereas the first two utterances were more or less theological statements about Israel and God's relationship with them, this third vision relates to Israel's presence in the Promised Land and their victory over their enemies.

Verse 5

"how beautiful…" — Rabbi Munk cites sources which indicate how hypocritical Balaam was here, uttering something good about Israel while secretly cursing them.[265] However, we cannot see that at this point Balaam was speaking anything other than what was really in his mind, especially seeing how caught up he was when he saw the entire camp of Israel. We know that the Torah describes him as the one who inspired the Moabites to seduce Israel's women. Perhaps that was a compromise for not cursing them as Balak instructed him. Maybe Balaam knew that while some Israelites would be seduced, the nation because of their God, would have resisted. At the same time, it seemed like a good way to placate Balak. In reality, who really knows, except the Holy One?

Verse 5

"how beautiful…" — Rabbi Hertz puts it so poetically: "He is swept away in rapt admiration of the Israelite encampments and homes arrayed harmoniously and peacefully, a picture of idyllic happiness and prosperity."[266] This phrase has become somewhat of a by-word among Jewish

---

263. Milgrom, *JPS: Numbers,* 200.
264. Wenham, *Numbers*, 176–177.
265. See Munk, *The Call of the Torah: Bamidbar,* 296–297.
266. Hertz, *Pentateuch and Haftarahs*, 678.

people, that it enjoys the honour of introducing one of the opening prayers in the Shacharit (morning prayer) service.

Verse 7

"**Agag**" — Agag was the king of the Amalekites during the time of King Saul in Israel (1 Samuel 15:8). Amalek was one of Israel's most dreaded enemies during Moshe's time. Milgrom has a good insight about the mention of Agag here when he comments, "Agag may remind the poet of *gag*, "roof," hence his wording "rise above Agag. The Septuagint and Samaritan [Pentateuch] read "Gog," the legendary future antagonist of Israel mentioned in Ezekiel 38–39, thereby giving the oracle an eschatological thrust."[267]

It is interesting to note that in the book of Esther (3:1), the infamous and evil Haman, is called "Haman son of Hammedatha, the Agagite." Therefore, Haman was a descendant of Agag, hence an Amalekite. King Saul, from the tribe of Benjamin was told by God to kill the Amalekites. He did not do it. About 700 years later, in Persia, Mordechai, also from the tribe of Benjamin, was about to suffer with the rest of his people at the hands of an Amalekite — Haman. However, through the courage of this descendant of Benjamin and his niece, Esther, the most famous Amalekite, Haman was destroyed, even in the midst of his plans to destroy Mordechai's people.

Verse 9

The promise to the patriarchs (Genesis 12:1–3) is now fulfilled, at least in part, by Balaam: "Those who bless you will be blessed and those who curse you will be cursed." The attempt to curse by Balak will backfire upon him and his kingdom.

Verse 10

Notice the progression of Balak's anger: 1) a mild rebuke, 2) more anger surfaced, and then here 3) open hostility. This is how uncontrolled anger usually progresses.

Verses 14–25

Balaam's fourth and last utterance — Now the prophecy turns against Balak and Balaam speaks about "what this people will do to your people in days to come "(24:14). This prophecy predicts that Israel will ultimately be victorious over her enemies such as the Moabites, the Edomites, the Kenites, the Assyrians and the Philistines. Moreover, this victory would not just come about partially through the successes of people like King David. The ultimate victory would come through the Messiah, as both traditional Jewish and Christian interpreters suggest.

Verse 17

"**a star**" — Please refer to the commentary above.

Verse 17

"**Moab**" — "A fitting and ironic conclusion to the Balaam story: Balak of Moab wished to curse Israel; instead, his hired seer, Balaam, curses Moab — a measure for measure principle."[268]

---

267. Milgrom, *JPS: Numbers,* 204.
268. *Ibid.,* 208.

Verse 21

"Kenites" — According to Judges 1:16 the Kenites must apparently have belonged to the Midianites because Jethro, Moshe's father-in-law, belonged to them. How they were Israel's enemies is not clear.

Verses 21–22

"**Asshur**" — Asshur is generally associated with the Assyrians, the fierce empire from the upper Tigris who ruled the Ancient Near East during the 7th to 5th centuries BCE. However, some scholars think that Assyria (the most natural choice for identification here), is not the people who are in view in this prophecy. Wenham, for example, suggests that it may have been a small tribe in the upper Sinai close to the Kenites. Our opinion is that the Assyrians are in view.

Verse 24

"**Kittim**" — this is usually a reference to Cyprus. It was also a word for Greece. On the other hand, it might be a veiled reference to the Philistines, a sea people from the region of the Aegean Sea. Yet, in Daniel 11:30, it appears that the ships of Kittim are referring to the Romans. In short, it is difficult to know who specifically is in view here.[269]

Chapter 25

Verse 2

It is difficult to imagine that while all of the drama was taking place in the mountains above, involving Israel receiving a blessing, that Israel would be playing the harlot with Moabite women and gods below. The close proximity of this story to what preceded it leads this commentator to the opinion that it was Balaam who attempted to set this situation up, realizing that it would not last long and Balak would also be satisfied. However, that is merely a conjecture.

Verse 2

Sacrificing to a god of the Ancient Near East sometimes also meant having illicit sexual relationships with the temple prostitutes connected with the worship of those gods.

Verse 3

"**Ba'al-peor**" — Ba'al is the name of the god. He was the god of storms and rain — a very precious commodity in that part of the world. Peor was the name of the location. Several places in Canaan also had Ba'al worship going on such as Ba'al-zephon (Numbers 33:7) and Ba'al-meon (Numbers 32:38). The word "Ba'al" itself means "lord, master or owner". The Ugarit and Mari tablets all confirm Ba'al's presence in the land of Canaan and that he was a powerful god near the second half of the second millennium BCE. This is the first time Israel met Ba'al and, therefore, was rather unprepared to meet him. Naturally, we are speaking of the demons manifesting as Ba'al.

---

269. Milgrom, *JPS: Numbers.*, 210.

Verses 4–5

"**leaders**" — The sin apparently involved all the different sections of the Israelite camp, so a death plague from the Lord broke out slaying 24,000 Israelites. To stop the plague, the leaders had to be executed. "In this case the whole nation, corporately though not individually, was involved in the offence, therefore representatives of all Israel had to atone for it. An additional reason for punishing the chiefs of the people was that they should have restrained their followers.[270]

Verses 6–8

We need to understand the nature of Pinchas' action in light of the fact that Moshe tried to water down God's sentence because the leaders were close to him and may, have been personally innocent of the crime. It was a rather awkward position for them to be in where they had to administer their own death penalty. Therefore, graciously, God raised up Pinchas to do what he did.

---

270. Wenham, *Numbers,* 186.

STUDY QUESTIONS

1. What is your impression of Balaam? How do you reconcile the account in Torah where he, at times, speaks blessings to Israel when "the Spirit of God was upon him", with the characterization of him in the Brit Hadasha and the Talmud?

2. What was it about Balaam that encouraged Balak to summons him to curse Israel?

3. Why did God send an angel to impede Balaam?

4. Why do you think that Balaam did not see the angel while the donkey did?

5. Do you think that the donkey literally spoke? Why or why not? If he spoke, why do you think that the Lord did that?

6. Why did Balak invite Balaam to the three different sacrifices?

7. What was the main content of each of Balaam's prophecies?

8. What was it about seeing the encampment of Israel that caused Balaam to speak his blessings?

9. What did Balaam mean about a certain "Star"?

10. What was Balaam predicting concerning Edom and Moab? What would have been the full impact of this prophecy to those listening to it?

11. Why could Balaam not curse Israel?

12. What did it mean to bless or to curse?

13. Why do you think chapter 25 relates the incident about the Israelites and the Moabite women?

14. Why did Pinchas act so decisively in executing the Israelite man and Moabite woman?

Parashat Pinchas פינחס

Torah: Numbers 25:10–30:1
Haftarah: 1 Kings 18:46–19:21

Parashat Pinchas פינחס

> Why was the Torah likened to a fig tree? Because, while the fruit of most other trees — the olive tree, the vine, and the date tree — is gathered all at once, that of the fig tree is gathered little by little; and it is the same with the Torah. One gathers little learning today and much tomorrow, for it cannot be learned in a year nor in two years. (Bamidbar Rabbah 21.15)

In this parasha, we are now back in the camp, instead of up in the Moabite mountains listening to Balaam. The Guardian and Protector of Israel has just thwarted a potentially major catastrophe in the unseen realm by stifling the curses of Balak and causing his prophet, the evil Balaam to utter blessings toward Israel instead. Now, the Holy One has some unfinished business to attend to, in order to fully prepare the new generation to take possession of the Land. That is the thrust of the remaining parashiyot in Numbers. As far as Parashat Pinchas is concerned, we will think through it this way:

I.   The Aftermath of the Baal-Peor Incident (25:10–18)
II.   The Accounting of a New Generation (26:1–27:11)
III. The Appointment of a New Leader (27:12–23)
IV.   The Additional Offerings (28:1–30:1)

I. THE AFTERMATH OF THE BAAL-PEOR INCIDENT (25:10-18)

A. The Reward for Pinchas (25:10–13)

The student might remember from the end of the previous parasha that the Israelites were having immoral relations with Midianite women. God subsequently disciplined them by sending a plague into the camp. In one incident, Pinchas, the son of Eleazar the High Priest, decided to take justice into his own hands and killed a particular Israelite leader and his Midianite harlot with a spear. This action prompted the Lord to end the plague.

This incident has several problems relayed to it. First, it was done without a trial. Pinchas literally took justice into his own hands and circumvented the judicial procedure outlined in the Torah. Another complication was the fact that since it was done spontaneously, the Israelite's family could easily have sought revenge on this zealous kohen.

Even though this incident, indeed, was done without the due process of law, nevertheless, the Lord saw things differently. To help to protect Pinchas, the Lord announced that He was entering into a "covenant of peace" with him because he had a "passion for Me" (25:11–12). This helped to save him from any personal revenge against him. It also served to vindicate him of any legal wrongdoing and assured that he and his descendants would continue in the Priesthood (25:13).

Professor Leibowitz sees an even deeper reason for this covenant of peace. She writes, "The Divine promise of a covenant of peace constitutes rather a guarantee against the inner enemy, lurking inside the zealous perpetrator of the sudden deed, against the inner demoralization that such an act as the killing of a human being, without due process of law is liable to cause."[271] If she is right, then what happened would be a commentary on the unfathomable kindness of God in order to help the person to accept himself if he is in fact innocent and not carry with him a guilty conscience.

There is something else about this covenant that the Holy One made with Pinchas. The text indicates that God was making an "eternal covenant" with Pinchas and his descendants. This was a covenant involving the Priesthood. There might be various ways of understanding this covenant but, in our opinion, Jacob Milgrom defines it best when he says, "the likelihood is that Phinehas is here promised that his line, later called the Zadokites (see Ezekiel 44:15–16) will be the exclusive officiates in the Temple."[272]

God made another dynastic covenant in Israel's history. He also made such a covenant with King David and his descendants, recorded in 2 Samuel 7. Here He promises that the descendants of David will occupy the throne of Israel forever; there will not be another family who will rightfully usurp this honour.

The prophet Jeremiah speaks about both of these families, the priestly family and the royal family in Jeremiah 33:17–18. He assures Israel that, "David will never fail to have a man sit on the throne of the house of Israel, nor will the priests, who are Levites, ever fail to have a man to stand before me continually to offer burnt offerings." Thus, the prophet confirms these covenants and through the prophet, God reiterates the fact that His covenants would never be broken.

To us it seems that there is no one left either of David or the sons of Levi to fulfil these two dynastic covenants that God made. However, we need to remember at least two things. First, the word "forever" *olam* (עולם), does not necessarily have to mean forever and ever without end. It could just mean "for a long-extended period of time". This was certainly true concerning both the Throne and the Priesthood. Secondly, however, the houses of both David and Pinchas, have never ceased to exist, even though we do not know for certain who are the proper descendants to fill their sacred offices. The important thing is that God certainly remembers! It is no problem for Him to sovereignly maintain the rightful descendants, even though we do not necessarily know who they may be.

B. The Discipline of Sin (25:14–15)

Both physical and spiritual harlotry was and has been a habitual problem for Israel through the centuries. To help deter this tendency the Lord made examples of the two perpetrators slain by Pinchas. The Holy One not only approved their execution, but also, He records their names and those of their families for all future generations. The Israelite was Zimri, from the tribe of Shim'on and the name of the Midianite woman was Cozbi. The recording of their names

271. Leibowitz, *New Studies in Bamidbar*, 331.
272. Milgrom, *The JPS Torah Commentary: Numbers*, 216–217.

undoubtedly brought humiliation upon their families — something which all would want to avoid. Rabbi Hertz, also picking up on this idea, adds, "Just as in the case of good men, so also are the names and families of evildoers recorded — an immortality of infamy is theirs."[273]

C. Wrath to the Midianites (25:16–17)

As another consequence of this episode, Moshe is instructed by the Lord to "treat the Midianites as enemies and kill them" (25:17). Even though the Midianites were not alone in afflicting the Israelites, having been in alliance with the Moabites, the Holy One singles them out for particular wrath. The Rabbis explain this by pointing out that, "No punishment is meted out to the Moabites because these had at least the excuse of their fear for their infamous conduct with the Israelites; whereas the Midianites were actuated by pure hatred."[274]

A question may be rightfully asked at this point, if the Israelites were so tempted to sin by the Moabites, why does the text relate that their war was to be against the Midianites and not against the Moabites? Jacob Milgrom has a helpful observation that may solve this problem for us. He says that historically, the Moabites and the Midianites were somewhat of a united kingdom that embraced all of Transjordan. When the Israelites defeated King Sihon in Numbers 21, it severed the major inland trade route, The King's Highway, thereby threatening the Midianites' hold on that vital spice trade which went along The King's Highway. "Thus Midian, Israel's erstwhile ally (10:20–21), now became its implacable foe."[275] Hence, this new political situation coupled with the sin from some of the Midianite women created an atmosphere of danger for the Israelites that may have prompted the battle described in 25:16-17.

II. THE ACCOUNTING OF A NEW GENERATION (26:1–27:11)

A. The Census

The Torah states that what God had promised concerning the fate of the generation of Israelites who came out of Egypt had come to pass. We now read in chapter 26 that God instructed Moshe to take another census of the people of Israel. He faithfully did so. When it was finished, the Holy One reminds us in 26:64–65, "Among these there was not one of those enrolled by Moshe and Aaron the priest when they recorded the Israelites in the wilderness of Sinai. For the Lord had said of them, 'They shall die in the wilderness.' Not one of them survived, except Caleb son of Jephunneh and Joshua son of Nun." Thus, it was an entirely new generation of Israelites that was encamped on the east bank of the Jordan River poised for an attack on the Land of Canaan.

We can discern at least two reasons, therefore, for this new census. The first was to emphasize the fact that God kept His Word. When He told the unfaithful generation that they would not see the Promised Land, He truly meant it. The second reason is similar to the purposes for the

---

273. J. H. Hertz, *The Pentateuch and Haftarahs*, 686.
274. *Ibid.*, 687.
275. Milgrom, *JPS: Numbers*, 218.

earlier censuses — to see how many men they could muster for the army.

B. The Assignment of Land (26:52–27:11)

Before Israel was able to march into the Promised Land, much had to be organized. As stated above, Moshe had to take another census of the people. In addition to that, however, the actual allotment of the land had to be done beforehand in order to avoid any last-minute squabbles among the families or tribes. This was an enormous task that required supernatural intervention by the Lord.

1. To the Israelites in General (26:52–65)

First, the inheritance had to be divided up for the nation as a whole. In general, at least two criteria went into allocating which tribes get which land. Larger portions were to be given to the tribes with the larger populations (26:52–54) and the specific piece of real estate was to be decided by lot (26:55). We do not learn of the actual division of the tribal territories until the Book of Joshua, when he leads the nation to dividing the land after much of it had been conquered. For a sneak preview, however, of how the lot took place, note the following Talmudic passage:

> Eleazar [the High Priest] was wearing the Urim and the Tummim, while Joshua and all Israel stood before him. An urn containing the names of the twelve tribes and an urn containing the descriptions of the boundaries were placed before him. Animated by the Holy Spirit, he gave directions exclaiming, "Zebulun is coming up and the boundary lines of Acco are coming up with it." Thereupon he shook well the urn of the tribes and Zebulun came up in his hand. Likewise, he shook well the urn of the boundaries and the boundary lines of Acco came up in his hand…And so was the procedure with every other tribe.[276]

Looking into the distant future, the prophet Ezekiel describes how the land will be allocated in the Messianic Age. In chapter 47 of his prophecy, Ezekiel tells us that not only will the Promised Land be divided into an inheritance for each of the 12 tribes, but there will also be non-Jews involved in it as well! He says,

> You are to distribute this land among yourselves according to the tribes of Israel. You are to allot it as an inheritance for yourselves and for the aliens who have settled among you and who have children. You are to consider them as native-born Israelites; along with you that are to be allotted an inheritance among the tribes of Israel (Ezekiel 47:21–22).

What a wonderful thought — that there will be a remnant from among the nations who will so desire to be identified with Israel that the God of Israel will even grant to them a physical inheritance within the Land!

2. To Sonless Families (27:1–11)

Our parasha records a second group of people who received an inheritance. The laws of inheritance demanded that the family's land and goods were to be passed on to the first-born son. This was also the case with most other nations in the Ancient Near East. However, in these

---

276. B. Talmud Bava Batra 122a.

verses, a case is brought before Moshe where a family had daughters, but no sons. Were they allowed to be the inheritors? Moshe took the case directly before the Lord, Who ruled in favour of the daughters. Then the Holy One continued to teach more about His wishes for inheritance in similar cases where there are no children.

One of the important points from this passage is to realize how revolutionary this instruction was. In similar Ancient Near East legislation, "Daughters do not usually appear to have shared in their deceased father's estate, apparently because they would be expected to be married and have their own husbands to provide for them."[277] This practice led to a rather unfair treatment of women in the ancient world. In contrast, the Torah provides care and protection for the women of Israel, often in stark contrast to their neighbouring nations. Hence, "God's decision showed that He was not willing to see the daughters of His people exploited or deprived of their legitimate holdings."[278]

Two additional points stand out about this episode. First, it teaches us "The land belongs to God, who assigned it to the Israelite clans for their use."[279] We have made this point elsewhere, but it never hurts to restate it. Moshe acknowledged God's ownership of the Land, which is why he took the case of the women to the Lord instead of using his own wisdom on the matter. In doing so, Moshe was clearly testifying to the fact that only God had the right to decide upon the use of the Promised Land.

Secondly, notice a subtle contrast here. Back in Numbers 13, the wayward explorers were all men, leaders, nonetheless. Yet, they categorically rejected the Land. On the contrary, here are three otherwise unknown women who boldly stepped forward to claim their right to the Land. There is certainly no place in God's covenant community for fleshly chauvinism!

III. The Appointment of a New Leader (27:12–23)

True to His Word, God reminded Moshe that because of the events at Kadesh Maribah, he was not going to lead the people into the Promised Land. Instead, the Lord told Moshe to climb a high mountain and look into the Land but not enter it.

At this point, rather than musing about why he could not enter, Moshe's mind turned to the care of his people, Israel. He asked the Lord about appointing a new leader. Notice, however, that Moshe did not suggest any of his own sons or relatives. His mind and heart were strictly on the will of the Almighty. Indeed, "There, Moshe exemplified the merit of the righteous who at the time of their death do not concern themselves with their personal deeds but with the deeds of the community."[280]

God's response was to choose Joshua, the son of Nun, Moshe's right-hand man, to lead the

277. R. K. Harrison, *Numbers*, 356.
278. *Ibid.*, 357.
279. Milgrom, *JPS: Numbers*, 230.
280. *Ibid.*, 234.

people after him. To help facilitate this transition to the new leader, Moshe was instructed to hold a public ceremony at the Tent of Meeting, rest his hand on Joshua, and "place some of your majesty upon him" (27:20). To confirm this choice before the people, Eleazer was to consult the urim and thummim, under the care of the High Priest.

It would still be a little while before Joshua actually took over the leadership, even though it is recorded here in this passage. What we mean is that Moshe still had a little more teaching of the Torah to impart to the people. In addition, he also had the speech of Deuteronomy (the whole book) to give to them. Consequently, the appointment recorded here is actually the same one recorded at the end of Deuteronomy after all of Moshe's instructions had been given to Israel. Both were written at the same time and the same place. The Book of Numbers is merely giving us a sneak preview!

The first thing the text does is to list God's qualifications for who would replace Moshe. Therefore in 27:16–17 Moshe, who was truly speaking God's heart, said to the Holy One, "May the Lord, the God of the spirits of all mankind, appoint a man over this community to go out and come in before them… so that the Lord's people will not be like sheep without a shepherd". The most outstanding qualification that was essential for a successor for Moshe was that he be a military man. This is indicated by the phrase, "go out and come in". This idiom was used to speak of army commanders. Israel's officers were "not like others … who send out their troops first and they come last." Rather, they were to lead their troops into the battle. In fact, even to this day, "the officers of modern Israel's defence forces are noted for their battle cry 'aharai (אחרי)'— 'follow me!'."[281]

The next most important qualification for the one who was to walk in Moshe's sandals was that he had to be a shepherd. It is hard to picture a man who would have the strength and boldness of a general yet possess the kindness and gentleness of a shepherd. Yet, the leader for God's holy community was to be just such a person. One of the best-known examples of these characteristics was King David, the shepherd king who made Israel into a formidable military power.

However, by far the best example of such a person was/is Yeshua, the Messiah. He Himself said that He is the Good Shepherd. As such He provides food, protection, community, and the comfort of His presence to guide His sheep. On the other hand, we know from Revelation 19 that this kind and tender shepherd is also the King of Kings and Lord of lords who will come back to planet earth as the general of God's armies and wage victorious war with the enemies of the Lord.

However, in Moshe's day, in our parasha, God had a certain someone in mind even before Moshe prayed about it. Interestingly enough, he also was Yeshua, or should we say, Yehoshua — Joshua. The list of Joshua's qualifications for this enormous task is seemingly endless. One

---

281. Milgrom, *JPS: Numbers,* 234.

characteristic, however, stands out in this parasha. In 27:16, Moshe asks the Lord for a successor who would be a shepherd over Israel. Even though Joshua was a military man, a capable leader, and protégé of Moshe, the one characteristic Moshe was concerned about was that Joshua be a true shepherd. Accordingly, this was apparently one of the main reasons that the Lord chose him.

The Midrash develops this theme and suggests that since Joshua was a shepherd, he must have been a student of Torah. In support of this idea, the Midrash cites Proverbs 27:18,

> "Who so keeps the fig tree shall eat the fruit thereof." And, remember, the Midrash says this: "Why was the Torah likened to a fig tree?" Because, while the fruit of most other trees — the olive tree, the vine, and the date tree — is gathered all at once, that of the fig tree is gathered little by little; and it is the same with the Torah. One gathers little learning today and much tomorrow, for it cannot be learned in a year nor in two years.[282]

What rich symbolism we see here. According to this midrash, Joshua was a great shepherd of Israel because he studied God's Word and kept it. We do not think that we needed this midrash, however, to tell us this! Ever since we first met Joshua, he was always at Moshe's side, especially at Mount Sinai. One cannot be that close to such a great Torah teacher as Moshe and not be a diligent student of God's Word. Moreover, just as his mentor was a great shepherd (both physically and spiritually) so also must his most dedicated student have been as well. We are sure that Joshua studied every move Moshe made as a shepherd of God's flock and learned his calling well. As far as his military training is concerned, almost from the very beginning of our knowledge of Joshua, he was in the leadership of Israel's army. Now, by the time that this passage was taking place, he has had intensive military experience for over 40 years.

Based on these two factors alone, no one among all of Israel had more qualifications for succeeding Moshe. However, the Holy One also sought to give him even more essential qualifications for the job. Hence, in 27:18–23, the Lord instructed Moshe to do two very special things to Joshua.

First, He told Moshe to lay his hands on him, symbolizing the fact that Moshe's authority was to now rest upon Joshua. This was done in front of all Israel so that there would never be any question that Joshua was the man who Moshe designated to succeed him. When Moshe placed his hands on him the Lord said that it was in order to "give him some of your authority" (27:20). It is difficult to ascertain precisely how to render the Hebrew term that the NASB translates as "authority". It is the word *hod* (חוד, pronounced with a long o). This word can mean weight, authority, splendour, or majesty.[283] Any of these translations would fit the context. Perhaps a good way to understand it is to phrase it like this: "place some of his (Moshe's) majestic authority upon him."

Rabbi Munk tells us that the midrash compares this to "a candle lighting another candle". He

---

282. Bamidbar Rabbah 21:15
283. HALOT, 241.

continues to explain that according to Rashi" Moses' face was like the sun, which is an inexhaustible source of energy. Joshua's face was like the moon which benefits from the sun's light and reflects its rays.[284]

Secondly, even though God specifically singled out Joshua and made His choice known to Moshe, nevertheless, the Lord told Moshe and Eleazar the High Priest that they were to visibly seek God's confirmation through the use of the urim and thummim. This was most likely done to confirm to all Israel that not only was Joshua Moshe's choice, but also that He was God's.

IV. THE ADDITIONAL OFFERINGS (28:1–30:1)

The remaining material in this parasha is about additional sacrifices and offerings which the Lord instructed to be offered at the *mo'adim*. From this new material, we learn that several kinds of sacrifices/offerings were brought to the Mishkan.

One kind was the personal offerings as outlined in the first 5 chapters of Leviticus. Individuals for the various reasons stated in that passage brought these. The second kind was those specifically required as part of the observance of a particular *mo'ed*. For example, on Pesach it was the Pesach Lamb and on Yom Kippur there were two special goats for atonement. The third variety of sacrifices was the continual or "*tamid*" offerings described in Numbers 28:1–8. This was to make sure that there was always a continual "pleasing aroma" in God's House. The last was additional or "*mussaf*" offerings which were to be offered on each Holy convocation. This parasha tells us specifically which ones were to be offered on each specific day. For easy reference, the *ArtScroll Chumash* offers a little chart on page 899 as a summary of what this sidra is teaching.

A. "For Me"

One of the most important features of the list of tamid offerings is that they were specifically for the Holy One. They are referred to in 28:2 as, "My offering, My food for My fires, My satisfying aroma…"(author's paraphrase). To appreciate the fullest import of this statement, remember that these sacrifices were to be offered in God's House, the Mishkan. This was the family dwelling where the "Husband" (God) met in intimacy and fellowship with his "wife" (Israel). The animals were offered to honour Him, they were eaten together facilitating close fellowship, and they produced the sweet aroma of atonement and praise that was to permeate this House.

B. When You Enter the Land

The Lord laid heavy stress on making sure that Israel knew exactly how to relate to Him once they were in the Land. Accordingly, the Torah instructed them to do a number of things once they were there. These included:

---

284. Munk, *The Call of the Torah: Bamidbar*, 342.

1) the implementation of the cycle of mo'adim in Leviticus 23:9

2) the supplementary sacrificial offerings listed in Numbers 15:1–12

3) these sacrifices listed in chapter 28 of Numbers.

Thus, Israel's first duty upon settling in its land is to establish the proper lines of communion with the Lord.[285]

We have a few other general observations concerning these sacrifices mentioned in chapter 28. First, the animals are all males, including lambs, rams, bulls, and goats. Second, at least as far as the lambs are concerned, for the most part the number seven is predominant. Seven, of course, is considered the perfect number, symbolic of God's perfect completion of His creation. Last, for whatever reason, notice that during Sukkot, the number of bulls offered decreases one per day as the week goes by, until it levels of with the number seven.

C. Messiah — Our Tamid Offering

The "*tamid*" offerings were rendered redundant by the offering of Yeshua, the Messiah. In Him we have close fellowship with God. In Him we smell the sweet aroma of atonement and praise. The word *tamid* (תמיד) means "always". We are told that Yeshua's sacrifice was a once-for-all sacrifice, or a "tamid" offering before the Lord (Hebrews 9:11–14). The difference is that instead of being offered all the time, it is effective all the time! Finally, like the "tamid", Messiah's offering, was not only for us, the needy recipients, but also for the Lord who desired sweet fellowship with His creation.

— EXCURSUS —

THE INHERITANCE

It has taken only a few paragraphs in the text for 40 years to pass, and just as the Lord had promised, a whole generation of Israelites has died off in the wilderness. As Parashat Pinchas unfolds, the next generation is now preparing to follow the Lord into the Promised Land. While they were encamped in the Jordan valley, on the east bank of the Jordan River, everyone's eyes began to look west, toward the Promised Land. Parashat Pinchas, accordingly, begins with a new census. Like the first census in Bamidbar, this second one is for military purposes. A war with the Canaanites needed to take place in order for the children of Israel to receive their inheritance.

Did we say, "Inheritance"? Yes, inheritance! Perhaps as they were thinking about the upcoming battles, many would have looked beyond the fighting toward settling the Land. Thus, an important part of this parasha discusses the process for the distribution of each tribe's inheritance.

Previously in the Torah, the Lord had made promises to Israel about the inheritance that He had planned for them. Our parasha shows how this promise was becoming a reality. Since we

---

285. Milgrom, *JPS: Numbers*, 237.

have not previously discussed the subject of "inheritance" in detail, this passage affords us an appropriate opportunity to do so. We will approach the subject with the following outline:

I.   The Promise of an Inheritance
II.   The Partakers of the Inheritance
III. The Procurement of the Inheritance
IV.   The Partition of the Inheritance

I. The Promise of an Inheritance

One of the most fundamental promises that God made with Israel was the promise of an inheritance. This promise is part of the covenant that God made with Abraham (Genesis 12 and 15) and confirmed with Isaac and Jacob. In addition to the inheritance, there were other equally significant features of that covenant, such as the promise of offspring and greatness. Our focus now, however, is on the promise of the inheritance — the promise of land to the descendants of Abraham.

The main Hebrew word that we render "inheritance" is *nachal* (נחל). In the Scriptures, this word has been used to describe an estate received by a child from his parents. Likewise, it is accordingly used to describe the land received by the children of Israel as a gift from God.[286] This promise of a piece of sacred real estate is also confirmed to Moshe and the children of Israel in Exodus 6:8, where the Lord gives encouragement to Moshe for the difficult task for which He has chosen him. This encouragement came in the form of promises to which God committed Himself out of His love and grace, for Israel. The last of these promises states, "I shall bring you to the Land about which I raised my hand to give it to Abraham, Isaac, and Jacob and I shall give it to you as a heritage — I am the Lord!"

II. The Partakers of the Inheritance

It was the custom in the Ancient Near East for the family inheritance to be passed on to the first-born son. However, as far as we can determine, nowhere was it a law written in the Word of God that the first-born *must* receive the inheritance. As we know, Abraham had two sons, Isaac and Ishmael. Isaac was always considered the son of The Promise, the inheritor of the covenant, the receiver of the Land. Yet, he was not Abraham's first-born. It is interesting to note that, while God promised of Ishmael, "I will make a great nation of him" (Genesis 21:18), as far as we can determine, God did not specifically promise a specific parcel of land to him, like He did to Abraham and Isaac. Though God promised that Ishmael would be a great nation (Genesis 21:13, 18), He did not promise a particular piece of land to him and his descendants. He merely said that they "lived in the wilderness of Paran." Apparently, his descendants were destined to wander throughout the Near East as Bedouins.

Likewise, Jacob was not Isaac's first-born, yet he also received the inheritance promised to his grandfather, Abraham and his father Isaac. it was the descendants of Jacob's twelve sons who

286. *The International Standard Bible Encyclopaedia*, vol. 2, 824.

were given the specific Land of Canaan as an inheritance upon which to settle. Esau was to be confined to the land east of Canaan (present-day southern Jordan)

The Holy One referred to Israel as His first-born son. We find this in Exodus 4:22, which reads, "So said the Lord, 'My first-born son is Israel'." As God's first-born, therefore, Israel stood in the position to receive a special inheritance from the Lord. This inheritance was the Land.

III. Procurement of the Inheritance

It is clear from Genesis that the inheritance was a grace gift to the children of Israel. However, in the sovereign plan of God, the Eternal One established that the Land was to be secured by battle and enjoyed by faithfulness to the Covenant. Let us explore these ideas further.

1. The Fighting Force

Numbers records that at least twice in the wilderness, Moshe took a census of the children of Israel. It is specifically stated that one of the purposes for these censuses was the organization of ex-slaves into an efficient fighting unit — an army. To be sure, Israel had to defend itself, but God made it equally clear that Israel would also be an offensive army. In short, He was preparing them to face the battles that they would have to endure in the process of taking the Land of Promise from the Canaanites.

2. Why Fight for the Inheritance?

It seems that we have encountered somewhat of a contradiction at this point. It has been stated that inheriting the Land was a fulfilment of the *promise* of an inheritance (in the similar context of the other promises that God made to Abraham as unconditional). In other words, these promises were a gift to Israel out of the grace and kindness of their Father who chose them to serve Him. (See our comments on Genesis chapter 15 for some important details about this gift and God's promises given by oath.) If, according to Genesis 15:7, God gave to Abraham and his descendants the Land as a gift, then why did Israel have to fight the Canaanites in order to possess the inheritance? Why did the Lord not just peacefully bring Israel to the Land where they could quietly enter into it and begin their normal lives?

3. Not Salvation!

In order to solve this problem, we need to understand our symbols and pictures. If God used Israel and His relationship with her to picture the believer's relationship with Him (and He did), then we need to have the correct symbolism.

As Israel was facing the battle for the Land — the inheritance — they did so as a redeemed community! The Land could not be theirs until they were first redeemed! Long ago, God promised that Land to them, but for that to happen, He had to first redeem them. Taking possession of the Land, then, was not redemption; it was the place where the redeemed community lived out their redemption. Hence, as far as symbols go, the Land does not represent our redemption and/or salvation. The Exodus pictures that. Instead, the Land pictures what our life would be like here on planet earth *as redeemed people* — the redeemed life as it is lived out.

Yet, the land was called Israel's inheritance. Accordingly, when we are spiritually redeemed, we also received an inheritance. To connect these two, we need to remember that the Land as it was then, and is now, is only a small part of the inheritance. There is yet a glorious future for this Land which God has in store for redeemed Israel. It has not yet come to pass. We can only catch small glimpses of it in this life.

In the same way, our present life on planet earth as redeemed people, as wonderful as it is to be new creations, is not all that will be of our eternal inheritance. We all await a glorious future with the Messiah when we will have new bodies to live on a recreated earth in a recreated heaven. As for our lives here and now, we can only catch little glimpses of what that glorious future inheritance may hold. Just as ancient Israel struggled, the experience of our inheritance now must be one of battle and trial in our serving the One Who redeemed us.

4. "Temporal" vs. "Glorious"

Thus, we can call the Land to which Israel was heading, their "temporary inheritance", as opposed to their "glorified inheritance". However, do not get hung up on the nomenclature. Call it what you want as long as we understand that the Land God gave Israel to live in was not the final expression of the glorious inheritance He had in store for them. In the same way, we believers can call our lives here a temporary inheritance. In it, we experience temporal joys in our relationship with God and with other "new creations", but we also await the permanent, glorious expression of our inheritance where the joy will be unspeakable!

5. Lessons on Life in the Temporary Inheritance

If all this is true, then we can learn a great deal about what it is to live as "new creations" in a land that is basically hostile to us, by merely observing how Israel was to live in their non-glorified inheritance. Here are some of these lessons.

Life is a Battle

Israel was poised for battle. It was real war. There were going to be casualties, blood, and trouble. Taking the Promised Land was not going to be easy. The temporary inheritance was going to be difficult to secure.

We can also remember that our temporary inheritance may be hard to live. We, too, face challenging battles. However, just knowing that battles are normal for our lives makes it a little easier to live them. Some people think that life for a believer should be easy or easier than what it seems. Sickness should not afflict us, they say, if we have faith. Financial problems should not overwhelm us, they contend, if we just believe God for more. Family troubles should not be a part of our living, they assert, if we just raise our kids God's way.

All of that sounds good on paper, but in actual practice, we all know life sometimes does not happen the way some well-meaning spiritual advisors say it should. Sometimes we can try to muster all the faith we can, but that disease or ailment just does not get healed. Other times we can trust to the best of our new creation ability, but even though we believe that God is able to provide for our needs, the money does not always seem to come! Finally, we may be practising all of the biblical principles of child raising, but then we learn that children are not computers that give the proper response when the correct buttons are pushed.

All of this has no reflection on any supposed inability on God's part or any feigned weakness of His Word. It is just that God calls us to listen to Him regardless of the results. God has called us to trust Him no matter what our circumstances.

The battle for Israel to win the Land was a lot easier to face once they knew that it was a battle that required the effort of the entire nation. Likewise, our battles can be easier to endure if we remember that fighting them requires our whole selves. Furthermore, Israel was called to follow their General Joshua even if they did not understand how his particular commands could result in victory. Hence, it is the same for us. We need to learn to follow our "General" — Yeshua, even when we do not understand how His instructions will be able to result in victory.

A Visible Enemy

From the beginning of the promise of the inheritance, God made it clear who the enemies were. He said in Genesis 15:18–21, "To your descendants I give this land, from the river of Egypt to the great river, the Euphrates-the land of the Kenites, the Kenizzites, Kadmonites, Hittites, Perizzites, Rephaites, Amorites, Canaanites, Girgashites, and Jebusites." These nations did not have the God-given right to be living on the Sacred Land. They were poachers! The Land was God's Land; it was His to give and no one else's. The Torah states it clearly in Leviticus 25:23, and the Prophet Isaiah confirms this in chapter 8 when he calls the Land of Israel, Immanuel's Land. It was the Owner's decision to let Israel be the caretaker of the Land. As such He designed Israel to be holy and set apart from the others. This Land, in short, was to be a little enclave where righteousness, justice, and love would be lived out for all to see and know what its Owner was like.

However, in the course of time, others came to live in the Land. They were the nations described in Genesis 15:18–21. They did not have a God-given right to live there. For one thing, God had decided that this was to be the place where His chosen people would dwell. Beyond that, however, these nations worshipped other gods. As if that were not bad enough, in worshipping those other gods, they committed some of the most repugnant religious, ethical, and moral atrocities the world has ever known. They were, in reality, spiritually polluting Immanuel's Land.

It is in this light that God warned Israel in Numbers 35:33 to not commit murder, for "the land will not have atonement for the blood that was spilled in it, except through the blood of the one who spilled it." Even though this is firstly a reference to Israel, the principle holds true for anyone who dwells in this sacred real estate. Since the illegal inhabitants continually shed innocent blood in their serving their idols, they had grossly polluted the Land. That blood had to be "atoned for". Hence, God used Israel as the means of "atonement" when He called Israel to wipe out all of the "sinful usurpers" of His land. Thus, the Canaanites and other people groups who were living in the Land of Promise were Israel's outward visible enemies. War had to be waged on these enemies because they were not willing to freely give up the territory they claimed for their own sinful end.

Believers also have outward enemies. We may think that these are the people who persecute us for our faith. In a sense, that may be true. However, we are not called to wage war on those people. Yeshua called us, instead, to pray for them. The real outward enemy of the believer is "the flesh". This, according to Romans 7 is that part of us where sin dwells. Sin used to be so much a part of us that we could be called sinners. However, things drastically changed when Messiah came into our lives. The "old man" died as stated in Romans 6, and we became new creations, alive in Messiah. Beyond that, however, sin lost its place of dominance. Before, we could hardly say "no" to sin. It ruled us. Now however, we can definitely resist its temptation. We are new people! Sin has lost its domineering grip on our lives and because of that, sin wages war against us. Resisting it can be a real battle. Romans chapter 7 describes how severe the struggle can be. However, the very fact that we are called upon to resist sin and yield our members to righteousness implies that God has given us the ability to do it with victory. This enemy can be defeated!

An Invisible Enemy

When Israel was fighting the Canaanites, they were fighting a much bigger enemy than they may have realized. They were, in reality, fighting the evil spiritual forces that empowered the Canaanites. Behind all of the Canaanite gods, idols, and fiendish practices, were innumerable demons calling all of the shots. Israel could see the Canaanites. The demons they could not always see. The way this unseen war was to be fought was rather interesting. God called Israel to wage war on the outward, visible enemy, the enemy that served as the tool for the invisible one. At the same time as that war was being fought, God's heavenly army fought on the spiritual, invisible level.

We get a glimpse of this spiritual battle in Joshua 5:13–15. Just as Joshua was to lead Israel in their first battle inside the land, he was suddenly confronted by "a man standing opposite him with his sword drawn in his hand" (5:13). When Joshua inquired about his identity, the man said, "I indeed come now as captain of the host of the Lord" (5:14). The Hebrew literally reads, "I am the head of the army of the Lord." From this encounter, we learn that another battle was going on in the invisible realm as the visible battle was taking place. Both battles were just as real, just as important and, equally essential to be fought.

It is exactly the same in our temporary inheritance. Our lives on planet earth as redeemed people will hold many battles in the visible realm, especially against our flesh. Paul also reminds us of the other battles taking place in the heavenly places that we cannot always see. He says in

Ephesians 6:12, "For our struggle is not against flesh and blood, but against the rulers, against the powers, against the world-forces of this darkness, against the spiritual forces of wickedness in the heavenly places".

After saying this, however, he provides us with an unusual hint regarding how to fight in this invisible realm. As for the Israelites, the head of the Lord's army identified Himself to the General of Israel's army. However, in this unseen battle which Paul is describing, he tells us to put the armour on and don the weapons! Why? It is simply because we also have the same Commander that the Joshua of old had. Only, this Commander is also inside of us! He indwells us! Moreover, He equips us to learn how to let Him fight the battles through us. That Commander is the Messiah!

God Keeps the War Going!

Israel conquering their inheritance teaches us yet another lesson. It was not just one battle that they had to fight. It was an ongoing war. It is true that they were called to wipe out their entire enemy, every man, woman, child, and beast. However, in Deuteronomy 7:22 God warned Israel, "The Lord your God will drive out those nations before you, little by little. You will not be allowed to eliminate them all at once, or the wild animals will multiply around you."

One reason why the war had to continue slowly and not be finished all at once was for a very practical reason. If all of the inhabitants had been wiped out at once, Israel would have been too overwhelmed with the wild animals who would be given free rein in the rather desolated land. Israel did not realize this. God had to tell them. It was an unforeseen danger. By informing them, God demonstrated that no matter what, He would always be looking out for His people, especially in their struggles.

The parallels to our lives are obvious. We sometimes get so caught up in our "wars" that we are unable to watch out for the many dangers that may be lurking right before our eyes. The Lord, however, does see them and He is "our rear guard", so to speak. "He neither slumbers nor sleeps," continually protecting us. Sometimes He seems to keep our battles going when we think they should have ended a long time ago. One reason He does so is to protect us when we are not quite prepared to handle life without a war!

To Learn and to Test

We see at least two additional lessons that we can learn from Israel conquering her inheritance. These lessons are both from Judges 3:1-4. Judges 3:2 says that God prolonged the war so that a new generation may be taught how to fight God's battles. That seems rather strange to the pacifists among us. However, the truth stands. Israel always needed to defend herself. That meant that she always needed to learn how to fight. Believers are the same. The struggles continue sometimes because God is continually in the process of training His spiritual army.

Those of us who live in the land of Israel today have a catch phrase that we use among ourselves to help us get through some of the extraordinary difficulties we face while living here.

Whenever a particular struggle comes, we remind each other "this is *haganah*." The Haganah was the illegal Israeli defence force while Israel was still Palestine and under the British Mandate. They had to learn to fight in order to survive the imminent war they would face with the Arabs once the British Mandate was over. However, the British would not let them legally exist. So, they had to surreptitiously train for war. It was a difficult, but necessary training and it encompassed every part of one's being. During the day, the Haganah volunteers were shopkeepers, waitresses, teachers, or mothers. At night, they sacrificially learned how to fight. Thus, we all need to be a "spiritual Haganah" and let God teach us how to continually fight His battles.

The second reason why the war was prolonged for the Israelites is stated in Judges 3:4. It says that God allowed some of the enemies to hang around in order "to test Israel, to find out if they would listen to the commandments…" (our translation). The Torah actually says that God allowed some of the enemy to remain. We need to remember this during our struggles. It is God who has purposely planned these difficult times in order to test us, to see if we would learn to obey Him and live life according to His teachings.

IV. The Partition of the Inheritance

The land was given to the nation of Israel as a possession. How did it become the possession of each of the twelve tribes and their families? Numbers gives us part of the answer. We are told in 26:52–56 that there were two criteria which had to be considered when the inheritance was distributed to the people of Israel. The first was the size of the tribe. "For the more numerous you shall increase his inheritance, and for the fewer, you shall lessen his inheritance, each one according to his count shall his inheritance be given." The second criterion was how the lot turned out. For we are told that once the land was divided according to size of the tribe, then they used lots to determine which tract of land should go to which tribe.

We assume that Jacob's prophecy (Genesis 49) about the particular tribe would also be considered in the distribution of the inheritance. In addition to all of that, Numbers 27:1–11 describes how the Lord gave additional instruction on how to give an inheritance to a family that has no sons.

It is not important for our purposes to go into what the Talmud says will be different about the inheritance in the world to come. It is important to note however, that the sages of old recognized that the inheritance would be different in the world to come. It will be similar, yet vastly different. As far as the land is concerned, there is every indication from the Scriptures that the redeemed remnant (saved Israel) will indeed, live in the same general geographic location as this present inheritance. Things however will be drastically different.

In the future world, the "lion will lay down with the lamb;" "swords will be beaten into ploughshares," and "nations will not learn war anymore." Moreover, there will be real justice and equity. There will be safety from all dangers and the Torah will be studied from Jerusalem and throughout the rest of the world.

The above is what the prophet Isaiah speaks of in chapters 2 and 11 of his prophecy. In addition, Ezekiel gives us more details about the permanent boundaries of the inheritance. He says, "And you shall divide it for an inheritance, each one equally with the other, for I swore to give it to your forefathers, and this land shall be to you as an inheritance." (47:14)

Why will anyone want to become part of that future inheritance? Perhaps they will so desire for at least two reasons. First, at that time Israel will be functioning and behaving according to all that the Torah said she would be. She will be the place where year in and year out all of the sacred and joyful festivals will be kept unto the Lord. She will be the place where there will be abundant fruit and produce will be reaped from the sacred soil of the land. She will be the place where all the treasures of the Torah and the rest of the Bible will be discussed, taught, and disseminated.

As wonderful as all of that sounds, there is yet one more compelling reason why non native-born Israelites will want a piece of this inheritance. Isaiah the prophet phrases it perfectly for us: "And many peoples will come and say, 'Come let us go up to the mountain of the Lord, to the House of the God of Jacob; that He may teach us concerning His ways and that we may walk in His paths…" (Isaiah 2:3). Why will believers want to live in the future glorious inheritance, the land of Israel, in the world to come? Simply, to be able to be in as close proximity as possible to the King who will be reigning in Jerusalem, to the Landlord Himself, Immanuel, the Holy One of Israel who died for us so that we can receive an imperishable inheritance. Believers will want to be here just because they want to be as near as possible to the Great Shepherd of the sheep, Messiah Yeshua.

ADDITIONAL NOTES

Chapter 25

Verse 11
"**My zeal**" — Pinchas was just as upset about the situation as God was.

Verse 12
"**covenant of peace**" — Literally this reads, "Covenant of Shalom", in Hebrew. This could mean that God guaranteed Pinchas personal safety against any possible revenge directed toward him for taking these lives. It is different from the next covenant God makes with him, the covenant of the priesthood.

Verse 13
"**covenant of a lasting priesthood**" — Gordon Wenham notes that "Israel had broken the covenant by worshipping foreign gods. Phinehas has restored that covenant by his deed and is therefore rewarded with the covenant of a perpetual priesthood, a reward that mirrors the sin

atoned for."[287] Milgrom and Wenham disagree about the nature of that covenant of priesthood. Milgrom says it does not refer to the High Priesthood because the text merely mentions "priesthood" and not "High Priesthood".[288] Wenham suggests that it does refer to the High Priesthood. Hertz, agreeing with Wenham, says that with the brief exception of Eli, the High Priesthood continued in Pinchas' family until the fall of the Jewish state.[289]

Verse 17

"**be hostile to…**" — The Hebrew word "be hostile to" is *tsarur* (צרור). It carries the idea of showing hostility toward someone or treating them as an enemy, not merely harassing them as if there is an occasional vexing.[290]

Chapter 26

Verse 1

This is the first time since the death of Aaron that Moshe and Eleazar are addressed together by the Lord.

Verse 2

The Census —This census here in Numbers 26 and that of Numbers chapters 1 and 3 have some differences. First in this census the family names are stated, and not just the numbers. Second, there is an obvious difference in the totals. Wenham notes that the total population at this point is almost the same as that when they were numbered at Sinai. Here it is 601,730 (26:51) and at Sinai it was 603,550 (1:46).[291] Remember that they are just counting men who are of military age (20 years old and older). The tribes of Reuven, Gad, Ephraim, Naphtali, and Simeon all decreased in size while the rest increased.

"**take a census**" — Rashi suggests two reasons for the new census. Firstly, he says it is because God wanted to show concern for his people in a similar way that a shepherd would take stock of his flock after an attack from wolves. Secondly, Rashi observes that when the Israelites were handed over to Moshe after they left Egypt, they were counted before he assumed leadership. So, likewise, as Moshe is about to die, he hands them back to the Lord but not before they are counted again.[292]

Verses 9–10

"**Dathan and Abiram**" — Despite the fact that this was a normal census to determine who was of fighting age, the Holy One saw fit to mention the marred family background of these people. The text refers to what happened to them as a *nes* (נס), a miracle/sign. "This event was a warning

---

287. Gordon Wenham, *Numbers* (TOTC), 188.
288. See Milgrom, *JPDS: Numbers*, 216–217, and Wenham, *Numbers*, 188, respectively.
289. Hertz, *Pentateuch and Haftarahs*, 686.
290. BDB, 865.
291. Wenham, *Numbers*, 190.
292. Rashi: *Bamidbar*, ArtScroll Edition, 323.

and a reminder for the future that no one should oppose the right of Aaron and his descendants to the priesthood."[293]

Verse 28

"**Manasseh and Ephraim**" — They are listed according to their order of birth rather than according to the order of blessing in Genesis 49. "This is probably because of the former's growth and the latter's diminution during the time between the two censuses."[294]

Verse 33

Daughters are rarely mentioned in genealogies. However, because Zelophehad had no sons, the mention of them was required for legal inheritance purposes.

Verse 53

How did the whole process of choosing lots for the Land actually work? The closest we can come to knowing how the partition actually may have happened in the Book of Joshua is by reading what both Bamidbar Rabbah and the Talmud say about it. They provide a similar description of the ceremony of allocating the land. We will quote the Midrash at length for us to get the fullest impact of what it says. (Bamidbar Rabbah 21:9; and the Talmudic reference is B. B. 122a.)

> Eleazar the son of Aaron was invested with the Urim and Tummim, while the urn for the lots stood before Joshua (Joshua 18:6). Before the lot ever came up Eleazar would say, inspired by the Holy Spirit: 'The lot of such-and-such a tribe is coming up and indicates that he shall receive his territory in such-and-such a place.' Joshua would put out his hand and the said lot would come up, as it says (Joshua 19:51). The following additional miracle happened, namely, that the lot as it came up would cry out: 'I am the lot of such-and-such a tribe and have come up to assign him to such-and-such a territory.' How do we know that the lot spoke? Because it is written, 'By the mouth of the Lord shall their inheritance be divided'."

The Talmud confirms this rendition but adds a few more details. For example, it tells us that the urim and tummim functioned to confirm what the lot said and that before Joshua drew from the urn it was shaken up. But the Talmud adds one further piece of information for us, which will lead our thinking to a different level. While discussing the procedure about the division of the land into inheritances for the tribes, the Talmud looks to the future. It says, "And the division in the world to come will not be like the division in this world…" (Bava Batra 122a).

Verse 57

The Levite census was taken separately from the rest of the nation because the Levites were exempt from military service.

Chapter 27

Verse 1

Wenham keenly observes, "From a legal point of view the case of the daughters of Zelophehad is extremely interesting. It shows how many of the laws in the Bible came to be enacted. When a problem arose without previous precedent, it was referred to Moses, who then sought the Lord's

293. Munk, *The Call of the Torah: Bamidbar*, 322.
294. Milgrom, *JPS: Numbers,* 223.

direction. The decision then became a precedent for future similar cases. It seems likely that many of the case laws in the Old Testament originated in a similar way."[295]

Verse 3

"**our father died**" — The daughters were careful to note that their father did not die in the Korach rebellion. Rather his death was part of the general penalty God put on that entire generation. Because of this they felt that their father's name should not be lost. Hence, their appeal for an inheritance since he had no sons or close relatives.

Verse 7

"**What ….the daughters are saying is right**" — Hertz comments, "Happy is that mortal, whose words are acknowledged to be true by God."[296]

Verse 7

"**property as an inheritance**" — The Hebrew reads, *ahzot nakhalah* (אחזת נחלה). Milgrom points out that *ahuzzah* (אחזה) [singular of ahzot] is a technical term denoting inalienable property received from a sovereign, while *nahalah* (נחלה) refers to inalienable property transmitted by inheritance. "The land seized by the Israelites ('ahuzzah) will become their inheritance (nahalah)."[297]

Verse 12

"**Abarim**" — Most scholars equate this with Mount Pisgah, one of the peaks of Mount Nebo, clearly visible as it rises high above the Jordan valley east of Jericho.

Verse 13

"**as your brother Aaron**" — "The rabbis explain this to mean that like Aaron he [Moshe] was to die 'by the mouth of the Lord', i.e. his also would be 'death by a divine kiss'."[298]

Verse 16

"**May the Lord, the God of the spirits of all mankind**" — The Hebrew can also be rendered "The Lord, the God of the spirits of all flesh…" "Moshe prays to God of the spirits to appoint as leader a man in whom is the feeling spirit, to bear each person with his individual temperament."[299] The only other time Moshe uses this expression of God is when he intercedes for the life of all Israel after the Korach incident (16:22). Hence, both here and there, he appeals to God "as the giver of life [who] must be specially concerned with the continued existence of His chosen people, Israel."[300]

Verse 18

"**lay your hand on him**" — This is the same process used in rabbinical and evangelical ordination. Here the verb is *samakh* (סמך), the basis for the Jewish term "ordination", *smikhah*.

295. Wenham, *Numbers*, 192.
296. Hertz, *Pentateuch and Haftarahs*, 692.
297. Milgrom, *JPS: Numbers*, 232.
298. Hertz, *Pentateuch and Haftarahs*, 692.
299. Munk, *The Call of the Torah: Bamidbar*, 340.
300. Wenham, *Numbers*, 194.

As this passage indicates, ordination must involve a laying on of hands, symbolically transferring authority and ability to the person who is being ordained.

Verse 20

"**some of your authority**" — The rabbis are quick to point out that the text indicates that Joshua was to receive only "some" of Moshe's authority. Perhaps this is because Moshe received instruction and directions directly from God whereas Joshua was to receive directions from God through the priest using the urim and tummim.

Chapters 28–29

These chapters deal with the sacrifices that are to be offered when they enter the Land of Canaan. To be sure, much of this material is presented elsewhere, so what are the differences in this presentation from the others? There are several.

First, these chapters describe the type and number of sacrifices that are to be offered on a daily basis by the priests for the people, whereas other listings of sacrifices dealt with what the people were to bring. Thus, secondly, here in Numbers 28–29, these sacrifices concentrate on the priestly duties as opposed to the obligations of the laymen. They list the minimum number of sacrifices on a daily basis for the entire year. Since they are daily offerings, then the list also includes the daily offerings required during the mo'adim. These chapters follow a very natural organization to these chapters in that we learn of daily, then weekly, then monthly, and finally annual offerings:

1. 28:2–8 | Daily burnt offerings
2. 28:9–11 | Weekly Shabbat offerings
3. 28:11–15 | Regular monthly offerings (on Rosh Hodesh, the New Moon)
4. 28:16–29:38 | The annual offerings for the mo'adim

STUDY QUESTIONS

1. What do you think the "covenant of peace" meant to Pinchas? What do you think was the purpose for it?

2. Was Pinchas justified to act without a trial? Why or why not? What principle can we draw upon for future zealots?

3. Why did God single out and publicly name a specific Israelite and Midianite who were playing the harlot with each other?

4. Why did God command the Midianites, and not the Moabites along with them, to be smitten by the Israelites?

5. How do you think Moshe felt about this since his first wife, Zippora was a Midianite?

6. Compare this census with the first one found in Numbers. What are the similarities and differences?

7. What is the reason for this second census?

8. How were the land allocations decided?

9. What do you think of using the "lot"? Should we still use it today or not? Explain.

10. How important is the physical inheritance of land compared to the spiritual inheritance believers possess? Explain.

11. If, as some would say, the physical inheritance is not important, then why does the Torah put so much emphasis on it?

12. Why do the prophets (i.e. Ezekiel) tell us about a future physical inheritance?

13. What attitude toward women do you discern from the Torah, especially in the light of 27:1–11?

14. Why was Moshe not permitted to enter the Promised Land?

15. Why do you think Moshe's sons were not considered as his successors?

16. What characteristics were Moshe and the Lord looking for in a potential successor?

17. Why do you think Joshua was chosen? Why not Caleb?

18. What do you think Moshe may have been thinking when he was standing on the mountain that God told him to ascend?

19. What was the procedure of succession?

20. What does it mean to have Moshe's "majesty" pass on to Joshua?

21. Why do you think that there is additional teaching on the offerings at this point in Numbers?

22. What "Torah Picture" do the tamid offerings paint?

23. What "Torah Picture" do the mussaf offerings paint?

PARASHAT MATOT מטות
PARASHAT MASEI מסעי

TORAH: NUMBERS 30:2–36:13
HAFTARAH: JEREMIAH 2:4–28; 3:4

Parashat Matot מטות, Parashat Masei מסעי

THE TRAVELOGUE

This double portion are the final parshiyot in the book of Numbers. They are often combined into a double portion, as we are doing here. The contents cover a variety of subjects such as the Levitical and refuge cities, the teachings about murder and manslaughter, the final borders of Israel, and the division of the Promised Land. The section, however, upon which we will focus our studies, is a travelogue that Moshe compiled through divine inspiration. It consists of the places the children of Israel stopped during their forty years of wandering after leaving Egypt.

We will use this list of locations in our commentary for much the same reason it was written — as a memorial to what transpired between Israel and the Lord at each given location. Of course, it is impossible to comment on every site because we do not know what happened at every place listed within this reading. However, as we come across these places in other parashiyot, we will comment on them.

By the end of this commentary, and the book of Numbers, we will have a great historical journal of the relationship between the Lord and Israel. Accordingly, we will also be afforded an opportunity to see what Israel learned about the Messiah in that early stage of their history as a nation. The outline for our study will be the three main divisions of travel that Moshe specifies in his journal. Hence, it will look like this:

I.   The First Division — The Exodus to Rephidim   33:1–14
II. The Second Division — Rephidim to the Death of Aaron (Mount Hor) 33:15–41
III. The Third Division— Mount Hor to the Plains of Moab   33:42–49

I. THE FIRST DIVISION: THE EXODUS TO REPHIDIM   33:1–14

The travelogue begins by informing us that the Israelites moved out "by divisions" (33:1). This is a clear indication that as God was moving them, He was also forming a great army, the army of the Lord.

A. Rameses (33:3–4) — Slavery/Redemption/Pesach

The name of the first location is Rameses. This, of course is where it all began. This is one of the places where Israel was enslaved and building a store city for Pharaoh. This also would have been the place where the slaying of the firstborn occurred. In addition, it was at Rameses that the first Pesach was celebrated. Then from Rameses, "The Israelites set out on the fifteenth day of the first month, the day after the Pesach. They marched out boldly in full view of the Egyptians, who were burying all their firstborn, whom the Lord had struck down among them; for the Lord had brought judgement on their gods" (33:3-4).

It was here that Israel came to know the misery of slavery and the feeling of desperation to be rescued. It was also here that they saw first-hand, the mighty things that their God, whom they thought was apathetic to their cause, could do on their behalf. Finally, at Rameses, they received their first serving of the nourishing Torah — the teaching about keeping Pesach.

Thus, this first part of Moshe's entry was therefore the place where the children of Israel had their first lessons on what it means to be redeemed people and a holy community. This was the first preparation for them to begin to understand about the redeeming and saving work of the Messiah.

For notes on the location referred to as "Rameses," please see the commentary on Exodus, Parashat Shemot. We summarize these comments here. "In the 13th century BCE, Rameses II built a great capital… and it became known as Rameses from that time on."[301] It was only named Rameses *after* Pharaoh Rameses II rebuilt it again some 200 years after the Israelites exited Egypt. Ancient cities were built and rebuilt over many centuries at this location. Spread over eight square miles beneath the modern villages of Tell el-Dab'a, Qantir and Ezbet Helmi, today are the consecutive ancient Egyptian cities of Rowaty, Avaris, Peru-nefer and Rameses.[302]

Referring to this location where the Israelites were living as "Rameses" in the Torah is a good example of the occasional "scribal updates" we see throughout the Bible. This is where scribes who were copying the Scriptures throughout history saw fit to call locations by the names that were used in *their* day, rather than calling those locations by their archaic names, which few people may have known. "The scribes of antiquity, with the exception of the Sumerians, regularly revised earlier literary material and made such changes in orthography, grammar, and syntax as would update it."[303] Other examples of scribal updates include Bethel (Genesis 12:8; 13:3; and 28:19), Dan (Genesis 14:14; Deuteronomy 34:1; and Judges 18:29), and Samaria (1 Kings 13:32; and 16:24).

Here is a summary of this biblical location called Rameses as it changed names over the centuries. These names all refer to the same location, where Israel was enslaved and living before The Exodus:

Name	Approximate Time Period	Possible Meaning of the Name
Rowaty	Up to about 1800 BCE	"The Door of the Two Roads"
Avaris	About 1800 BCE to about 1550 BCE	"The Royal Foundation of the District"
Perunefer	About 1550 BCE to about late 1200's BCE	"Happy Journey"
Rameses	Mid to late 1200's BCE	The name of a Pharaoh

B. Sukkot and Etham (33:5–6) — Freedom, the Cloud and Fire

With the wonder of Pesach freshly engraved on their minds, the Israelites began to travel. Their first stop was apparently at Sukkot, and then they moved on to Etham. Most scholars generally

301. Bryant Wood, "Recent Research," *Bible and Spade*, Fall 2008, 103.
302. Gary Byers, "New Evidence from Egypt on the Location of the Exodus Sea Crossing: Part II*," Bible and Spade,* August and September 2008. (biblearchaeology.org, search for 'new evidence exodus crossing'.
303. *The International Bible Encyclopaedia*, [ISBE], vol. 1, 226.

understand these places to be located between Lake Timsah and the Bitter Lakes, southeast from where they began their journeying and approximately where the present-day Suez Canal is. See the map 8 below.

We do not know how long they stayed at these places, but it could not have been for more than a few days. However, the buzzword in everyone's mind was surely, "What kind of God do we have? He judges the wicked, He rescues His own, He does miracles, and He wants to be remembered for who He is and the great things He has done."

The Torah also informs us that sometime, beginning either at Sukkot (the location, not the holy day!) or at Etham, the Holy One began to show His sovereign care for them, "By day the Lord went ahead of them in a pillar of cloud to guide them on their way and by night in a pillar of fire to give them light, so that they could travel by day or night. Neither the pillar of cloud by day nor the pillar of fire by night left its place in front of the people" (Exodus 13:21).

C. Pi-Hahirot (33:7) — Crossing the Sea, God's Power

It was unusual for Israel to have passed through this rather obscure place. By all rights, most would have thought that they would have continued a northeast trek along the international coastal trade route, later called the *Via Maris* by the Romans. This most famous ancient trade route which connected Egypt and Africa with Damascus and the East followed the Mediterranean coast as it went through the Promised Land. In Egypt it was called the "Horus Highway." Between Egypt and the southwest coast of Canaan it was called the "Highway to the Philistines." This was, indeed, the most direct route to Canaan. Or, since they found themselves in Midbar Shur (Exodus 15;22) after miraculously crossing the Reed Sea, perhaps another direct route would have been the Shur Highway, which led from Goshen, across northern Sinai Peninsula, to Be'er Sheva.

However, God had other things up His sleeve! We learned in Exodus 14:2–3 that the Lord was tricking Pharaoh into believing that Israel was, "wandering about the land in confusion, hemmed in by the desert." When Pharaoh was thinking this, the Lord said, "I will harden Pharaoh's heart, and he will pursue them. But I will gain glory for myself through Pharaoh and all his army, and the Egyptians will know that I am the Lord" (Exodus 14:4).

Egypt most certainly found out that He was God! Hence, it was at Pi-hahirot that God skillfully orchestrated the miracle of the dividing of the Reed Sea, permitting Israel to cross on dry ground and yet destroying Pharaoh's army, which tried to pursue them. It is noteworthy that (as stated earlier in our studies in Exodus) that Pi-hahirot means either, "Mouth of Freedom" or "Mouth of Canals." Here, Israel chose freedom rather than submission again to slavery.

Map 8: Eastern Nile Delta. Follow the dotted line to see a possible route for the Exodus

Undoubtedly, when Israel thought of this place, they, therefore, thought "Salvation! Miracle! Judgment for Egypt! Deliverance for us"! This then, became the paradigm for all future lessons on salvation and deliverance, including the salvation of Messiah.

D. Marah (33:8) — Testing

From the crossing of the water, they went further south to one of the places that they would have liked to forget. They came to the bitter waters of Marah. We are not sure if it was originally called Marah or if Israel named it such. The Hebrew word *marah* (מרה) means "bitter". It referred to the water that was found there ". . . For they [the waters] were bitter; therefore, it was named Marah" (Exodus 15:23). The name Marah also referred to the reaction of the thirsty Israelites when they found that the water was unfit. They became embittered and, "So the people grumbled at Moshe. . ." (Exodus 15:24).

However, this is where the Almighty's training began. The bitter waters were no accident for Him! For, "there He tested them" and He taught them by saying, "If you will listen carefully to the voice of the Lord your God and do what is right in his eyes, if you pay attention to his commands and keep all his decrees, I will not bring on you any of the diseases I brought on the Egyptians, for I am the Lord who heals you" (Exodus 15:26). Bitterness is one of the "diseases of Egypt."

Hence, Marah became a place where the Israelites would remember that they began to grumble against the Lord who had just redeemed them. They also would have remembered it as the place where He lovingly tested them and taught them some of their first lessons as a redeemed community.

E. Elim (33:9) — Relief, Sweetness of God's Rest

As bitter as both the waters and the lessons were at Marah, the Holy One countered that experience by leading them to Elim, "where there were twelve springs of water and seventy date palms, and they camped there beside the waters" (Exodus 15:27).

Many suggest that the present-day site called Uyum-Musa or "Springs of Moshe", a large oasis just south of the Suez Canal on the east side, is the place where they were. What a pleasant memory that site must have been for them. In this memory, they would have thought of the Lord as the one who refreshes their life with sweetness. They would have considered that the Holy One was indeed, their Good Shepherd providing for them. Furthermore, Rabbi Alan Ullman suggests that Elim, with its 70 date palm trees and 12 springs of water, may have also reminded the Israelites of their beginnings.[304] They were 12 tribes and 70 people when they came down to Egypt. Now they are still 12 tribes and greatly multiplied as they exit from slavery to head back home to the Land of Promise.

F. The Reed Sea (33:10) — Thought and Contemplation

Nothing is mentioned elsewhere about this particular trip to the sea. It is, apparently, a return to the body of water that was the scene of one of the most memorable miracles in Israel's history. Perhaps upon their return, however brief, the Lord wanted them to think and contemplate on what He did here to release them from the Egyptians. However, this was not the section of the body of water where the great miracle occurred. The reference here in Numbers is therefore a little confusing.

G. The Wilderness of Sin (33:11) — Quail and Manna, God's Provision

So it came about at evening that the quails came up and covered the camp, and in the morning there was a layer of dew around the camp. When the layer of dew evaporated, behold, on the surface of the wilderness there was a fine flake-like thing, fine as the frost on the ground. When the sons of Israel saw it, they said to one another, "What is it?" For they did not know what it was. And Moshe said to them, "It is the bread which the Lord has given you to eat" (Exodus 16:13–15).

After another brief stopover at the Sea, God led the children of Israel to the Wilderness of Sin (מדבר סין). To English speakers, this sounds as if it must have been a very bad place, for it was a Wilderness of "sin". However, do not be confused because of the languages! The English word "sin" in this instance is just a transliteration of the Hebrew word (סין) and has nothing to do with sin!

Here we recall the giving of the quails and the manna. This was to be their diet for about the

---

304. Rabbi Alan Ullman is the former director of Rodef School of Jewish Studies, Newton, MA (USA). This suggestion was made in a class on Exodus 15-19 many tears ago as s student.

next forty or so years, until they reached the Promised Land.

Having said all of that, however we must report that it was in the Wilderness of Sin, that Israel gravely sinned! For, when they got hungry for some of the foods they left behind in Egypt, "...the whole congregation of the sons of Israel grumbled against Moshe and Aaron in the wilderness" (Exodus 16:2). In response, the Lord made a special appearance of His glory and promised that He would feed them with special provision that they would never forget.

H. Dophkah, Alush, Rephidim (33:12–14) — Water from the Rock and "The Lord is My Sign"

It is not often that we find a comment in this journal about what happened at a particular location. However, in 33:14 we read, "They left Alush and camped at Rephidim, where there was no water for the people to drink."

Modern Wadi Refatid might be the location for ancient Rephidim. It is about thirty miles from the southern tip of the Sinai Peninsula on the western shore of the peninsula. On the other hand, others suggest even more emphatically that "Rephidim can almost certainly be identified with Wadi Feiran, a long, lush valley that leads into the peninsula [Sinai] from the coastal plain."[305]

At this location, the people once again complained to Moshe. When Moshe brought his problem to the Lord, God said,

> Behold, I will stand before you there on the rock at Horeb; and you shall strike the rock, and water will come out of it that the people may drink. And Moshe did so in the sight of the elders of Israel. [As a result, Moshe] . . .named the place Massah and Meribah because of the quarrel of the sons of Israel, and because they tested the Lord, saying, "Is the Lord among us, or not?" (Exodus 17:6–9, NASB),

The testing of the Lord was not the only memorable event that happened at Rephidim. (Although, for some reason, that is the only event that Numbers 33:14 records.) We read in Exodus, "Then Amalek came and fought against Israel at Rephidim" (17:8). According to the account in Exodus, this attack was singled out particularly for an everlasting memory!

What happened was that when Israel went to defend herself against Amalek, Moshe and two others watched Joshua lead Israel victoriously into battle against them. However, the victory was contingent on Moshe holding up his staff,

> So it came about when Moshe held his hand up, that Israel prevailed, and when he let his hand down, Amalek prevailed. But Moshe' hands were heavy. Then they took a stone and put it under him, and he sat on it; and Aaron and Hur supported his hands, one on one side and one on the other. Thus, his hands were steady until the sun set. So, Joshua over-whelmed Amalek and his people with the edge of the sword (Exodus 17:11–13).

The next statement from God, however, truly revealed where His heart and mind were concerning the safety of His chosen people.

---

305. Leen and Kathleen Ritmeyer, *From Sinai to Jerusalem: The Wanderings of the Holy Ark,* 5.

Then the Lord said to Moshe, "Write this in a book as a memorial, and recite it to Joshua, that I will utterly blot out the memory of Amalek from under heaven."' And Moshe built an altar and named it "the Lord is my Banner." And he said, "The Lord has sworn; the Lord will have war against Amalek from generation to generation" (Exodus 17:14–16).

The phrase "the Lord is my Banner" became the byword for this occasion. That particular translation may, however, not be the best. We suggest that it (*Adonai Nissi,* יהוה נסי) be rendered "the Lord is my Miracle", or "the Lord is my Sign".

II. THE SECOND DIVISION: REPHIDIM TO THE DEATH OF AARON

A. Wilderness of Sinai   (33:15) — The Torah

Nothing is said in Numbers chapter 33 about what happened in the Wilderness of Sinai. Then again, probably nothing needed to be said! Just the very mention of the word Sinai was enough to bring to remembrance the major events that took place there.

The actual location of Mt. Sinai has been the source for much discussion. The consensus of most reputable scholars is that Jebel Musa, in the west central Sinai Peninsula, seems to be the best candidate for its location. Leen Ritmeyer says, "At Ras Safsafeh, the peak at the northern extremity of Jebel Musa, one can best visualize the events of the giving of the Torah." Ritmeyer does more than just visualize things. Like most good scholars, he provides what he considers evidence for his position. In the last of his arguments, Ritmeyer suggests, "Most convincing of all is the wide, surrounding plain of Er Rahah, which provided ample space for the terrified Israelites to retreat from the spectacle of the smoking mountain." [306] Finally, Ritmeyer concludes his arguments in favour of the traditional location for Mount Sinai, by saying something not so traditional about its location. He writes, "Although later tradition had chosen the "true Mount Sinai" to be the highest peak of Jebel Musa, with the Monastery of Saint Catherine at its base, it was actually Ras Safsafeh that the early Byzantines identified with the biblical Horeb."[307]

Jacob Milgrom, along with Professor Meneshe Har-El, one of Israel's leading geographers and an expert on the Sinai Peninsula, provides some good reasons why the site called Jebel Sin Bisher (and not the more traditional Jebel Musa in southern Sinai), still in the southwest Sinai, should be identified with Mount Sinai. We quote Milgrom at length about this issue out of deference to this great scholar.

> The identification of Sinai with Jebel Sin Bisher, about 48 kilometers (30 mi.) southeast of Suez, has much to commend it. At 579 meters (1,900 ft.) high and 305 meters (1,000 ft.) above the plain, it alone fits the two distances specified in Scripture: a three-day journey from Egypt (Exod. 3:18) and eleven days from Kadesh-barnea (Deut. 1:2). The widely accepted identification of Mount Sinai with Jebel Musa in southern Sinai has been effectively refuted by Harel on the following grounds: (1) The area cannot support many people; (2) fishing is good here (whereas 11:5 bewails the lack of fish); (3) the many Egyptian-owned mines that were in the area at the

---

306. Ritmeyer *Wanderings*, 5.
307. *Ibid.*

time were guarded by Egyptian troops; (4) Jebel Musa is more than a three-day trip from Egypt (Exod. 5:3) and an eleven-day trip to Kadesh (350 km.; 210 mi.).[308]

Another popular suggestion for the location of Mt. Sinai is in the northern Sinai Peninsula, at a place called Mount Karkom, sometimes referred to as Jebel Ideid. See map 9.

This suggestion is perhaps best stated by Israeli Emanuel Anati. While his research is extensive and seems plausible, in our opinion, it seems to fall short of the evidence for the traditional location in the Southern Sinai. For two excellent essays comparing both possible locations for Mt. Sinai, we suggest reading "Is Mount Karkom the Mountain of God?" by Tali Erickson-Gini and "The Location of Mount Sinai: A Southern View (Jebel Musa)" by Gerald L. Mattingly in the *Lexham Geographic Commentary on the Pentateuch*. (See our Bibliography on page 232).

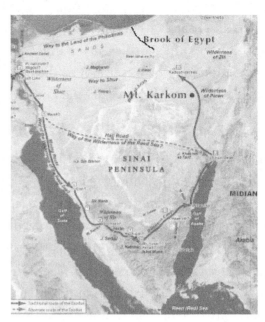

Map 9: Mt. Karkom – Brook of Egypt

Another possible location for Mt. Sinai has been asserted, especially by some pseudo scholars who try to assert that Mt. Sinai is in the western part of the Arabian Peninsula. This theory seems to have gained popularity in some circles of believers in Yeshua. That is why we provide a few comments about it.

We disagree with this theory on many grounds. For one, Milgrom writes, "A location in Edom or Midian (northwestern Arabia) is equally improbable since it would place Mount Sinai too far from Egypt and would also render absurd Hobab's wish to return to his homeland (Numbers 10:29). He would already have been there!"[309] Furthermore, Exodus states that when the Israelites finished crossing the water, "Then Moshe led Israel from the Reed Sea, and they went out into the wilderness of Shur…" (Exodus 15:22). It is well-known that the Wilderness of Shur is in the northwest Sinai and connected Israel's southwest Negev with Egypt. That alone rules out an Arabian Mt. Sinai.

Perhaps the most scholarly refutation of the Arabian Theory might be found in the Fall 2000 edition of *Bible and Spade*, written by Gordon Franz. We do not have the space to treat this subject with the detail that it deserves. However, we will summarize Franz's arguments against Saudi Arabia being the location of the Biblical Mount Sinai.[310] Franz builds his arguments by

308. Jacob Milgrom, JPS: *Numbers,* 280.

309. *Ibid.*, 280.

310. All of the material From Gordon Franz is from the Fall 2000 edition of *Bible and Spade*, 101–113.

attacking the theory's false assumptions.

False Assumption # 1: The Sinai Peninsula was considered the Land of Egypt.

To this Franz retorts, "Egypt exploited the natural resources of Sinai and controlled certain roads in the northern part of the peninsula, but it [The Sinai] was not within the borders of the Land of Egypt."

False Assumption # 2: Mount Sinai is in the Land of Midian.

Franz counters this argument by using the Torah that contradicts this assumption. The first is in Exodus 18:27, where we read that Jethro, Moshe' father-in-law, was only visiting Moshe at Mount Sinai; it was not his home: "Then Moshe sent his father-in-law on his way, and Jethro returned *to his own country*" (italics ours). The second passage is in Numbers 10:30, which says essentially the same thing.

False Assumption # 3: Galatians 4:25 says Mount Sinai is in Saudi Arabia.

This one is easy to refute. First, one needs to realize that Saudi Arabia did not exist in Moshe's day. Secondly, all one needs to do is to study ancient Greek and Roman geography, the geography prevalent during the time that Paul wrote to the Galatians. Geographers and ancient historians such as Strabo, Herodotus, among others, including the translators of the Septuagint, all place the western border of ancient Arabia anywhere between the Nile River and the present-day Gulf of Suez.

Of course, Franz also deals with the so-called archaeological evidence used to support the Saudi Arabian Theory. Citing all of his evidence, including his documentation is beyond the scope of this commentary. We suggest that the student contact the web site of the *Associates for Biblical Research*.[311] So much for Mount Sinai being in the present Saudi Arabian Peninsula.

The most outstanding event that took place at Sinai was, of course, the giving of the Torah. The Lord revealed a good portion of the Torah to Moshe at this location. He received further revelation on the wilderness journey during the next 40 years and then the rest was spoken to him on the Plains of Moab, across from Jericho. Moshe wrote all that God spoke. Because of this revelation, in the wilderness of Sinai, Israel began to "build a house", so to speak. That is, God entered into a sacred marriage with Israel at Sinai. In doing so, He instructed her to do all of the things which are part of setting up a new household: building the "house" (the Mishkan), providing for intimacy in the marriage (sacrifices and priests), establishing special "family" days (the Mo'adim), and so on.

All was not joyful at Sinai, however. Just as Moshe was descending from the mountain and his encounters with God, Israel was engaged in committing spiritual adultery and worshipping the golden calf. In the same way as it was not necessary to mention the giving of the Torah here in this travelogue, so it was also not necessary to mention the golden calf incident. All Israel needed to hear was the word "Sinai" and both would have come to the people's minds.

---

311. *The Associates for Biblical Research*: www. Christian Answers.net/abr/abrhome.html

B. Kibrot-Hatta'avah (33:16): Quail Coming from their Noses!

According to Numbers chapter 11, the people rebelled again at Kibrot-Hattaavah. In this rebellion, the people, once again, complained about their food. This time they wanted more meat. In response, it is recorded,

> Therefore, the Lord will give you meat and you shall eat. You shall eat, not one day, nor two days, nor five days, nor ten days, nor twenty days, but a whole month, until it comes out of your nostrils and becomes loathsome to you; because you have rejected the Lord who is among you and have wept before Him, saying, "Why did we ever leave Egypt?" (Numbers 11:18–20, NASB)

As a result, the Israelites named this location Kibrot-Hattaavah, which means, "the graves of lust". This was so named because they "gorged themselves" on the quail meat.[312] Some memory!

C. Hazerot (33:17): The Humility of Moshe

From Kibrot-Hattaavah the people set out for Hazerot, and they remained at Hazerot, a beautiful valley (Numbers 11:35). The text gives us the impression that it was while they remained at Hazerot, that Miriam and Aaron gossiped against Moshe and challenged his right to lead. In recalling this location therefore, the children of Israel would have remembered the Lord's defence of Moshe when the Lord said, "But this is not true of my servant Moshe; he is faithful in all my house. With him I speak face to face, clearly and not in riddles; he sees the form of the Lord. Why then were you not afraid to speak against my servant Moshe?" (Numbers 12:7–8).

Numbers 33:18–21 mentions several rather obscure places along the Israelite itinerary. "Many of these reference local geographical features (oasis, wadis, wells, rocks, mountains, etc.) where the travellers camped for a time."[313] Examples include this line of campsites visited in sequence: Hazerot in 33:17, meaning "grassy places", Ritmah (33:18), meaning "place of broom trees"), Libnah (33:20, which translates as "white places", and Rissah in 33:21, meaning "moist spot."[314] Paul H. Wright adds: "Unsurprisingly, the majority of these place names, erased by the sands of time, can no longer be identified, although church and local Bedouin traditions help to keep some of the memories alive."[315]

D. Moserot/Moserah (33:31): Aaron's Death

This location of Moserot poses a small problem. According to Numbers 33:30–31, Israel travelled from Moserot to Bene-jaakan. "Moserot" (מוסרות) is in the plural in the Hebrew. However, according to a similar account in Deuteronomy 10:6, they went from Bene-jaakan to Moserah, wherein "Moserah" is spelled in the Hebrew singular. Are "Moserot" and "Moserah" two different locations? It is possible; but one cannot know for sure. If they were two different places, then it would be easy to explain the apparent discrepancy in the order in which they

312. Ritmeyer, *Wanderings*, 15.
313. Paul H. Wright, *Holman Illustrated Guide to Biblical Geography: Reading the Land*, 108.
314. *Ibid.*
315. *Ibid.*

travelled according to Numbers and Deuteronomy. If they are the same location, then we do not know how to explain the difference. What is important, however, is that it was here that Israel would have remembered the death of Aaron.

Aaron's death is mentioned in three passages: Numbers 20:22–29; Deuteronomy 10:6; and here in 33:37–39. From these three passages we learn that Moshe, Aaron, and Eleazer ascended Mt. Hor together. After Aaron died, Eleazer was commissioned as the new High Priest. Mt. Hor has not been positively identified as yet. Both linguistics and geography have presented some problems. One prominent possibilitiy is a very high mountain west of Petra. This would have placed Aaron's tomb in Edomite territory, outside of the Promised Land. Yet the Torah says that not any part of Edom was to be part of Israel's inheritance (See Deuteronomy 2:5). However, it is noted that "this exclusion need not be classified as a territorial concession. Certainly Jebel Haroun [the modern name for this site] was not 'in the midst of Edom,' as frequently suggested."[316]

A second possible location places Mt. Hor with modern Jebel el-Medhra, about 12–15 km (7.5–9.3 mi) northeast of Kadesh-barnea, on the route toward Arad in the Negev. Such eminent authorities subscribe to this suggestion as Yohanan Aharoni and Nelson Glueck. Yet we are still not certain.[317]

E. Jotbathah (33:33): The Levite's Inheritance

Deuteronomy 10:7–9 reports that Jotbathah, "a land with streams of water", was "where the Lord set apart the tribe of Levi to carry the ark of the covenant of the Lord, to stand before the Lord to minister and to pronounce blessings in his name, as they still do today. That is why the Levites have no share or inheritance among their brothers; the Lord is their inheritance as the Lord your God told them." We are sure that the Levites would have recalled this location on many occasions, when their right to serve in the Mishkan or the Temple may have been questioned. Today the location is a modern Israel kibbutz called Yotbatah (spelled the same way in Hebrew), about 40 km. (25 mi.) north of Elat.

F. Ezion-Geber (33:35): Skip Edom, Pass through Moab

Leen Ritmeyer observes that it was only an 11 days' journey from Mount Sinai to Kadesh-barnea, in the northern Sinai (assuming a southern Sinai location). However, the Torah indicates that it took the Israelites almost a whole year to reach Kadesh-barnea. "This accords well with a detour over to the coast of the Gulf of Eilat touched on by Deuteronomy 1:1."[318]

There are no particular outstanding memories about Ezion-Geber, other than it was the place where there was a minor directional adjustment. From here they were to circumvent the Edomites, travel to their east, and then go through Moab as they headed north.

---

316. Martin H. Heicksen, "Aaron's Tomb," *The New International Dictionary of Biblical Archaeology*, 1.
317. Ritmeyer, *Wanderings, 15.*
318. *Ibid.*

Ezion-Geber was located right on the Red Sea (not the Reed Sea!) next to Eilat. It is the southernmost tip of modern Israel. The ancient Israelites would not have guessed that in a few hundred years from their passing through it, King Solomon would build, a fleet of ships in Ezion-geber, which is near Eilat on the shore of the Red Sea, in the land of Edom (1 Kings 9:26).

G. Kadesh-barnea (33:36): Bad News for Moshe

Kadesh-barnea apparently went by several names: Kadesh-barnea (32:8), En-mishpat (Genesis 14:7), Meribah (Numbers 20:13), or Meribath-kadesh (Numbers 27:14). It forms part of the southern boundary of the Promised Land (34:4) and, hence, of the territory of Judah (Joshua 15:3). It is located either in the wilderness of Paran (Numbers 13:26) or Zin (Numbers 20:1). Perhaps it is to be located on the border of these two adjoining wildernesses.[319] It is more likely that the people of the wilderness wandering stayed most of the time near the springs in the vicinity of Kadesh-barnea,[320] though ironically, Israel complained about water there!

Kadesh-barnea has been identified today with a large degree of certainty with the modern valley of Ein el-Qdeirat,[321] just over the modern Israeli-Egyptian border in the southern Negev. As the Torah indicates, several things happened here, things both Moshe and Israel would rather have forgotten. First, it was here that Israel rebelled against the Lord and accepted the evil report of the spies. Hence, Kadesh-barnea will always be remembered as the place where the fate of the generation of the Exodus was sealed for death, being condemned to 40-years of wilderness wandering (Deuteronomy 9:23). It was also at Kadesh-barnea that Miriam died and was buried (Numbers 20:1).

Moreover, as if her death was not enough for Moshe to handle, at Kadesh "there was no water for the community, and the people gathered in opposition to Moshe and Aaron" (Numbers 20:2–3). Because of this, Moshe, once again, went to the Lord. God gave him specific instructions about how to solve the problem, but somehow when Moshe carried them out, he failed to properly glorify God amidst the people. Hence, it was at Kadesh in Zin that the Holy One told Moshe, "Because you did not trust in me enough to honour me as holy in the sight of the Israelites, you will not bring this community into the land I give them." (Numbers 20:12).

Kadesh-barnea would have been a good place to begin the occupation of the Land of Canaan. It was situated at the very southern end of the central mountains, the "back bone" of Israel, where a good portion of the population resided further north. Furthermore, a good route upon which to travel originated from there. Israeli biblical geographer, Yohanan Aharoni identified this route as the Atarim Road mentioned in Numbers 21:1. It "led from Kadesh-barnea, [northeast through] Tell Malhata and Tell Arad into southern Judah."[322] Then it connected with the central mountain road. Thus, it cut right through the Negev of Israel. As it is, entry into the

319. Milgrom, JPS: *Numbers,* 104.
320. Alfred J. Hoerth, *Archaeology of the Old Testament*, 202.
321. *Ibid.,* 19.
322. David Dorsey, *The Roads and Highways of Ancient Israel*, 124–125.

Land through Jericho was also a great idea!

H. Mount Hor (33:37): Aaron's Death

Deuteronomy 1:46 says that Israel stayed at Kadesh for many days then headed north to Mount Hor. Here we have a real problem. Deuteronomy specifically tells us that Aaron died at Moserah: "From Moserah, Israel travelled to Jotbathah", but Numbers 33 tells us that it was not until Israel reached Mount Hor, near Edom — *apparently* well after Jotbathah — that Aaron died. Deuteronomy 32:50 confirms that Aaron died on Mount Hor. The only explanation we have to offer is that Moserah, may have been a name for the *region* of Mount Hor. Furthermore, it is also possible that the term "Edom" may have applied to more than just what is in southern modern-day Jordan, as many biblical geographers assert. Indeed, sometimes in Israel's history, "Edom frequently extended its control westward across the Aravah [into the eastern or even central Negev], thus enlarging the region thought of as Edom." [323]. Hence, perhaps Moshe is referring very loosely to Edomite territory in the Aravah or eastern Negev and not just to the traditional Edomite homeland in the mountains of southern modern-Jay Jordan. Thus, we place Mount Hor, not in Transjordan, but somewhere in the eastern Negev. See the notes above when we commented on Moserot/Moserah in 33:31.

What would Israel have remembered about Mount Hor? Since Aaron died there, they would have certainly remembered his passing. Chapter 33 specifically mentions it as the most important part of their stay there. It was quite an unforgettable moment. We are told that when he died, "the entire house of Israel mourned for him thirty days". (Numbers 20:29)

The text in Numbers provides us with some important information about the death of Aaron. First, we are told his age at the time of his death, 123 years old. Second, it provides the date on which he died: the 1st day of the 5th month of the 40th year (of their freedom). This means that the journey from Rameses in Goshen to Mount Hor completes their 40 years of wilderness wanderings.

Aaron's death marked the passing of a great man. Ronald Allen notes, "His death came at a great age — a mark of God's blessing in his life. By the mercy of the Lord, his time was extended to the very last year of Israel's desert experience; his own sin (Num. 20) kept him from living into the time of the conquest of the land."[324]

The mention of Mount Hor in the text brought another memory to the Israelites besides the death of Aaron. The passage in Numbers also mentions the fact that while Israel was around Mount Hor, they were challenged in battle with the Canaanite King of Arad. This was a great victory for the Israelites. Coming at the end of their wilderness wanderings, this first victory of

---

323. Elaine A. Phillips, "Edom and Israel's Wanderings from Kadesh to the Plaines of Moab," *Lexham Geographic Commentary on the Pentateuch*, 635.

324. Ronald B. Allen, "Numbers" in the *Expositor's Bible Commentary* ("EBC"), comments on Numbers 33:38-40.

the Israelites was a "promise for a new generation being different than their fathers." [325]

III. THE THIRD DIVISION: MOUNT HOR TO THE PLAINS OF MOAB

A. Zaknibah (33:41) Punon (33:42) Ovot (33:43): The Bronze Serpent

We do not know exactly where it happened, but according to Numbers 21:10, between the time they left Mount Hor and when they arrived at Ovot, further north in Transjordan, the Israelites had yet another rebellion. This time the Lord sent fiery serpents against them. In order to stop it, God instructed Moshe to make a bronze serpent "and set it on the standard; and it came about, that if a serpent bit any man, when he looked to the bronze serpent, he lived" (Numbers 21:9–10). This most likely happened in Transjordan.

Without a doubt the information about the locations in the text are complicated to follow, especially when we compare the locations found here in Numbers 33 with those of Deuteronomy chapters 1–2.

While there is stunning ambiguity in regards to both of these recitals [the one in Deuteronomy chapter 1 and this one in Numbers 33} one possible way of interpreting them would be that God redirected Moses and the Israelites from their circuitous route that would have taken them further south and east….It would be just too long; they were in the wilderness and broken by the serpent calamity.[326]

From the names of the locations, it is clear that the text has Israel now in Edom, especially with the mentioning of Punon in 33:42. We might remember from Numbers 20 that Edom refused Israel passage on their trek north toward the Promised Land. Just a few more notes regarding Edom. Edom was located on the east side of the Rift Valley, in the southern part of modern-Day Jordan. Its southern border was near Eilat. Throughout history, Edom attempted to dominate the desert trade-routes going west, through the Negev toward the Mediterranean Sea.

The request to pass through Edom was denied upon a show of force from the Edomites, as recorded in 20:20–21. The refusal was possibly because of past family history between Jacob and Esau. The text does not tell us, so we need to be a little cautious in our interpretation.

Some scholars have a disagreement about the northern border of Edom. Up until recently this commentator believed that the issue was rather clear-cut. Almost everyone places Edom's northern border at the Zered River, as it flowed into the southern end of the Dead Sea. Along these lines, Yoel Elitzur says, "the identification of Wadi Zered with Wadi al-Hasa is also accepted in all encyclopedias, in modern exegesis, and in scholarly literature."[327]

According to Yoel Elitzur, geographers may have made a mistake, identifying the Zered

325. B. Allen, *"Numbers" in the Expositor's Bible Commentary ("EBC"), comments on Numbers 33:38-40*

326. E. Phillips, "Edom and Israel's Wanderings," 644.

327. Yoel Elitzur, *Places in the Parasha: Biblical Geography and its Meaning*, 481.

River with Wadi al-Hassa, which flows east-west into the southern end of the Dead Sea. He suggests a more northern location. The arguments for and against the traditional location for the Zered River (Wadi al-Hasa) are too lengthy to treat in this commentary. We urge the student to read Elitzur's treatment of this subject in his comments on Parashat Chukkat where he devotes a whole chapter on Wadi Zered.[328]

However, for now, we should note this about the Zered. According to Deuteronomy 2:8–25, …the crossing Wadi Zered is portrayed here as a festive event possessing historical significance. Wadi Zered represents the end of the period of Israel's wanderings, the termination of thirty-eight years of wandering that were decreed following the sin of the spies…it is the final event before entering the land of the Amorites, which is part of the land of Israel, as it was bequeathed to the tribes of Israel.[329]

After the event of crossing the Zered, the most logical route to proceed north in Transjordan would have been via the King's Highway (20:17), which went basically from Eilat in the south all the way to Damascus. However, Israel was forced by Edom to travel slightly east in the land that bordered on the Arabian desert. The specific route is not known.

B. Dibon-Gad (33:45): The Place Gad Built

Dibon-Gad was in the territory just north of Moab, on the east side of the Jordan River. It was while the Israelites were getting ready to begin the conquest of the Land of Canaan, that the tribe of Gad, particularly after Israel was victorious in some battles in the region, settled in some of the cities of Bashan. Dibon was one of them, for it says, "But we have overthrown them; Heshbon is destroyed all the way to Dibon. We have demolished them as far as Nophah, which extends to Medeba. So, Israel settled in the land of the Amorites" (Numbers 21:30–31).

Israel would have remembered this place as one of the locations in which they first began to settle after their traumatic exodus and forty-year trek through the wilderness. These would have been happy thoughts for the children of Israel!

C. Almon-Diblatathaim (33:46)

No Comments.

D. Mountains of Abarim, Near Nebo (33:47–48): The Death of Moshe

One of the final localities in this travelogue was the Mountains of Abarim, near Nebo. This is the mountain range in present day Jordan that overlooks the Jordan River Valley, opposite Jericho and near the northern section of the Dead Sea. It was while Israel camped here that, "the Lord said to Moshe, "Go up this mountain in the Abarim Range and see the land I have given the Israelites. After you have seen it, you too will be gathered to your people, as your brother Aaron was" (Numbers 27:12–13).

The Torah specifies that the Lord did not want the exact location of Moshe's grave in these

---

328. Yoel Elitzur, *Places in the Parasha: Biblical Geography and its Meaning.*, 481–493.
329. *Ibid.*, 484.

212 Briteinu Numbers | במדבר בריתנו

mountains to be known. Hence, all we can say is that somewhere in these craggy mountains, Moshe is buried. When Israel heard these words in chapter 33, so many different thoughts would undoubtedly have gone through their minds. At the very least, this place would have reminded Israelites of every generation of their prophet, deliverer, teacher, and shepherd.

E. The Plains of Moab (33:49–56): The Last Stop Before Their Inheritance!

The Plains of Moav is the place from where this travelogue was being written. Israel spent a fair amount of time encamped on the Plains of Moab. While they were there, unknown to them, an unseen battle was being waged in the mountains above and to the east of them when Balak summoned the pagan prophet Balaam to curse them. However, God intervened for them. In the valley where they were living, during the same time period, they faced rampant sin when the daughters of the Midianites and Moabites began enticing some of their men. Pinchas, the son of Eleazar and grandson of Aaron, stood firm for the Lord and slew all the wrongdoers. From here, Moshe ascended the mountains to die, and Joshua took over the leadership of the nation and made preparations to begin the battle for their inheritance.

SUMMARY AND CONCLUSION

As the new generation of Israelites listened to the travelogue, not only would they have remembered the historical events that took place at each location, but in doing so, they also would have remembered their God, and the many things He had done for them. Perhaps they would have repeated the stories that happened at each location as they sat around their evening campfires. When they did, they would have discussed all the different things that these places would have reminded them about their God.

This is a great exercise for anyone to do. All of us need, on occasion, to go through our personal or congregational history to see the many lessons that God has taught us over the years. As we talk about them, we would inevitably talk about the greatness and goodness of our God and the Messiah.

The Book of Numbers finishes in a rather inglorious way. One would think that a more appropriate manner of concluding it would have been with the teaching on the promises and borders of the Land. Instead, it concludes with a legal discussion about the daughters and their inheritance in the event of their marriage.

This, however, reminds us that the Torah was meant to be very practical. It was, after all, the teaching for the redeemed who not only live in the Land, but for all of God's redeemed. It was not meant to be merely theological. It was meant to be lived out by the believer, especially (although not exclusively) as he resided in the Land of Israel. In short, the Torah if applied by means of the Spirit of God, was designed to make us strong believers walking in holiness. With this in mind, therefore, we conclude this book as the rabbis do, repeating with meaning the words:

חזק חזק ונתחזק
"Chazak! Chazak! Venitchzeik!"

Be strong! Be strong!
And may we be strengthened!

ADDITIONAL NOTES

Chapter 30

Verse 2 (Hebrew verse 3)
making vows — Two Hebrew words have to do with making vows in these verses. The first is *neder* (נדר). It is a general word denoting anything that a person promises to God either as a votive offering or even promising himself for some special service. Wenham suggests that it is a vow to do something positive such as offering a sacrifice.[330]

This second word is *shevuah* (שובעה). It is a word that is used is in combination with the verb that is usually rendered "to bind". It means "a sworn oath". It is a very strong vow, carrying legal connotations and is sometimes accompanied by a pronouncement of covenantal difficulties for failure to keep this oath.[331] It is combined with the word "to bind" in this verse (*asar*, אסר), Asar is a term that has to do with binding oneself to do something. Actually, asar is also used to speak of fetters in a prison or binding someone with cords.[332]

Verse 2 (Hebrew verse 3)
"**he must not break his word**" — The word translated "break", is apparently from the word *chalal* (חלל). This word means to break or pierce as with a sword. The idea here is that someone should not pierce or wound, so to speak, his/her promises. However, in this verse the verb is in the *Hiphil* stem. When it is used in that verbal stem, it carries the idea of profaning something. Thus, the text is warning people not to desecrate their words or break their vows.[333]

Verse 2 (Hebrew verse 3)
"**he must do everything he said**" — The Hebrew literally reads, "all that goes out of his mouth." A vow or oath is a promise that a person voluntarily obligates himself to do. It is through speaking that a vow is made. God charges us to let our words be true and only let come from our mouths those words which we intend to keep. The text, having stated the general principle, now applies it to several different cases:

1) Vows made by single women 30: 3–5
2) Vows made by married women, 30: 6–8
3) Vows made by widows and divorcees, 30:9–15

Case One

Note: The verse numbering in Hebrew is slightly different.

Verses 3–5
"**if a woman makes a vow**" — This first case involves a woman making a vow while she is still under the authority of her father because she is still in her youth. The word "youth" is *na'ariah*

---

330. Gordon Wenham, *Numbers* (NICOT), 231.
331. HALOT, 1335.
332. BDB, 68.
333. Rashi: *Bamidbar*, ArtScroll Edition, 372.

(נעריה). This word, according to Rashi, describes a woman who is young and even marriageable but still in her father's house.[334]

We are not sure under what circumstances a father would oppose such a vow, nor does the text indicate it. However, the Torah does teach that if he so thought, her vow should be nullified, and gave him the legal right to do so. When he did oppose the vow, we are told that the Lord forgave the girl who made the vow. From this we can learn at least two lessons. One is that this passage indicates that this teaching puts obedience to parents above voluntarily undertaken religious obligations. Second, the text says that the Lord would forgive the girl if her father annuls the vow.

Case Two
Verses 6–8
"if she should marry" — The second case involves a situation where a woman made a vow before she was married and finds out that her husband does not approve of it and wants it invalidated. What should happen then? The teaching is that when her husband learns of the vow, if he approves, she is still obligated. If he opposes her from fulfilling that vow, then the Lord will forgive her. It is important to note that, in 30:15, the husband only has one day to think about it. In fact, the usual rabbinic interpretation is that he must annul the vow or oath on that day but not thereafter.

Case Three
Verses 9–15
The vow of a widow or of a divorced woman — While she is still married the principle stated in 30:6–8 is still in effect. However, if her husband died and has not annulled any previous vow, the Torah states, "whatever she has imposed upon herself, shall be binding upon her."

Verse 16
"these are the laws" — The text indicates that we have been talking not about *torah* (תורה), that is teachings, but rather strictly legal matters. Hence, 30:17 calls these passages we have just reviewed *hukim* (חוקים), which are laws.

For what purposes did God see fit to legislate for the women of Israel? In general, this teaching considers that a vow or an oath is a sacred obligation that can only be nullified through legal means. Women particularly were very vulnerable and needed extra measures of protection. This passage focuses on vows women may have made. The point of the matter is that sometimes when the woman made a vow, she may have had her single state in mind, or she may have made it in the immaturity of her youth. Thus, the unmarried female was under the special care of her father, who would protect her interests until she had a husband to care and provide for her. In the case of a husband nullifying a woman's vow, he could not do so just to assert any chauvinistic whim. He had to have the care of his wife in mind.

---

334. Rashi: *Bamidbar*, ArtScroll Edition, 372–373.

This was given to give the women a legal "out" of the vow. The two possibilities of negating her vow are through her father, if she is still under his guardianship, or through her husband. Both the father and the husband are given the authority to legally release the vulnerable woman from her vow providing they do it as soon as they learn about it.

One of the great lessons to be gleaned from this passage is that in the redeemed community, women are to be cared for and protected. The authority of the father or husband over a woman is not to be perceived as one of a dictator or tyrant, but one of gentle and protective care for one who is especially vulnerable.

Chapter 31

Chapter 31 discusses the fate and treatment of one of Israel's nemesis, Midian. The Lord commanded Moshe that before he died, he must lead Israel to "take vengeance for the children of Israel against the Midianites" (31:1). We find several points of importance here.

Verses 1–2 | The War Against Midian

avenge the Israelite people — In the previous section, we saw God as the defender of women and the upholder of honesty and integrity. Now, we see a different aspect of God, the Avenger. Here God will act as Israel's defender. The people were not to take vengeance; it was only the right of God to do so. The people of Israel were the tools for working out God's vengeance.

Jacob Milgrom takes issue with the translation of *nakam* (נקם), as "vengeance". He says that "the verb *nakam* bears two closely associated meanings: to redress past wrongs and to exact retribution."[335]

Verse 2

"against the Midianites" — Why against the Midianites and not the Moabites? Rashi suggests two possible reasons. First, it is because the Moabites harassed Israel "out of fear" while the Midianites "were angry with the Israelites for a quarrel which was not theirs." A second suggestion by Rashi is that God was sparing the Moabites because, "I expect to bring Ruth from among them."[336]

Verse 3

"arm some of your men" — Moshe was to pick out armed men for a battle against Midian. The phrase "armed for battle" is one word in Hebrew, *hekhaletzu* (החלצו). This word is associated with the idea of "withdraw".[337] It carries the idea of having men who are withdrawn from everything and trained for war, as opposed to just an ordinary militia. They would be specially trained soldiers. Milgrom suggests that they "must comprise the bravest and most skilled and, hence, are 'picked out'."[338] Only a thousand from each tribe were chosen for this special attack on Midian (31: 5).

---

335. Milgrom, *JPS: Numbers*, 255.
336. Rashi, *Bamidbar*, ArtScroll Edition, 378.
337. BDB, 322–323.
338. Milgrom, *JPS: Numbers.*, 256.

Verse 6

"with Pinchas son of Eleazer" — We find at least two items of interest here. The first is the fact that the priests were associated with the troops. They were to go along "with the sacred utensils and the trumpets for sounding the blasts". The instructions for the priests in battle are described in Deuteronomy 20:2 ff. Essentially, they were there to represent the Lord's presence with the army. The priests were to encourage Israel before and during the battle. The second item of interest is that it was Pinchas who was chosen to go with Israel. He had a special interest in this battle because of his actions in slaying the Israelite and his harlot.

Verse 7

"and killed every man" — The context would suggest that they slew every adult male who was in the battle and not every male of the entire Midianite tribes. We know this also because Judges 6–8 indicates that the Midianites were, once again, troublers of Israel.

The destruction of Midian was to set the pattern for the destruction of the rest of the inhabitants of Canaan. It is critical to understand the reason for this. We need to remember chapter 25 and what happened to the Israelites when they came upon the Midianite women. They were lured away into idolatry. In the process, they were committing gross immorality, which was so characteristic of idol worship.

However, it was even worse than that. The Torah only shows us the tip of the iceberg! We know from archaeology how extensive idolatry was in the Ancient Near East. We also know how participation in this paganism was participation in demons, which were represented by the idols. Therefore, the inhabitants: men, women, and children of Canaan and its surrounding territory were literally infested for the most part with demons. If such a brief exposure to this idolatry enticed Israel away from the Holy One, imagine what living right next door to it would be like. The only solution was to do as the Lord directed, total destruction of the Midianites — and eventually, the Canaanites.

Verse 16

"through the council of Bilaam" — These verses confirm the fact that Bilaam was not such a good guy as might have first appeared. It is true that he refused to curse Israel, claiming that he had to listen to the Lord. I believed him! Our own opinion is that Bilaam needed to "save face" somehow from the incident with Balak. Finding that he could not destroy Israel via the curse, he figured out a safe way to do some damage to Israel and at the same time appease Balak who might have sought his life over the episode.

Our opinion is that apparently, Bilaam knew that introducing some harlots along with idol worship would not completely destroy Israel, so he helped manipulate the situation. At the same time, he did enough damage to make Balak happy and, thus, spare his own life. In the end, his actions proved wrong. Much of Israel did go after the women and the sin. Therefore, God had to destroy Bilaam.

Verses 9–54 | The Aftermath of the Battle with Midian

1. The Captives: verses 9–18

The victory over the Midianites was clearly a decisive one. The Israelites took the women and the Midianite wealth as booty and brought them back to the Israelite camp.

Verse 15

"**allowed every woman to live**" — Formally in battle against the Canaanites, the Israelites were not permitted to take any women captives, but these are not Canaanites. However, Moshe is concerned that it was the Midianite women who seduced the Israelites before and that they could do it again. So, he justly orders all who are not virgins to be put to death.

How were they to know who had had relations or not? Milgrom says that the midrash suggests that Moshe offered a test: "Every female child you shall stand before the holy crown (the gold frontlet of the high priest) and cross-examine her. And whoever has slept with a man, her face will pale; and whoever has not slept with a man, her face will blush like a fire, and you shall spare."[339]

Verse 18

"**but save**" — What did they do with the women whom they spared? Wenham says, "They were allowed to marry the Israelite warriors, thereby being incorporated into the elect nation of Israel."[340] Hertz, on the other hand, says that they spared the women to employ them as domestic servants.[341] We do not know.

2. The Purification of the Soldiers: verses 19–24

Verse 19

"**you shall stay outside the camp...and your captives**" — The ritual instructions required that the ashes of the red heifer (Numbers 19) be applied to the people or things which had come into contact with a corpse. This would especially apply to soldiers. It is interesting that the law also applied to non-Israelites (their captives) who came into the camp after touching a corpse. Hertz observes that it was, "in order to prevent the spread of their contamination by the Israelites' contact with their garments."[342]

Verses 22–23

"**anything else that can withstand fire**" — It appears that this chapter adds to the instructions of purification described in chapter 19 by insisting that not only must they be sprinkled with the water of immersion, but in addition, they must be passed through fire or water. The metal objects are listed in descending order according to their value. Pottery and earthenware are not listed because they are porous and, therefore, cannot be purified; they had to be destroyed.

---

339. Milgrom, *JPS: Numbers.*, 259.
340. Wenham, *Numbers,* 236.
341. J. H. Hertz, *The Pentateuch and Haftarahs*, 705.
342. *Ibid.*

Verse 24

"on the seventh day" — Entrance back into the camp was not permitted until the seventh day after their return from battle. They were to wash their clothes. It is assumed that they also took a bath, though not stated explicitly. Milgrom noted that the Dead Sea Scrolls mention this bodily immersion specifically in the War Scroll. It reads, "In the morning they [the soldiers] shall launder their garments and wash themselves of the blood of the guilty cadavers."[343]

3. Distribution of the Spoils of War:

Verses 25–47

This next section concerning the battle with the Midianites has to do with the equitable distribution of the spoils of war among the Israelites. The booty was shared equally between those who fought and those who stayed behind. This would imply that the whole community shared equally in the responsibility of war, either in fighting or in supporting it. Finally, there was also a tenth of a share for the priests and Levites. It broke down to 1/500 of the soldiers' share to the priests and 1/50 of the civilians' share.

4. The Ransom for the Living: vv. 48–54

Verse 49

"not one of us is missing" — It was such a miraculous victory which God gave to the Israelites that no one was killed! This was unheard of in war. Rabbi Munk adds, "It should not be surprising that the Jews came away from the battle without suffering any losses. Rambam teaches that as a rule no man was lost in battle in Moshe's time."[344] This is a nice thought, however, we must remember that they did loose miserably when they fought on their own, after the spy incident.

Verse 50

"to make atonement for ourselves" — Milgrom says that this should be rendered, "to ransom our lives."[345] It is most likely that this ransom was really a thanksgiving for not losing a single life in the battle, although the word used is *kaphar* (כפר), which usually means "atonement" or "ransom" and not "thanksgiving". Hertz stays with the thanksgiving idea, as does Wenham.

Chapter 32

The Geography of Transjordan Settlement

Transjordan can be divided into three discrete geographical regions: (1) Mishor (rendered "Tableland") from the Arnon to wadi Hesban (Joshua 13:9,21; Jeremiah 48:20), (2) Gilead, and

---

343. Milgrom, *JPS: Numbers*, 261–262.
344. Elie Munk, *The Call of the Torah: Bamidbar*, 381. Notice that Munk uses the word, "Jews." This is rather anachronistic. The descendants of Abraham, Isaac, and Jacob were called "Israelites" or children of Israel back then. They were not called "Jews" until mainly the Second Temple Period.
345. Milgrom, *JPS: Numbers*, 264–265.

(3) Bashan (Deuteronomy 3:10; 4:43; Joshus 13:9–12; 20:8). The boundary between Gilead and Bashan is not definite, alternating in the sources as either the Jabbok or the Yarmuk.[346]

Population of Transjordan

This chapter deals with the request of the Gadites and the Reuvenites to possess the land east of the Jordan River as their inheritance. It is the first time we hear of any of the Israelites expressing a desire to inherit the land. Up until now it has always been assumed from the text and from the mouths of the leadership. Now finally we hear what the tribes are thinking.

Verse 1

"**the children of Reuven and the children of Gad came and said to Moshe**" — At first glance it seems that their request is quite reasonable, as is Moshe's immediate negative reaction to it. Some commentators, however, see an evil motive behind their request, as Moshe did at first. Rabbi Munk is one of these. His interpretation is: Moshe, however, "recognized the selfish and inappropriate motivations hidden in their words. Thus, when they said, sheep pens shall we build here for our flocks and cities for our children (verse 16); he saw that they valued their property above their children."[347] This seems to be a very unfair judgment from a commentator who lived centuries removed from the situation. Therefore, we do not think that their motives were wrong. In the end, neither did Moshe.

Wenham sees a different problem with their request. He says that the land east of the Jordan was not to be included in the Promised Land, according to Numbers 34:47. Once more, in the end, their request was approved thereby signifying that God also approved of this territory as legitimate land for Israel to settle.

We know from Joshua 13:15 ff that eventually Reuven occupied the land immediately east of the Dead Sea and Gad occupied the land east of the Jordan River between the Dead Sea and the Sea of Galilee. However, at this stage of occupation, there is some intermingling of the tribes.

Verse 1

"**livestock**" — The Hebrew word here is *miqneh* (מקנה) and it is broader than just cattle (as some translations render it). It can refer to any kind of domesticated livestock. The Tribe of Reuben, in particular, was later characterized by its investment in grazing animals, as is clear from Judges 5:16 and 1 Chronicles 5:9. If Gad and Reuven had a lot of livestock before, their supply was certainly increased after the Midianite war.

Verse 4

"**the land the Lord subdued before the people of Israel**" — So now the debate continues. Did God intend Israel to have this land or not? We have already stated some of the opening arguments in our comments on verse one. Now we have more. Milgrom, for example sees this tension. On the one hand, he states that it appears that since this land across the Jordan was originally Moabite and Ammonite it was "forbidden territory from the beginning" and even

---

346. Milgrom, *JPS: Numbers,* 494.
347. Munk, *The Call of the Torah: Numbers,* 382.

impure for Israel.[348] He also cites the rabbinic tradition that this land was exempt from the law of first fruits because "Israel took it on its own volition (See. Deut. 29:8)."[349] Yet, on the other hand, Milgrom also gives evidence for the other side of the argument, the Reuvenite and Gadite contention. This evidence comes from Genesis 15:16–21 and Exodus 23:31.

Verse 17

"we ourselves will be armed"— The JPS renders this phrase as, "we will go out as shock-troops." — The word in question is the verb *nachaletz*, נחלץ). It is the *niphal* form of the verb *chalatz* חלץ . This is the same word used in 31:3 to describe the kind of soldiers that went out to fight Midian. Here it seems to be used somewhat in the sense of "commandos". Since they would not be burdened with family or livestock, they were free to be used for specially trained missions into Canaan. This Hebrew word is used seven times in this chapter. When the text says that Gad and Reuven actually sent a fighting force to join their brothers in possessing the Land, the Hebrew word used to describe that fighting force of "armed men", found in 32:29 is also the same word. The plural noun associated with this verb is in modern Hebrew *chalutzim* (חלוצים).

This is a famous word in modern Israeli history. It describes the early pioneers who came to settle the land. They came, giving up careers, wealth, and education to come before the rest of their brothers to "conquer" the Land for them and to settle in it.

> This term has now entered the everyday vocabulary of Jews the world over and has come to represent the pioneer who deliberately forsakes all considerations of career for the mission of building with his own hands the future of his people in Eretz Yisrael. It is now a platitude to say that the State of Israel was built up by the generations of such halutzim.[350]

Today there is a different kind of halutzim, the Jewish believers in Yeshua. They are pioneers who have come to the Land before the rest of their brothers. Some have made incredible sacrifices to come. They are settled in *Eretz Yisrael*, helping to build a spiritual environment. These Jewish believers in Yeshua have been sent here by the Lord to help pave the way for the building of the body of Messiah here in Eretz Israel.

Verse 22

when the land is subdued before the Lord and before Israel — Notice man's two responsibilities in order to walk with a clear conscience. First, he is to be clear before the Lord but second he is to be clear before his fellow man. As a result of this verse there is a famous maxim among the rabbis that states, "Man should be clear not only before God, but also in the estimation of his fellowmen."[351]

Verses 29–30

the valid condition — Moshe, the Reuvenites, and Gadites went through the conditions of their agreement twice before it was finally approved. From this, the rabbis have derived what is

348. Milgrom, *JPS: Numbers,* 266–267.
349. *Ibid.*
350. We apologize but for technical reasons, we are not able to provide the source for this quotation.
351. Hertz, *The Pentateuch and Haftarahs,* 709.

known as "principles for a valid condition". The way that Gad and Reuven agreed to what was asked of them became in rabbinic thinking the paradigm for making conditions and agreements. The rabbis say that such conditions must have the four elements, which are observed in the text here in chapter 32. They are:

1) It is stated twice, as a positive and a negative
2) The positive precedes the negative
3) The condition precedes the consequence
4) The condition is capable of being fulfilled[352]

Verse 33

the half-tribe of Manasseh — How did Manasseh come into the picture all of a sudden? Wenham suggests "It could be that the representatives of Manasseh took no part in the negotiations until Moshe had approved in principle a settlement in Transjordan."[353] At any rate, we should not take the phrase "half-tribe" as mathematically literal. It merely denoted a portion of the tribe. We learn from 26:29–32 that there were eight sub-divisions of Manasseh, six of which settled in the main part of Canaan, in the west of the Jordan.

Chapter 33

Verse 2

"Moshe recorded" — This is the only place in Numbers that claims to have Moshe specifically as the author. This does not mean that he was not the author of the rest of the book, but we know definitely that he was for this one section. There is nothing about the doctrine of Divine Inspiration that would prohibit the book from having been written by someone other than Moshe, unless, of course it specifically indicates that Moshe wrote it entirely. Nor does the doctrine prohibit Moshe from being an editor. Divine inspiration says that what is recorded was done so with 100% accuracy from the mouth of God.

Verse 8

"three days' journey" — This is the only place in the travelogue which provides a time period for one of the marches.

Verse 9

"Elim" — Milgrom observes that "This comment is typical of Ancient Near Eastern military itineraries: an account of the sources of water and food."[354] Up to this point all we can glean from the text is that the line of the march was southward.

Verse 53

"to you (in the Hebrew)" — This expression comes first in this phrase, showing emphasis: For to *you* i.e. Israel, "I have given this land!"

---

352. Milgrom, *JPS: Numbers*, 272.
353. Wenham, *Numbers,* 240.
354. Milgrom, *JPS: Numbers.*, 279.

Chapter 34

Without going into any great detail about each boundary marker, here are the general limits to the Land of Promise: It includes the mountains of Lebanon, Damascus and Bashan (Golan Heights). It includes the Sea of Galilee and a little below it along the Yarmuk River, which comes into the Jordan River close to the southeast side of the sea of Galilee. It seems to include the area east of the Jordan River as far south as the Arnon River. The western boundary is the Mediterranean Sea. The southern border runs from the Dead Sea up to the Ascent of Akrabbim, through the wilderness of Zin and south of Kadesh-Barnea. Then the southern border turns northwest to the "Brook of Egypt" (34:5). "Brook of Egypt" is not the Nile River. It is "Nahal Mitzraim," a small seasonal stream or stream valley in the northeast Sinai or southwest Negev. See map 9 on page 204.

Yochanan Ahroni, says,

> The Biblical description matches perfectly the boundaries of the Egyptian district of Canaan during the second half of the thirteenth century. This is one of the most instructive examples of ancient sources being preserved among the geographical texts of the Bible, because we have here a document which makes no sense whatever in later periods.[355]

The nation of Israel has never yet fully occupied this whole geographical entity.

Chapter 35

Verse 2
"to live in" — The Levites were to have the right to dwell in those cities, but the possession of them was vested in the tribe in whose territory the particular city was situated.

Verse 5
"2,000 cubits" — The rabbis assert that 2,000 cubits is the Shabbat walking distance from a city. This verse does not teach this. This passage is merely measuring the pastureland allotted to the Levitical cities. The 2,000 cubits became known as "a shabbat-Day Journey," is rabbinic invention in the late Second Temple Period. It is not a biblical instruction.

Verse 12
The city of refuge is not to be understood as a place where anyone may go for refuge for any crime, nor can it be assumed that the one who fled there is exempt from justice. Instead, only manslayers could flee to one. There they were to await trial and not escape the law. To appreciate these cities fully, we really need to grasp the reality of the blood avenger in the Near East — both ancient and modern. It was (and still is in some places) a legal right for the next of kin (the "redeemer", 35:12, to take matters into his own hands and avenge the death of his relative.

---

355. Yohahan Aharoni, *Land of the Bible*, 69.

224 Briteinu Numbers | בריתנו במדבר

Verse 15

"**accidently**" — this is what separates the murderer from the manslayer. One person cannot determine this motive. This is why a court with witnesses, cross-examination, and judges is necessary — for the good of the accused and the justice of the avenger.

Verse 28

"**until after the death of the High Priest**" — Why must a manslayer remain in the city of refuge even though he is innocent of murder until the High Priest dies? Milgrom suggests that

> As the high priest atones for Israel's sins through the cultic service in his lifetime, so he atones for homicide through his death. Since the blood of the slain, although spilled accidentally, cannot be avenged through the death of the slayer, it is ransomed through the death of the high priest.[356]

Hertz, on the other hand says that since the cities of refuge were mentioned in connection with the Levitical cities, the death of the High Priest rather than the death of the king was a natural point to terminate the exile of the innocent manslayer.[357] Wenham agrees with Milgrom and offers this concluding remark: "Thus the high priest of ancient Israel anticipated the ministry of our Lord, not only in his life of offering sacrifice and prayer on behalf of the people, but also in his death."[358]

Chapter 36

The book of Numbers concludes with the touching sequel to the story of the daughters of Zelophechad. The children of Israel lived in the wilderness for forty years because their national leaders, for the most part, rejected the gift of the Promised Land. Numbers relates this story and discusses the events of those forty years.

Now, at the end of the journey, when Israel is about to enter the Land, we have the account of a few single women whose sole desire was that they would receive an inheritance for themselves and their family in the Land. From this we see that not everyone in Israel wanted to reject the Land. God always had His righteous remnant who were faithful to Him. Although the rebellious generation died out, these women stand as a lasting testimony that indeed, there were godly people among the ancient Israelites, especially among the women.

---

356. Milgrom, *JPS: Numbers,* 294.
357. Hertz, *The Pentateuch and Haftarahs,* 722.
358. Wenham, *Numbers,* 266.

STUDY QUESTIONS

1. Why do you think Moshe made a travel journal? What purposes would it have served Israel to have it with them?

2. Is there any apparent organization to this travelogue? If so, what is it?

3. Why did Moshe leave out of this journal some of the most important events in Israel's history?

4. What notation does Moshe himself make in his journal?

5. Go through this journal for yourself and identify what they would have learned about Messiah at each location.

SOME HELPFUL MAPS

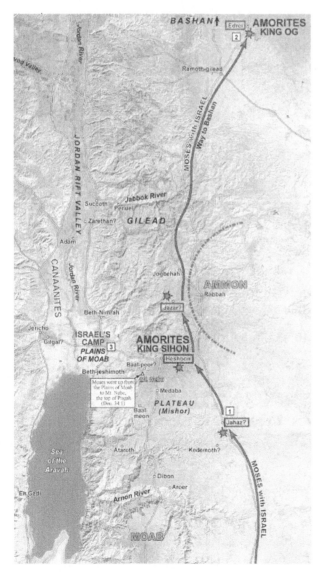

Map 11: The Biblical Borders of Israel

Map 10: Travel Route in Transjordan

Torah and Haftarah Readings

The following are the generally accepted weekly Torah and Haftarah readings. In the Haftarah section, "A" stands for the generally accepted Ashkenazic tradition and "S" denotes the generally accepted Sephardic tradition. There are some variants within each tradition. Furthermore, the Haftarah readings also vary according to whether the Shabbat is during a Holy Day season, or a Rosh Chodesh (New Moon).

Table 1: Torah and Haftarah Readings

		Torah Readings	Haftarah Readings
Genesis			
Bereshit	בראשית	Genesis 1:1–6:8	A. Isaiah 42:5–43:10
			S. Isaiah 42:5–21
Noach	נח	Genesis 6:9–11:32	A. Isaiah 54:1–55:5
			S. Isaiah 54:1–10
Lekh Lekha	לך לך	Genesis 12:1–17:27	Isaiah 40:27–41:16
Vayera	וירא	Genesis 18:1–22:24	A. 2 Kings 4:1–37
			S. 2 Kings 4:1–23
Chayei Sarah	חיי שרה	Genesis 23:1–25:18	1 Kings 1:1–31
Toledot	תלדות	Genesis 25:19–28:9	Malachi 1:1–2:7
Vayetzei	ויצא	Genesis 28:10–32:2	A. Hosea 12:13–14:10
			S. Hosea 11:17–12:12
Vayishlach	וישלח	Genesis 32:3–36:43	Book of Obadiah
Vayeshev	וישב	Genesis 37:1–40:23	Amos 2:6–3:8
Mikketz	מקץ	Genesis 41:1–44:17	1 Kings 3:15–4:1
Vayigash	ויגש	Genesis 44:18–47:27	Ezekiel 37:15–28
Vaychi	ויחי	Genesis 47:28–50:26	1 Kings 2:1–12
Exodus			
Shemot	שמות	Exodus 1:1–6:1	A. Isaiah 27:6–28:13, 29:22–23
			S. Jeremiah 1:1–2:3
Va'era	וארא	Exodus 6:2–9:35	Ezekiel 28:25–29:21
Bo	בא	Exodus 10:1–13:16	Jeremiah 46:13–28

		Torah Readings	Haftarah Readings
Beshalach	בשלח	Exodus 13:17–17:16	A. Judges 4:4–5:31
			S. Judges 5:1–31
Yitro	יתרו	Exodus 18:1–20:23	A. Isaiah 6:1–7:6; 9:5–6
			S. Isaiah 6:1–13
Mishpatim	משפטים	Exodus 21:1–24:18	Jeremiah 34:8–22, 33:25–26
Terumah	תרומה	Exodus 25:1–27:19	1 Kings 5:26–6:13
Tetzaveh	תצוה	Exodus 27:20–0:10	Ezekiel 43:10–27
Ki Tisa	כי תשא	Exodus 30:11–34:35	A. 1 Kings 18:1–39
			S. 1 Kings 18:20–39
Vayakhel	ויקהל	Exodus 35:1–38:20	A. 1 Kings 7:40–50
			S. 1 Kings 7:13–26
Pekudei	פקודי	Exodus 38:21–40:38	A. 1 Kings 7:51–8:21
			S. 1 Kings 7:40–50
Leviticus			
Vayikra	ויקרא	Leviticus 1:1–6:7	Isaiah 43:21–44:23
Tzav	צו	Leviticus 6:8–8:36	Jeremiah 7:21–8:3; 9:22–23
Shmini	שמיני	Leviticus 9:1–11:47	A. 2 Samuel 6:1–7:17
			S. 2 Samuel 6:1–19
Tazria	תזריע	Leviticus 12:1–13:59	2 Kings 4:42–5:19
Metsora	מצרע	Levitcus 14:1–15:33	2 Kings 7:3–20
Acharei Mot	אחרי מות	Leviticus 16:1–18:30	Amos 9:7–15;
			Ezekiel 22:1–19
Kedoshim	קדשים	Leviticus 19:1–20:27	A. Ezekiel 22:1–19
			S. Ezekiel 20:2–20
Emor	אמור	Leviticus 21:1–24:23	Ezekiel 44:15–31
Behar	בהר	Leviticus 25:1–26:2	Jeremiah 32:6–27
Bechukotai	בחקתי	Leviticus 26:3–27:34	Jeremiah 16:19–17:14

		Torah Readings	Haftarah Readings
Numbers			
Bamidbar	בְּמִדְבַּר	Numbers 1:1–4:20	Hosea 2:1–22
Nasso	נָשֹׂא	Numbers 4:21–7:89	Judges 13:2–25
Beha'alotkhah	בְּהַעֲלֹתְךָ	Numbers 8:1–12:16	Zechariah 2:14–4:7
Shelach	שְׁלַח	Numbers 13:1–15:41	Joshua 2:1–24
Korach	קֹרַח	Numbers 16:1–18:32	1 Samuel 11:14–12:22
Chukat	חֻקַּת	Numbers 19:1–22:1	Judges 11:1–33
Balak	בָּלָק	Numbers 22:2–25:9	Micah 5:6–6:8
Pinchas	פִּינְחָס	Numbers 25:10–29:40	1 Kings 18:46–19:21
Mattot	מַטּוֹת	Numbers 30:1–32:42	Jeremiah 1:1–2:3
Mas'ei	מַסְעֵי	Numbers 33:1–36:13	A. Jeremiah 2:4–28, 3:4
			S. Jeremiah 2:4–28, 4:1–2
Deuteronomy			
Devarim	דְּבָרִים	Deut. 1:1–3:22	Isaiah 1:1–27
Va'etchanan	וָאֶתְחַנַּן	Deut. 3:23–7:11	Isaiah 40:1–26
Ekev	עֵקֶב	Deut. 7:12–11:25	Isaiah 49:14–51:3
Re'eh	רְאֵה	Deut. 11:26–16:17	Isaiah 54:11–55:5
Shoftim	שׁוֹפְטִים	Deut. 16:18–21:9	Isaiah 51:12–52:12
Ki Tetze	כִּי תֵצֵא	Deut. 21:10–25:19	Isaiah 54:1–10
Ki Tavo	כִּי תָבוֹא	Deut. 26:1–29:9	Isaiah 60:1–22
Nitzavim	נִצָּבִים	Deut. 29:10–30:20	Isaiah 61:10–63:9
Va-Yelekh	וַיֵּלֶךְ	Deut. 31:1–30	Isaiah 55:6–56:8
Ha'azinu	הַאֲזִינוּ	Deut. 32:1–52	2 Samuel 22:1–51
Ve'zot Habrakhah	וְזֹאת הַבְּרָכָה	Deut. 33:1–34:12	Joshua 1:1–18

Torah Readings for Festivals

Table 2: Torah Readings for Festivals

Festivals / Fast days	Torah Readings	Haftarah Readings
Rosh Chodesh (weekday)	Numbers 28:1-15	
Rosh Chodesh (Shabbat)	Numbers 28:9-15	Isaiah 66:1-24
1st Day of Rosh Hashanah	Genesis 21	1 Samuel 1:1-2:10
2nd Day of Rosh Hashanah	Genesis 22	Jeremiah 31:2-20
Fast of Gedaliah	Exodus 32:11-14	Isaiah 55:6-56:8
Shabbat Shuvah		Hosea 14:2-10; Micah 7:18-20
Yom Kippur - Shacharit	Leviticus 16; Numbers 29:7-11	Isaiah 57:14-58:14
Yom Kippur - Minchah	Leviticus 18	Book of Jonah; Micah 7:8-20
1st Day of Sukkot	Leviticus 22:26-23:44	Zechariah 14:1-21
2nd Day of Sukkot	Leviticus 22:26-23:44	1 Kings 8:2-21
Shabbat of Sukkot	Exodus 33:12-34:26	Ezekiel 38:18-39:16
Hoshanah Rabbah	Numbers 29:26-34	
Shemini Atzeret	Deut. 14:22-16:17	1 Kings 8:54-9:1
Simchat Torah	Deut. 33:1-34:12; Genesis 1:1-2:3	Joshua 1:1-18
8 Days of Hanukkah	Numbers 7:1-8:4	
1st Shabbat of Hanukkah		Zechariah 2:14-4:7
2nd Shabbat of Hanukkah		1 Kings 7:40-50
Fast of Esther	Exodus 32:11-14; 34:1-10	Isaiah 55:6-56:8
Purim	Exodus 17:8-16	
Shabbat HaGadol	Malachi 3:4-24	
1st Day of Pesach	Exodus 12:21-51	Joshua 3:5-7; 5:2-6:1, 27
2nd Day of Pesach	Leviticus 22:26-23:44	2 Kings 23:1-9, 21-25

Festivals / Fast days	Torah Readings	Haftarah Readings
Shabbat of Pesach	Exodus 33:12-34:26	Ezekiel 37:1-14
Shabbat of Pesach	Exodus 33:12-34:26	Ezekiel 37:1-14
7th Day of Pesach	Exodus 13:17-15:26	2 Samuel 22:1-51
1st Day of Shavuot |	Exodus 19:1-20:23	Ezekiel 1:1-28; 3:12
17th of Tammuz	Exodus 32:11-14; 34:1-10	Isaiah 55:6-56:8
Tisha BAv	Deuteronomy 4:25-40	Jeremiah 8:13-9:23

The Five Megilot

Table 3: The Five Megilot

Festival Day	Megilah
Purim	Esther
Pesach	Song of Solomon (Shir haShirim)
Shavuot	Ruth
Tisha B'av (9th of the month of Av)	Lamentations
Sukkot	Ecclesiastes (Kohelet)

Briteinu Bibliography

Since the *Briteinu Torah Commentaries* is a series, encompassing all five books of the Torah (Genesis to Deuteronomy) we think it is better to provide a comprehensive list of sources, rather than giving a separate list for each of the volumes. Hence, the following bibliography is for the entire *Briteinu Torah Commentary* series.

Commentaries

Alfred, Henry. *The Greek New Testament*, 4 vols. Chicago: Moody Press, 1958.

Anderson, Sir Robert. *Types in Hebrews*. Grand Rapids: Kregal Publications, 1978.

Ashley, Timothy R. *The Book of Numbers (New International Commentary on the Old Testament,* "NICOT"). Grand Rapids: Eerdmans, 1993.

Baldwin, Joyce G. *Haggai, Zechariah, Malachi (Tyndale Commentaries)*. Downers Grove, IL: Inter-Varsity Press, 1972.

Beastly-Murray, G. R. *Revelation (The New Century Bible Commentary)*. Grand Rapids: Eerdmans, 1974, 1981.

Barrett, C. K. *The First Epistle to the Corinthians: Black's New Testament Commentary*. London: A & C Black, 1968, 1986.

Boice, James M., *The Gospel of John,* 5 vols. Grand Rapids: Baker, 2005.

—— *God and History*, volume IV of the series Foundations of the Christian Faith. Downers Grove, IL: InterVarsity Press, 1981.

—— *The Minor Prophets.* Vols. 1 and 2. Grand Rapids: Kregel, 1996.

Bonchek, Avigdor. *Studying the Torah: A Guide to In-Depth Interpretation*. Northvale, NJ: Jason Aronson Inc., 1996.

Brown, Raymond. *The Message of Deuteronomy*. Leicester, UK, Inter-Varsity Press: 1993.

Buksbazen, Victor. *The Prophet Isaiah: A Commentary*. Bellmawr, NJ: The Friends of Israel Gospel Ministry, 2012.

Cohen, A. *The Soncino Chumash. With Introduction and Commentary.* 2nd edition. London: Soncino Press, 1947.

Cole, Alan. *Exodus (Tyndale Commentaries)*. Downers Grove, IL: InterVarsity Press, 1973.

Cook, F. C., ed. Barnes Notes: *Exodus to Esther*. 1st Edition. Grand Rapids: Baker, 1965.

Craige, Peter C. *The Book of Deuteronomy* (NICOT). Grand Rapids, Eerdmans, 1976.

Drazin, Israel and Wagner, Stanley M. *Onkelos on the Torah: Understanding the Bible Text. Exodus.* Jerusalem: Gefen, 2006.

Durham, John I. *Exodus (Word Biblical Commentary)*. Waco, TX: Word Books, 1987.

Edersheim, Alfred. *The Life and Times of Jesus, The Messiah*. Grand Rapids: Eerdmans, 1971, 1990.

France, R. T. *Matthew (Tyndale Commentaries)*. Downers Grove, Il: Intervarsity Press, 1985.

Freedman, H. *Midrash Rabbah*. New York: Soncino Press, 1983.

Fried, Lisbeth S. "Why Did Joseph Shave?" in *Exploring Genesis: The Bible's Ancient Traditions in Context*. Washington, DC: Biblical Archaeology Society, 2013.

Friedman, David. *They Loved the Torah*. Clarksville, MD: Lederer, 2001.

Gaebelein, Frank E., gen. ed., *The Expositor's Bible Commentary*, vols. 1–7. Grand Rapids: Zondervan, 1985.

Harrison, R. K. *Leviticus (Tyndale Commentaries)*. Downers Grove: InterVarsity Press, 1980.

—— *Numbers*. Grand Rapids: Baker Book House, 1992.

Hebershon, Ada R. *Outline Studies of the Tabernacle*. Grand Rapids: Kregel, 1974.

Hendricksen, William. *New Testament Commentary: Matthew*. Grand Rapids: Baker Books, 1977.

Hamilton, Victor. *The Book of Genesis: Chapters 1–17* (NICOT). Grand Rapids MI: Eerdmans, 1990.

Hertz, J. H. *The Pentateuch and Haftarahs*. 2nd ed. London: Soncino Press, 1987.

Hirsch, Samson Raphael. *The Pentateuch*. New York: The Judaica Press, 1997.

Isaiah, R Ben, Abraham and Sharfman, Benjamin. *The Pentateuch and Rashi's Commentary*. Brooklyn, NY: S. S. & R. Publishing Co., 1949, 1976.

Kaiser, Walter C. Jr. *Exodus (The Expositor's Bible Commentary)*. Grand Rapids: Zondervan, 1990.

—— *Toward Old Testament Ethics*. Grand Rapids: Zondervan, 1983.

Keener, Craig S. *IVP Bible Background Commentary: New Testament*. Downers Grove, IL: InterVarsity Press, 2014.

Keil, C.F. and Delitzsch, F. *Commentary on the Old Testament*, 10 vols. Grand Rapids: Eerdmans, 1973 reprint.

Kidner, Derek. *Genesis (Tyndale Commentaries)*. Downers Grove, Ill: InterVarsity Press, 1979.

Lachs, Samuel Tobias, *A Rabbinic Commentary on the New Testament*. Hoboken, NJ: Ktav Publishing, 1987.

Leibowitz, Nechama. *Studies in the Weekly Parasha*, 7 vols. Jerusalem: Eliner Library, The World Zionist Organization, 1993.

Lightfoot, John. *Commentary on the New Testament from the Talmud and Hebraica: Matthew — 1 Corinthians*, vol. 2, *Matthew — Mark*. Grand Rapids: Baker Books, 1979, reprint from 1859 edition.

Newsome, James D. Jr., ed. *A Synoptic Harmony of Samuel, Kings and Chronicles*. Grand Rapids: Baker, 1986

Morris, Leon. *The Genesis Record*. Grand Rapids: Baker Book House, 1976, 1982.

MacRae, Allen A. *Studies in Isaiah*, Hatfield, PA: Interdisciplinary Biblical Research Institute, 1995.

—— *The Gospel of Isaiah*. Chicago: Moody Press, 1977.

Munk, Elie. *The Call of the Torah*, 5 vols. Translated by E.S. Mazer. Brooklyn, NY: Mesorah Publications, 1992.

Nachshoni, Yehudah. *Studies in the Weekly Parashah: Devarim*. Brooklyn: Mesorah Publications, 1989.

Prager, Dennis. *The Rational Bible: Commentaries on Genesis, Exodus, Leviticus, Numbers, and Deuteronomy*. Washington, DC: Regency Faith, 2019±.

Rashi, ArtScroll Edition. Brooklyn, NY: Mesorah Publications, 1994.

Ross, Allen P. *Creation and Blessing: A Guide to the Study and Exposition of Genesis*. Grand Rapids: Baker, 1998.

Sacks, Jonathan. *Covenant and Conversation: Commentaries on Genesis through Deuteronomy*. Jerusalem: Koren Books, 2010±

Sarna, Nahum N., Gen. ed. *The JPS Torah Commentary*. Philadelphia: The Jewish Publication Society, 1991.

Schaeffer, Francis A. *Genesis in Space and Time*. Downers Grove, IL: InterVaristy Press, 1972.

Scherman, Nosson, ed. *The ArtScroll Chumash*, The Stone Edition. Brooklyn, NY: Mesorah Publications, Ltd., 1994.

Scherman, Nosson, and Zlotowitz, Meir *Sefer Bereshis*, Vol. III. Brooklyn, NY: Mesorah Publications, 1978.

Silbermann, A.M. ed. *Chumash with Rashi's Commentary*. Jerusalem: Feldheim Publishers Ltd, 1934.

Slotki, I.W. *Isaiah*. London: Soncino Press, 1983.

Soltau, Henry W. *The Holy Vessels and Furniture of the Tabernacle*. Grand Rapids: Kregel Publications, 1851, 1982.

Sosevsky, Moshe C. *Samuel II*. New York: The Judaica Press, Inc. 1992.

Soltau, Henry W. *The Holy Vessels and Furniture of the Tabernacle*. Grand Rapids: Kregel Publications, 1851, 1982.

Sterman, Baruch. *The Meaning of Tekhelet*. Jerusalem: P'Til Tekhelet, ND. This booklet originally appeared as an article in B'Or Hatorah, November 11, 1999.

Stern, David H. *Jewish New Testament Commentary*. Jerusalem: Jewish New Testament Publications, 1992.

Thiele, E. R. *The Mysterious Numbers of the Hebrew Kings*. 3rd edition. Grand Rapids: Zondervan, 1983

Thompson, J.A. *Deuteronomy* (Tyndale Commentaries). Leicester, UK: InterVarsity Press, 1974.

Tiller, Lawrence V. *Garments for Glory and for Beauty*. Cheltenham, Glos. England: Greenhurst Press: 1981.

Walton, John H.; Matthews, Victor H.; and Chavalas, Mark W. *IVP Bible Background Commentary: Old Testament*. Downers Grove, Ill: InterVarsity Press, 2000.

Watts, John D. W., gen. ed. *Word Biblical Commentaries: Genesis-Deuteronomy*. Dallas: Word Books, 1994+.

Wenham, Gordon. J. *The Book of Leviticus* (NICOT). Grand Rapids: Eerdmans, 1979.

—— *Numbers* (Tyndale Commentaries). Downers Grove, IL: InterVarsity Press, 1981.

Whitcomb, John C. Jr. and Morris, Henry M. *The Genesis Flood*. Philadelphia: The Presbyterian and Reformed Publishing Co., 1961, 1974.

BIBLICAL GEOGRAPHY

Aharoni, Yohanan, *The Land of the Bible: A Historical Geography*. Philadelphia: Westminster Press, 1979.

Aharoni, Yohanan; Avi-Yona, Michael; Rainey, Anson F.; and Safrai, Ze'ev. *The Macmillan Bible Atlas*, Completely Revised, Third Edition. New York: Simon & Schuster & Macmillan Company, and Jerusalem: Carta, 1993.

Atlas of the Bible Lands. Maplewood, NJ: C. S. Hammond & Co., 1959.

Beitzel, Barry J., ed. *Lexham Geographic Commentary on the Pentateuch*. Bellingham, WA: Lexham Press, 2023.

Beitzel, Barry J. *The Moody Atlas of Bible Lands*. Chicago: Moody Press, 1985.

Bolen, Todd. *Pictorial Library of Bible Lands*: *Original High-Quality Photographs of the Bible*, categorized and labelled. See: www.bibleplaces.com.

Bolen, Todd; Cook, Randy; Schlegel, William. *From Dan to Beersheba* — Unpublished Field Studies prepared for use in "The Land and The Bible," a historical geography course taught by the authors as part of the Israel-Bible-Extension Campus ("IBEX") of the Master's University.

Bolen, Todd and Schlegel, William. *The Geography of Transjordan* — Unpublished Field Study Notes prepared for use in "Transjordan," a historical geography course taught by the authors as part of the Israel-Bible-Extension Campus ("IBEX") of the Master's University.

Dailey, T.J., G. Brubacher, and D. Rappe. *The Biblical Garden*, Booklet # 8. Jerusalem: Bible Resource Study Center, 1990.

Dorsey, David A. *The Roads and Highways of Israel*. Baltimore: The Johns Hopkins University Press, 1991.

Elitzur, Yoel., Daniel Landman, trans. *Places in the Parasha: Biblical Geography and Its Meaning*. Jerusalem: Maggid Books/Yeshiva University Press, 2020.

Hareuveni, Nogah. *Tree and Shrub in Our Biblical Heritage*. Kiryat Ono, Israel: Neot Kedumim, Ltd. 1989.

Pfeiffer, Charles F. and Vos, Howard F. *The Wycliffe Historical Geography of Bible Lands*. Chicago: Moody Press, 1967.

Rainey, Anson and Notley, R. Stephen. *The Sacred Bridge*. Carta: Jerusalem, 2006.

Ritmeyer, Leen and Kathleen. *From Sinai to Jerusalem: The Wanderings of the Holy Ark*. Jerusalem: Carta, 2000.

Schlegel, William. *Satellite Bible Atlas, 2nd Edition*. Skyland, Jerusalem, 2016.

Shanks, Hershel, ed. *Ancient Israel*. Revised and expanded. Washington: Biblical Archaeolog Society. 1999.

Smith, George Adam. *Historical Atlas of the Holy Land*. London: Hodder and Stoughton, Ltd., 1936.

Smith, Randall. *Journey Through the Bible: A student's field manual for exploring Israel*. The Jerusalem Institute, 1996.

The Illustrated Bible Atlas. Jerusalem: Carta, 1994.

Wright, Paul H. *Holman Illustrated Guide to Biblical Geography: Reading the Land*. Nashville, TN: B&H Publishing, 2020.

INTRODUCTIONS AND HISTORY

Archer, Gleason L., Jr. *A Survey of Old Testament Introduction*. Chicago: Moody, 1964.

Archbold, Norma. *The Mountains of Israel*. Israel: Phoebe's Song Publications, 1993.

De Vaux, Roland. *Ancient Israel*, vol. 1. New York: McGraw-Hill, 1965.

Dothan, Trude and Moshe. *People of the Sea: The Search for the Philistines*. New York: Macmillan,1992.

Finegan, Jack. *Light from the Ancient Past*, vol. 1. Princeton: Princeton University Press, 1974.

Gulston, Charles. Jerusalem: *The Tragedy and the Triumph*. Grand Rapids: Zondervan, 1978, 1987.

Harrison, R.K. *Introduction to the Old Testament*. Grand Rapids: Eerdmans, 1969.

Hoerth, Alfred J. *Archaeology and the Old Testament*. Grand Rapids: Baker, 1998.

Hoerth, Alfred J., Mattingly, Gerald L., and Yamauchi, Edwin M. eds. *The Peoples of the Old Testament World*. Grand Rapids: Baker Book House, 1994.

Hoffmeier, James K. *Israel in Egypt: The Evidence for the Authenticity of the Exodus Tradition*. Oxford: Oxford University Press, 1996.

Mazar, Benjamin, gen. ed. *The World History of the Jewish People*, vols. 1–3, Tel Aviv: Massada Publishing Co., 1970.

Merrill, Eugene H. *Kingdom of Priests: A History of Old Testament Israel*. Grand Rapids: Baker Books. 1987.

Mulder, Martin Jan. *Mikra: Text, Translation, Reading and Interpretation of the Hebrew Bible in Ancient Judaism and Early Christianity*. Philadelphia: Fortress Press, 1988.

Naim Ateek, Walker, P.W.L. ed. *Jerusalem Past and Present in the Purposes of God*. Cambridge: Tyndale House, 1992.

Packer, James I., Tenney, Merrill C., and White, William Jr. *Everyday Life in the Bible*. New York: Bonanza Books, 1989.

Pinch, Geraldine. *Egyptian Mythology: A Guide to Gods, Goddesses, and Traditions of Ancient Egypt*. Oxford: Oxford University Press, 2002.

Porten, B. *Archives from Elephantine*. Berkley: University of California Press, 1968.

Pritchard, James B. ed. *The Ancient Near East*, vols. 1 & 2. Princeton, NJ: The Princeton University Press, 1958.

Richman, Chaim. *The Holy Temple of Jerusalem*. Jerusalem: Carta and The Temple Institute, 1997.

Robinson, H. Wheeler. *Corporate Personality in Ancient Israel*. Edinburgh: T. & T. Clark, 1981.

Schiffman, Michael. *Return of the Remnant*. Baltimore: Lederer Messianic Publishers, 1992, 1996

Schultz, Samuel J. *The Old Testament Speaks*. San Francisco: Harper, 1990.

Shanks, Hershel, ed. *Ancient Israel*. Revised and Expanded. Washington: Biblical Archaeology Society. 1999.

Unger, Merrill F. *Israel and the Arameans of Damascus*. Grand Rapids: Baker Book House, 1980.

Von Soden, Wolfram. *The Ancient Orient*. Grand Rapids: Eerdrmans, 1985, 1994.

Walton, John H. *Ancient Israelite Literature in its Cultural Context*. Grand Rapids: Zondervan, 1989.

—— *Chronological and Background Charts of the Old Testament*. Grand Rapids: Zondervan, 1978.

Wiseman, D. J., ed. *Peoples of Old Testament Times*. Oxford: Clarendon Press, 1973.

JEWISH STUDIES

Blackman, Philip. *Mishnayoth*, vol. 2. New York: The Judaica Press, Inc., 1963.

Blech, Benjamin. *Understanding Judaism*. Northvale, NJ: Jason Aronson, 1991.

Bloch, Abraham P. *The Biblical and Historical Background of the Jewish Holy Days*. New York: KTAV Publishing House, 1978.

Cardozo, Nathan T. Lopes. *The Written and Oral Torah: A Comprehensive Introduction*. Northvale, NJ: Jason Aronson, Inc., 1997.

Cohen, A. *Everyman's Talmud*. New York: Schocken Books, 1975.

Danby, Herbert. ed. & trans. *The Mishnah*. London: Oxford University Press, 1933, 1983.

Davidovitch, David. *The Ketubah: Jewish Marriage Contracts Through the Ages*. Tel Aviv: E. Lewin- Epstein, Ltd., 1959.

Donin, Hayim Halevy. *To Be a Jew*. New York: Basic Books, Inc., 1972.

Eliach, Yaffa. *Hasidic Tales of the Holocaust*. New York: Vintage Books, 1982.

Epstein, ed. *Babylonian Talmud*, New York: Soncino Press, 1989.

Flusser, David. *Judaism and the Origins of Christianity*. Jerusalem: The Magnes Press of the Hebrew University, 1988.

Gurary, Nosson. *The Thirteen Principles of Faith: A Chasidic Viewpoi*nt. Northvale, NJ: Jason Aronson, 1977.

Heschel, Abraham Joshua. *The Sabbath*. New York: The Noonday Press, 1951.

Jacobs, Louis. *The Book of Jewish Belief*. West Orange, NJ: Behrman House, Inc.,

Kaplan, Aryeh. *Made in Heaven*. Jerusalem: Moznaim Publications, 1983.

Kehati, Pinchas, trans. and commentator, Nahman Kahana, trans. *The Mishnah*, vol. V. Jerusalem: Eliner Library, Department for Torah Education and Culture in the Diaspora, 1994.

Kolatch, Alfred J. *The Jewish Book of Why*, vols. 1 and 2. Middle Village, NY: Jonathan David Publishers, 1985.

Lutzke, Harvey. *The Book of Jewish Custom*. Northvale, NJ: Jason Aronson, Inc., 1986.

Nachman, Rebbe of Breslov, Mykoff, Moshe ed. *The Breslov Haggadah*. Jerusalem, Israel Breslov Research Institute, 1989.

Neusner, Jacob. *What is Midrash?* Philadelphia: Fortress Press, 1987.

Raphael, Chaim. A Feast of History: Passover through the Ages as a Key to Jewish Experience. New York: Simon & Shuster, 1972.

Rodkinson, Michael, ed. *Babylonian Talmud*. Boston: Talmud Society, 1918.

Scherman, Nosson. *The Complete ArtSroll Machzor: Yom Kippur*. Brooklyn, NY: Mesorah Publications, 1986.

Strassfeld, Michael, *The Jewish Holidays: A Guide and Commentary*. New York: Harper & Row Publishers, 1985.

Touger, Eliyanhu. *Maimonides, Mishnah Torah*. Brooklyn, NY: Moznaim Publishing Corporation, 1990.

—— *Kitzur Shulchon Oruch*, Jerusalem: Mozanim Publishing Corporation, 1991.

—— *Maimonides, Mishnah Torah*. Brooklyn, NY: Moznaim Publishing Corporation, 1990.

Waskow, Arthur. *Seasons of Our Joy*. New York: Summit Books, NY, 1982.

Weinberg, Yaakov. *Fundamentals and Faith*. Southfield, MI: Targum Press, Inc., 1991.

DICTIONARIES, ENCYCLOPEDIAS, LANGUAGE STUDIES

Arndt, William F. and Gingrich, F. Wilbur, eds. *A Greek-English Lexicon of the New Testament* by William Baur. Chicago: University of Chicago Press, 1957, 1979.

Bivin, David. *New Light on the Difficult Words of Jesus*. Ein-Gedi Resource Centre, Inc.: Holland, MI, 2005.

Botterweck, G. and Johannes and Ringgren, Helmer, eds. *Theological Dictionary of the Old Testament*, vol. 2. Grand Rapids: Eerdmans, 1986.

Bromiley, Geoffrey W. gen. ed. *The International Standard Bible Encyclopaedia*, 4 vols. Grand Rapids: Eerdmans, 1979.

Brown, Colin, ed. *The Dictionary of New Testament Theology*, 3 vols. Grand Rapids: Zondervan, 1967, 1979.

Brown, Francis, Driver, S. R., and Briggs, Charles A. The New Brown, Driver, Briggs, *Gesenius Hebrew and English Lexicon* ("BDB"). Peabody, MA: Hendrickson Publishers, 1979.

Dana, H. E. and Mantey, Julius R. *A Manual Grammar of the Greek New Testament*. Toronto: The Macmillan Company, 1927, 1957.

Deissmann, Adolf. *Light from the Ancient East*. Grand Rapids: Baker Book House, 1978.

Douglas, J.D. organizing editor, *The New Bible Dictionary*, 2nd ed. Wheaton, IL: Tyndale House Publishers, 1987.

Encyclopaedia Judaica. Jerusalem: Keter Publishing, 1972.

Freedman, David Noel, ed. *The Anchor Yale Bible Dictionary*, 5 vols. Yale University Press, 1992.

Harris, R. Laird, ed. *Theological Wordbook of the Old Testament*, 2 vols. Chicago: Moody Press, 1980.

Koehler, Ludwig and Baumgartner, Walter. *The Hebrew and Aramaic Lexicon of the Old Testament* ("HALOT"). Leiden, The Netherlands: Koninklijke Brill, 2000.

Payne, J. Barton. *Encyclopedia of Biblical Prophecy*. New York: Harper and Row, 1973.

The American Heritage Dictionary. New York: Houghton Miffin Co., 1992.

GENERAL AND THEOLOGICAL WORKS

Bacchiocchi, Samuele. *Shabbat to Sunday*. Rome: The Pontifical Gregorian University Press, 1977.

Berkowitz, Ariel & D'vorah. *Take Hold*. Richmond, MI: Shoreshim Publishing, 2020

—— *Torah Rediscovered*. Richmond, MI: Shoreshim Publishing, 2012.

Carlebach, Shlomo. *Shlomo's Stories*. Northvale, NJ: Jason Aronson, Inc., 1994.

Chaikim, Dov, "*After the Order Of*," Tishrei, vol. 1, No. 2, pp. 29–30.

Fischer, John, "Covenant, Fulfilment and Judaism in Hebrews," an unpublished paper.

—— Private Conversations over many years!

Flusser, David. *Jewish Sources in Early Christianity*. Tel Aviv: MOD Books, 1989.

Frydland, Rachmiel. *What the Rabbis Know About the Messiah*. Cincinnati, Ohio: Messianic Literature Outreach, 1993.

Goldberg, Louis, "Atonement According to Moses and The Traditional Writings," Tishrei Winter 1993/1994, Vol. 2, No. 2.

Hegg, Tim. *It is Often Said: Comments and Comparisons of Traditional Christian Theology and Hebraic Thought*. 4 volumes. Tacoma, WA: TorahResource, 2013.

—— "Gentile Believers & Pesach in the Pre-Destruction Era," A paper published by TorahResource.com.

Hengstenberg, E.W. *Christology in the Old Testament*. Grand Rapids: Kregel Publications, 1970, reprinted from the 1847 edition.

Juster, Daniel. *Due Process*. Shippensburg, PA: Destiny Image, 1992.

Juster, Daniel, and Intrator, Keith. *Israel, the Church, and the Last Days*. Shippensburg, PA: Destiny Image, 2005.

Longenecker, Richard N. *The Christology of Early Jewish Christianity*. Grand Rapids: Baker Books, 1970.

Murray, John. *Redemption Accomplished and Applied*. Grand Rapids: Eerdmans, 1974.

Nassi, Tzvi. *The Great Mystery: How Can Three Be One?* Cincinnati, OH: Messianic Literature Outreach, 1990.

Netanyhu, Benjamin. *A Place Among the Nations: Israel and the World*. New York: Bantam Books, 1993.

Pritz, Ray. *Nazarene Jewish Christianity*. Jerusalem: The Magnes Press of the Hebrew University, 1992.

Rosen, Moshe. *Christ in the Passover*. Chicago: Moody Press, 1978.

Rosenberg, David. Private conversations, Long Island, NY. August 1996.

Santala, Risto. *The Messiah in the Old Testament*. Jerusalem: Keren Ahvah Meshihit, 1992.

Steele, Paul E. and Ryie, Charles C. *Meant to Last*. Wheaton, IL: Victor Books, 1984.

Yancy, Philip. *Where is God When It Hurts?* Grand Rapids: Zondervan, 1977.

BIBLES

Accordance 7.1. OakTree Software, 2006. This electronic resource includes a host of materials we used for Briteinu including Bibles, Bible Atlas, Biblical Archaeology Review pictures, and much more. Contact www.accordancebible.com

Biblia Hebraica Stuttgartensia. Stuttgart, Germany: Deutsche Bibelgesellschaft, 1990.

Charlesworth, James H. *Old Testament Pseudepigrapha Apocalyptic Literature and Testament*, 2 vols. Garden City, NJ: Doubleday & Co., 1983.

New American Standard Bible, The International Inductive Study Bible (Eugene, OR: Harvest House Publishers, 1993.

NIV Archaeological Study Bible: An Illustrated Walk Through Biblical History and Culture. Grand Rapids, Zondervan, 2005.

Tanakh — The Holy Scriptures. The New JPS Translation. Philadelphia: The Jewish Publication Society, 1988.

The Greek New Testament, 3rd ed. Stuttgart, Germany: United Bible Societies, 1983.

The NET Bible, Second Edition Notes. Nashville, Tennessee. Biblical Studies Press/Published by Thomas Nelson, 2019.

The New International Version. Colorado Springs, CO: International Bible Society, 1984.

PERIODICALS

Archaeology Odyssey

Bible and Spade (www.biblearchaeology.org)

Biblical Archaeology Review

Biblical Archaeology Today. Jerusalem: Israel Exploration Society, 1985.

Journal of the American Oriental Society

About the Author

Ariel Berkowitz (B.S. West Chester State University and Philadelphia Biblical University; M.Div. (Biblical Theological Seminary) is, with his wife D'vorah, a teacher and writer with Torah Resources International (TRI). In addition, Ariel has been an Adjunct Instructor at The Master's University Israeli Campus "IBEX" (Israel Bible Extension) Program from 1995 and an Adjunct Instructor at Torah Resource Institute from 2012. Ariel and D'vorah have four grown children and seven grandchildren, and they live in the Negev in Israel.

Ariel's style of writing and teaching makes biblical scholarship very accessible to students and promotes a deeper understanding of the Torah, while inspiring further study of the Scriptures. Ariel (with his wife, D'vorah) brings over forty years of teaching experience in east Asia, the Philippines, Australia, Europe, UK, Ireland, South Africa, the U.S., Suriname, and Israel to produce this lucid, learned, and easy-to-read commentary.

Other books by Ariel and D'vorah

Torah Rediscovered

Take Hold

"Open My Eyes" (גל עיני):
Studying & Teaching the Bible Made Simple

The Good News of The Good News
Knowing our Identity in the Messiah

The Briteinu Torah Commentary:
Vol. 1 — Bereshit: The Foundations of Covenant
Vol. 2 — Shemot: The Written Covenant
Vol. 3 — Vayikra: Living the Covenenant
Vol. 5 — D'varim: Renewing the Covenant

Studies in the Book of Deuteronomy:
(Self-Studies)
Books 1, 2 & 3: Renewing the Covenant

Studies in the Book of Joshua:
The Covenants in Action

The Torah of the Sages:
A Simple Introduction to the Oral Torah

The Twelve Overlooked Prophets (ספר תרי עשר):
A Survey of Hosea to Malachi

A Week in the Life of the Lamb

Hanukkah in the Home of the Redeemed

MBTA: Modular Biblical Training Academy
The Academy offers Biblical training as a unique place of learning for all ages. The style of learning helps to develop a Biblical vocabulary and build fundamental concepts needed for learning Torah found at torahtruths.com

To order any of these books, please see our website:
torahresourcesinternational.com
or visit Amazon.com

Made in United States
North Haven, CT
15 May 2025

68878909R00135